MAKING IT ON YOUR OWN

SURVIVING AND THRIVING ON THE UPS AND DOWNS OF BEING YOUR OWN BOSS

SARAH and PAUL EDWARDS

JEREMY P. TARCHER, INC.
Los Angeles

Library of Congress Cataloging-in-Publication Data

Edwards, Sarah (Sarah A.)
    Making it on your own : surviving and thriving on the ups and downs of
    being your own boss / Sarah and Paul Edwards.—1st ed.
        p.   cm.
    Includes index.
    ISBN 0-87477-636-8 (pa.)
1. New business enterprises.   2. Self-employed.   3. Success in business.
I. Edwards, Paul, 1940–   . II. Title.
HD62.5.E393   1991
658 ' .041—dc20   91-3065
                                                                CIP

Jeremy P. Tarcher, Inc.
5858 Wilshire Blvd., Suite 200
Los Angeles, CA 90036

"Twelve Characteristics of Tough-Minded Optimists" is reprinted with permission from *The Power of Optimism* by Alan Loy McGinnis, New York:
Harper and Row, 1990.

Distributed by St. Martin's Press, New York

Manufactured in the United States of America
10   9   8   7   6   5   4   3   2   1

First Edition

C O N T E N T S
■■■■■■■■■■■■■■■■■■■■■■

Introduction   1

Part 1: Making the Mental Shift from Payroll to Profit   7

1. *We're Not Taught to Make It on Our Own*   *11*

The Classical Entrepreneur versus Today's New Propreneur   12
   The New Breed of Entrepreneur   14
   Are You an Entrepreneur or a Propreneur?   17
Propreneuring Requires a Different Approach   18

2. *Thinking Like Today's Successful Propreneurs*   *20*

   Twelve Mental Shifts from Paycheck Thinking to Profit Thinking   22

The Odds Have Changed in Your Favor: Shifting from Pipe Dreams
   to Practicalities   23
   The Force Is With You   23
   You Have Profit Potential   24

Ambiguity Means Opportunity: Shifting from Certainties to Possibilities   25
   Security Is an Illusion   26
   Ambiguity Is Our Only Hope   26
   Being on Your Own Is Perhaps the Ultimate Security   27
   Trust Is a Decision; You Can Put It Where You Want   28

Your Security Lies Within: Shifting from Waiting for a Break to Making
  Your Breaks   28
  There's No One to Blame   29
  Developing Your Self-Management Muscle   29
  Trust Comes from Experience   30
  Give Yourself the Break You've Been Waiting For   31
  You Make the Magic   31

Success Is an Experiment: Shifting from Following Rules to
  Following Results   32
  Making It on Your Own Is an Experiment   33
  There Is No Right Answer Until You Find It!   33
  The Lack of a Clear Path Is Never a Sign to Turn Back   33
  Confusion Is Normal   34
  No Results—No Reward   35
  Let the Results Be Your Guide   35

Being Good Is Not Enough: Shifting from Mastery to Marketing   36
  You Have to Toot Your Horn   37
  Toot about What You Can Do, Not Who You Are   37

Failure Is a Stepping-Stone: Shifting from Dreading Mistakes to
  Building on Them   39
  There's Nothing Wrong with You   40
  Success Is More Important Than Being Right   41
  Make Your Mistakes Where They Won't Hurt   41
  What to Do When You Make a Mistake   42

Excess Is Essential: Shifting from Playing It Safe to Keeping Your
  Options Open   42
  A Deal Isn't a Deal Until It's Done   43

It Gets Better and Better: Shifting from Boundaries to Breakthroughs   44
  Success Has a Momentum of Its Own   45
  Success Takes Time   46
  The Suffering Is Temporary   47
  Finding a Cash Cushion   48

Money Is a Multiplier: Shifting from Earning to Spend to Spending
  to Earn   48
  You Have to Support Your Business before It Will Support You   49
  You Have to Spend Money to Make Money   49
  The Money You Spend Needs to Make Money   50
  Credit Sources   51

The Only Authority You Have Is What You Can Command:
Shifting from Position Power to Personal Power   52

Success Is a Joint Venture: Shifting from Help Me to How Can I Help?   54

You Can't Afford the Luxury of Bad Morale:
Shifting from Employee to Coach, Colleague, and Cheerleader   56
Twelve Ways to Keep Yourself Charged Up   57

Part 2: Managing Everything That Needs to Be Done   59

3. *Having the Time of Your Life*   *61*

Making Time for It All   62
A New Outlook on Time   64

Putting First Things First   65

Following the 80/20 Rule to Quadruple Your Results   67
How to 80/20 Your Life   68

Working on Purpose   68
The Power of Knowing Why You're Doing What You're Doing   69
Three Steps to Getting on Purpose   70
Using a Purpose Poster to Stay on Track   73

Clearing Out the Backlog   74
The Four Essential Activity Centers   78

Scheduling for Results   79
Operating from Goals   80
Bringing Goals into the Moment   82
Making Time for Your Personal Life   84
Making Time to Work As Much As You Want   85
Interruption Busters   87

4. *Getting the Business to Run Itself So You Can Do What You Do Best 89*

Nine Principles for Getting Everything Working for You   90
When to Hire Help   93
Ask Your Way to Success   94
Your Personal Information Network   96
Little Things That Make a Big Difference   98
Making Light Work of the Most Time-Consuming Tasks   101

The Critical Mass Marketing Alternative to Having to Constantly
    Sell Yourself   102

    Thirty-five Ways to Get Business to Come to You   103

    Boldly Standing Out from the Crowd   104

    Becoming Self-Generating   104

    Making Your Marketing Efforts Self-Liquidating   105

    Letting Your Work Market Itself   105

    Four Steps to Building Your Critical Marketing Mass   105

Using Technology to Reduce Administrivia   107

    Equipping the Ideal Do-It-Yourself Office   108

    Fifty Jobs a Personal Computer Can Do for You   109

    Breaking Down Myths and Resistances to Technology   113

    Cutting Down on Cleaning Up   115

    60-Second Cleaning Secrets   116

You're the Boss   117

Part 3: Becoming the Boss You've Always Wanted to Have   119

5. *Motivating Yourself to Do What Needs to Be Done*   *121*

Becoming Your Own Coach, Mentor, and Adviser   122

    Three Steps to Becoming an Effective Self-Manager   122

    Making Sure You Can Count on Yourself to Do What You Say You'll Do   123

Identifying What Motivates You   124

    What Motivates You?   125

    Knowing What You Need to Hear and Saying It in Such a Way That
      You'll Listen   126

    What to Do When You Don't Feel Like Doing What Needs to Be Done   127

Getting in Peak Condition and Keeping Yourself There   128

    What Makes the Magic?   129

    Are You Ready for Success?   131

A Five-Step Regimen for Peak Performance   130

    Step One: Remain Relaxed under Pressure   131

    Musical Valium   133

    Step Two: Get Energized! Stay Energized!   134

    How to Have a Good Night's Sleep with Everything Hanging
      over Your Head   137

    Instant Energy Builders   138

    Step Three: Build Your Concentration   138

Step Four: Become an Optimist   140
Creating a Supportive Work Environment   141
Twelve Characteristics of Tough-Minded Optimists   142
Step Five: Be There Now   143
A Stay-Up Music Guide   144
A Five-Minute Warm-Up for Peak Performance   146

Making Success Automatic   147

Taking Care of the Coach   147

6. *Riding the Emotional Roller Coaster*   *151*

A New Perspective on What to Do with Your Feelings   153
Emotions as Valued Messengers   153

The Emotional Roadmap   158
From Angry to Satisfied   159
From Depressed to Encouraged   161
From Disappointment to Hopeful   162
From Discouraged to Feeling Encouraged   164
From Feeling Like a Failure to Feeling Like a Success   165
From Fear or Anxiety to Anticipation   166
From Guilt to Self-Confidence   174
From Hopeless to Determination or Acceptance   176
From Inadequacy to Self-Confidence   177
From Feeling Irresponsible to Assuming Responsibility   180
From Lethargic to Motivated   181
From Feeling Overwhelmed to Feeling Capable   182
From Feeling Stuck to Making Progress   182

When You Don't Like the Way You Feel   186
Working Your Emotional Throttle   186

Designer Emotions: Preselecting Your Feelings   189
Checking Your Premise   191
Adjusting Your Premise   192
A Premise for All Occasions   192

7. *Staying Up No Matter What Goes Down*   *194*

Eight Things to Do When You Don't Know What to Do   195
Thirteen Whacky Ways to Generate Workable Possibilities   198
Questions That Help Solve Problems   199

Getting the World to Take You Seriously   199
Four Available Sources of Power   203

Position Power: Using Your Title   203
Historical Power: Using Your Past   204
Cultural Power: Using Your Credentials   205
Personal Power: Using Your Charisma   207
You Don't Have to Fake It to Make It   209
Five Attitudes That Get in the Way of Being Taken Seriously   210

What to Do When You Don't Have Enough Money   213
The Only Three Reasons for Not Having Enough Money   214
Diagnosing What You Need to Do to Get More Business   214
Lifesaving Measures to Turn Tough Times Around   216
How to Know If You're Doing a Good Job   217
Avoiding Slow Times   218
Five Ways to Get Business Fast   219
What to Say to Others When Things Aren't Going Well   220
Who to Pay When There's Not Enough to Go Around   222
Collecting What You're Due   222
Can You Raise Your Prices or Fees?   224
Do You Have to Cut Costs and Living Expenses?   226

What to Do When You Feel Like Quitting   227
Does It Have to Take So Long and Be So Hard?   228
Success Has a Schedule of Its Own   229
Two Factors That Determine Your Success Rate   231
Is Your Market More or Less Receptive?   232
Are You More or Less Ready?   235

Moving Mountains   237
Taking a Personal Inventory   238

Conclusion: Enjoying Your Success   239

The Five Stages of Success   240
Starting Again with Confidence   242
Success Is Supposed to Feel Good   243
Keeping Success in Scale   243
Knowing Your Success Is Here to Stay   244
Adjusting Your Relationships to Your Success   244
Feeling Worthy   245
Acknowledging Yourself   245
Success Is a Beginning, Not an End   246

Index   247

ACKNOWLEDGMENTS

■■■■■■■■■■■■■■■■■■■■■■■

We're told that it's unusual for authors to have three books published at the same time by the same publisher. Yet this book is proof that it can happen and it is due to the extraordinary team of people at our publisher, Jeremy P. Tarcher, Inc. To Jeremy Tarcher we owe a continuing debt for his vision that resulted in his publishing *Working From Home* when it was regarded as something short of a fad in 1985, because he recognized that people are seeking alternatives to the 9-to-5 routine and that it's both possible and profitable to make it on your own working from home.

We thank Rick Benzel, our editor for our three new books, *Best Home Businesses for the 90s, Getting Business to Come to You,* and *Making It On Your Own.* Rick's support, creativity, good sense and problem-solving ability has come through many times in the course of developing these books.

We are especially grateful to Robert Welsch for his special vision and role in bringing these books about. We don't know how many hours of sleep Paul Murphy and Susan Harris will have lost to get these books out on time, and we are grateful. To Mike Dougherty, Lisa Ives, Michael Graziano, Lisa Chadwick we say "thank you" for helping us to get our message out that there are positive alternatives for people in a rapidly changing world.

We appreciate the hundreds of people we interviewed for these books, many of whom came to us by way of the Working From Home forum on CompuServe and our radio shows.

INTRODUCTION
■■■■■■■■■■■■■■■■■■■■■■■

If you were an Olympic athlete, enthusiastic audiences would cheer you on to great feats. Your coaches would encourage, prod, and guide you to success. If you were part of a top sales team for one of the nation's leading corporations, you'd attend regular seminars and training programs from experts to charge you up and build your skills and confidence.

But if you are one of today's growing number of self-employed individuals, who cheers you on? Who picks you up? Who gives you the boost you need? Chances are you have to do most of that for yourself.

Your family, friends, and colleagues may think you're crazy to have gone out on your own, even though they wish they could do it themselves. They may be telling you that what you're doing isn't practical, and when problems arise they may not be that sympathetic. After all, what can you expect when you don't play it safe?

Even if those around you are understanding and supportive, you may hesitate to discuss your concerns with them. They have their own problems and you don't want to add to them, at least not repeatedly. Sometimes it's even hard to share the excitement of your victories. Your success is often a reminder to others of what they wish they were doing.

If you've had any of these experiences, you're certainly not alone. All people who set out on their own feel the isolation of taking the road less traveled. And even though that road is taking you toward your dreams and the journey is exciting, it can also feel long and bumpy enroute. That's why we wrote this book. It's the collective voice of thousands of people like you who have left the familiar comforts and bothersome discomforts of a salaried job to venture into the unfamiliar but enthralling world of being your own boss.

If you think of making it on your own as similar to running a marathon, and many would agree it is, then this book is like a crowd of eager fans that line the road, cheering you on, calling out to encourage you along the way.

1

These fans, however, have run the race themselves, so you'll overhear them yelling out the precise words you need to hear at the very moment you need to hear them.

We've written this book because we've been there. We've felt both the exhilaration and the apprehension of leaving behind the security of a paycheck to pursue our ideas and manifest our dreams. We've lived through the lean years; we've felt the pain of Heartbreak Hill. But we also know the tremendous joy and satisfaction that come from knowing you've made it—that you've done what you set out to do and accomplished what others told you could not be done.

Over the past eleven years, through our consultations, seminars, call-in radio show, and the Working from Home Forum we manage on CompuServe Information Service, we've also met and shared journeys with thousands of others who have undertaken the challenge to make it on their own, sometimes by choice, sometimes as a result of unexpected circumstances. In the process we've found that success or failure on your own is no accident. Those who succeed approach the challenges with a different attitude and react to them in a different manner from those who do not.

Success is much more than simply knowing the basics of business start-ups and having a positive attitude. While having a positive attitude is important, very important, success also means knowing what to do with negative attitudes (both yours and others,) and what to do when the bills exceed the business. It's knowing when to invest money you don't have so that you will ultimately have it. It's knowing when to persist and when to change. It's knowing what to do and what to think when the money runs out. In many ways how you respond to and handle the apparent negative aspects of being on your own is even more important than how you handle the opportunities and routine aspects of making it.

In fact, we wrote this book to address the most common questions and challenges that we and other self-employed individuals encountered after taking the plunge, once all the standard logistics and basic business details were taken care of. Our focus here is on the many, many things that no one ever talks about, the things most business books and college courses leave out, the many subtle and not so subtle challenges that arise without warning, and the delightfully clever options that can get you over, around, or under any obstacle.

Through this book, you'll gain the experience of people who've done what others told them couldn't be done: people like Ellie Kahn, who earns a living creating videos that document family and corporate histories; people like Judy Wunderlich, who gets to stay home with her two small children while she works twenty-five hours a week and grosses nearly two hundred thousand dollars per year from her home-based employment agency for graphic designers; people like the photographer Dean Tucker, who turned his hobby into a quarter-of-a-million-dollar business by traveling across the country doing multi-media presentations; people like the comedian Kevin Hughes, who found a unique and profitable way to earn over one hundred thousand dollars a year by making people laugh, both on college campuses and in his own workshops for couples.

At one time, ventures like these might have been considered impractical, yet now they are thriving. Was it easy? Of course not. All these people started on a shoestring. They all had doubts. They all had challenges. But was it worth it? These individuals and those whose lives are improved by their services answer with a resounding *yes*!

It's from such experiences and those of other successful self-employed individuals, however, that we've learned of the rich array of practical strategies you can use to meet the most challenging aspects of being your own boss. It's through experiences like theirs that you can learn how to proceed with confidence through uncertainty, to overcome financial barriers and difficulties, and to remain relaxed and positive under the pressure of deadlines. It's with experiences like theirs that you can learn how to keep your energy up and perform in the midst of crises, how to position yourself to recognize and seize opportunities while you're keeping the wolves at bay. These are prerequisites for directing your own future that anyone can learn to master.

For years, we've been asked what kind of people are able to make it on their own. Can anyone do it, or are there certain characteristics someone must have in order to succeed? Over and over again, we've replied that you can make it on your own if you have a strong desire and the willingness to learn how to become a goal-directed, self-motivated person.

But let's face it: most of us were not taught how to be goal-directed, self-motivated individuals. We're given far too few opportunities to think for ourselves, to take initiative, to run with our own ideas, make mistakes, and learn from them how to get where we want to go. As a result, many people who set out on their own don't feel like they have what it takes at first, and yet they succeed nonetheless because everyone can develop these abilities. In fact, going out on your own provides the perfect opportunity to develop them. And actually that's what this book is about: how to develop the attitudes, skills, and confidence of a self-motivated, goal-directed person so that you can accomplish whatever you set out to do on your own.

We've found that these attitudes and skills will enable you not only to survive on your own, but to thrive. They will enable you to do the three things that can assure your success:

1. *Adopt a new, self-reliant mindset.* As you may already have discovered, working successfully on your own requires a new mental outlook. You must begin to think about yourself, your work, and your life in a new way as you leave behind the familiar world of the paycheck and enter a world in which you must rely upon yourself to produce the profits you need to live well.

In Part 1 of this book, "Making the Mental Shift from Payroll to Profit," we outline the vital and sometimes surprising mental shifts being on your own requires. You'll learn how to leave the paycheck mentality behind forever and permanently adopt a successful profit orientation.

In this section, you'll also learn the reasons some self-employed individuals succeed where others fail. You'll discover how most of these failures can be averted. And you'll learn the difference between today's new breed of self-employed individuals and the classical entrepreneur of the past. You'll understand why much of the business advice you've received has not been as useful as you might have liked. And best of all, you'll discover why your chances of success are greater today than ever before.

2. Put your show on the road. We all have dreams of how we'd like to spend our lives. We know how we'd like things to go. But to make it on your own, you have to take the next step. You have to know where you're going and set your life up so you will get there. You have to take charge and start directing the many things that need to be done so that you're running your life instead of it running you. You must literally *have the time of your life.*

You didn't go out on your own to spend most of your time acting as the secretary, receptionist, salesperson, bookkeeper, and cleaning service. But these tasks do need to be done, and you're probably the one who will have to do them. In Part 2 of this book, "Managing Everything That Needs to Be Done," you'll discover how to get organized so that your business can essentially run itself while you spend most of your time earning a living from doing what you do best and enjoy most.

You'll learn how to take strategic advantage of technology and support services and make marketing yourself and your work a part of what you're already good at. You'll also learn tactics for how to turn around slow times and make the most of limited resources.

3. Become your own boss. Once you know where you're going and you're set up to get there, you've got to learn to manage yourself to make sure that you do get there. You've got to literally be your own boss, motivating, inspiring, and preparing yourself to function at your peak as you ride the emotional roller coaster of being on your own. You can't let the ups and downs get you down. You have to direct and guide yourself through whatever challenges and problems arise along the way.

In Part 3, "Becoming the Boss You've Always Wanted to Have," we provide a mini-course in how to assume the role of effectively managing yourself. We deal with common motivational issues like staying focused, handling rejection, giving yourself ample time off, and performing well under the presssure of deadlines, setbacks, and too many things to do. We address what to do when you don't know what to do and how to respond when you feel like quitting. We provide guidelines for dealing with some of the most difficult issues self-employed individuals encounter—like not being taken seriously, running out of money, and not having enough clients or customers.

You'll discover how people who are willing to make the needed mental shifts to put their show on the road and to direct themselves to persevere until they get where they want to go are going to succeed. But there is one other essential ingredient for making it on your own—living well with success. Have you ever noticed that sometimes *successful* people are not *happy* people? In fact, sometimes success itself becomes overwhelming and demanding. Instead of feeling fantastic, you can become enslaved to your own success. So in the closing section of this book, "Enjoying Your Success," we talk about the unexpected aspects of achieving your goals and what's involved in making sure success is worth all the time and effort it takes to achieve.

Essentially, we've designed this book to help you make a revolutionary shift in the way you look at yourself and your work. As you read through it, picking those topics of most interest to you, we feel certain you will begin to see more clearly than ever before that your fate does not depend on chance, the whims of others, or even the ups and downs of the marketplace. Indeed, you will undoubtedly come to believe ever more strongly that you hold the power to create your own future and the quality of life you desire. We look forward to your thoroughly enjoying amazing results from making it on your own.

PART 1

■■■■■■■■■■■■■■■■■■■■■■■■

Making the Mental Shift
from Payroll to Profit

*Can success change the human mechanism
so completely between one dawn and another? Can it make one feel taller, more
alive, handsomer, uncommonly gifted, and
indomitably secure with the certainty that
this is the way life will always be? It can
and it does!*

MOSS HART

Have you ever noticed the transforma-
tion that takes place when someone becomes a champion? One day they're
struggling to get to the top of their game. They clutch in the clinch. They
almost make it. They're inconsistent—brilliant at moments and disappointing
at others. And then one day, with dogged determination and after much
effort, they do it. They get a perfect ten. They win the title. They break a
record. They take the gold medal. And somehow, almost miraculously, at that
point they *become* a champion. They step onto the field with a different gait.
They project a new aura of confidence. They begin thinking and walking and
talking like a champion. Something has shifted. And everyone knows it.

For me, Sarah, going out on my own was just like that. One day I was
working for someone else, dreaming about being my own boss, about writing
books and doing many things I'd always wanted to do. Then one day I
couldn't wait anymore and I did it. I quit my job. I went out on my own. It

7

was exciting and exhilarating—at first. I was like the rookie on opening day basking in the cheers of the crowd. Then came the next day and the next day and so on, and soon I realized what it meant to have stepped into the big league.

Suddenly I was called upon to *be* far more than I had ever been before. I was called upon to *do* far more than I had ever done before. There was so much I had not expected. So much I didn't know. I was playing with the pros. It was faster and harder than I had ever imagined. I loved it...but I felt small, inadequate, confused, and scared. Still, I was determined and committed: I wanted to make it.

That's when I became interested in studying champions. Not just the champions we see in sports, but people in all walks of life who are thriving on their own, doing work they've chosen to pursue. I wanted to think and walk and talk like those champions. I needed to know what enabled them to thrive while others seemed to struggle and flounder or even give up. I was determined to discover how these highly successful individuals have such seeming good fortune while others with similar talent, experience, and capability never make the shift.

It is tempting to think that these successful self-employed individuals are the lucky ones, the ones who had more money to begin with or knew more of the right people. Yet as I looked deeper into their stories, I found that those are rarely the real reasons some people thrive on their own, while others don't survive.

The business journals will tell you that the most common reasons for business failure are undercapitalization, poor business management, unfavorable economic conditions, and lack of business experience. But how can that be? Haven't you heard stories about people who went out on their own with no business experience whatsoever, some without even a high-school diploma, and were able to turn $65 into a six-figure income? We've not only heard about such individuals, we've met them. We've also met people with virtually unlimited funds and extensive business experience, Ph.D.'s and M.B.A.'s, whose ventures never got off the ground.

Of course, the opposite is true as well. We've talked with people who had limited funds and experience and fell flat on their faces, while still others have thrived with ample funds and a strong academic or business background. Furthermore, each of these varied outcomes has occurred under identical economic conditions.

So what made the difference? The fact that we can't find an easy answer to why some people succeed while far too many still fail is the very reason so many people fear going out on their own. It's this lack of clarity that keeps so many of us chained to a paycheck. It's this lack of certainty that sometimes makes being on your own more of an ordeal than a dream come true. The survival rate for small businesses, although improving, is still lower than most people are comfortable with.

In my quest for success, I've spent many hours contemplating this dilemma and I've concluded that nobody talks much about what's really involved. There seems to be a mystique surrounding the idea of leaving the security of a paycheck, a mystique rooted in ancient fears of desperate but determined immigrants and memories of economic hardships suffered through the Great Depression. These amorphous fears linger in the recesses of our minds and are passed on from generation to generation. Basically they arise from a fear of the unknown and the fact that most people still don't know how to make survival, let alone success, a certainty without a paycheck.

In talking with many hundreds of people who are successfully making it on their own, however, we've found that the reasons some people fail or barely survive while others thrive are usually not the ones we hear about or even the ones people talk about when asked why they've met with success or failure. Basically, two reasons emerged for why people don't make it on their own. The first is that we've had virtually no preparation for how to be our own boss. In fact, what we are taught about how to succeed in life is often diametrically opposed to what we need to do if we're going to succeed on our own. From the moment we're born, we're busy learning how to do what we're told. We're fed on schedule—told when and what to eat. Before long the teacher takes over where our parents left off, and by the time we get out of grade school we're masters at taking orders and following rules—or at breaking them. We've learned how to get in line, be quiet, speak only when called upon, and raise our hands if we need to go to the bathroom. In the process, we've been prepared to become good workers. Or we've rebelled against this regimentation and learned to become terrible workers.

Once we graduate from school, our employers quickly step into the role played by our parents and teachers. We're still expected to show up on schedule, eat on schedule, and work on schedule. We're still basically expected to stay in line and do what's asked of us.

As children we learn that if we're good boys and girls and do what we're told, mommy and daddy will be pleased and we'll be rewarded. In school we're taught more of the same. If we follow the rules, work hard, know the right answers, and do what the teacher says, we'll get good grades. These lessons have prepared us perfectly for what we call *the payroll mentality:* come to work on time, work hard, do a good job, do what the boss or the job description says, and in return you'll receive your paycheck on a regular basis. If you produce what's expected of you well enough, you may even get a raise!

But the minute you leave the job to go out on your own, you're free of all such regimen. You can do anything you want. No one will tell you when to get up, when to eat, when or if to take breaks, how long to work, where to work, or even whether to work. There aren't any rules. Or at least there's no one to oversee whether you follow any particular rules. And even more importantly, there's no paycheck! There's only the *prospect of a profit.*

Suddenly the whole world works differently. In fact, we've found a dozen fundamental mental shifts you need to make in how you think about yourself and your work if you want profits to materialize in place of the missing paycheck. Each of these mental shifts is diametrically opposed to a way we've been trained to think from the time we were born. Is it any wonder the success rate has been so low?

In this section, we'll outline these shifts and demonstrate how, in reality, the reasons for success or failure on our own are not in your pocketbook or on your résumé. They're in the way you think about yourself and your work. Undercapitalization, lack of experience, setbacks due to unfavorable economic conditions—these are situations that almost everyone faces at one time or another when out on their own. The problems someone has in responding to these challenges are the visible symptoms of the real ailment: trying to produce a profit with a payroll mentality. Responding to these challenges successfully requires a new set of attitudes, beliefs, and actions that are quite distinct from how we used to respond to problems at school or on the job.

In fact, if you think and make decisions like an employee, being on your own becomes an agonizing experience. The characteristics that make for a good employee are often the exact opposite from those that make for a successfully self-employed individual. And to make matters worse, when someone goes out on their own, much of the standard advice they get about how to proceed isn't particularly helpful, either. Not even all the positive thinking in the world can get people through treacherous and unknown waters they're totally unprepared to navigate.

That's the second reason some people don't make it on their own: much of the traditional information available about how to become your own boss does not apply to the new breed of individuals who want to become self-employed today. It doesn't address the needs of the majority of today's 16 million self-employed professionals, free-lancers, home-based businesspeople, craftspeople, consultants, and contract workers whose numbers are still growing.

In this section you'll find, however, that increasing numbers of these pioneering individuals are literally *making it on their own* and carving out of their experience new understandings, new tools, and new ways of thinking that will make it possible for everyone who wants to follow in their footsteps to do so with a confidence and certainty that wasn't possible in the past.

CHAPTER
ONE
■■■■■■■■■■■■■■■■■■■■■■■

We're Not Taught to Make It on Our Own

*There are so many places I wouldn't have
gone, so many people I wouldn't have seen
and met, so many expeditions I wouldn't
have led if I had only known in advance
what I was to experience.*

DOUCHAN GERSI

"I don't know what to do," a computer
consultant told us. "I've taken four business courses already, and so far I still
don't have a clue how they relate to the consulting business I want to start. I
don't have money for market research. I don't have any staff. I work from
home, so I don't need to pick a location. But the successful computer consultants I've met don't have these things, either."

Many members of today's new self-employed work force have had a similar experience. They find plenty of information about the technicalities of
getting into business, from getting a license to setting up an office and writing
a business plan, but when it comes to the strategies for how to do business
successfully, they instinctively sense that the tactics and concepts outlined in
traditional courses and books on small business don't help much.

In fact, many of the people who are making it on their own today don't
even consider themselves to be in business. When asked if they're in business
for themselves many tell us no. They consider themselves to be self-employed,
free-lancers, independent contractors, contract workers, artists, home-based
businesses, and so forth. In this sense, being self-employed is a commercial
hybrid. And that's why it can be such a challenge.

Self-employment, in its current form, is a relatively recent phenomenon. It has not been researched and studied by business scholars and analysts the way traditional business has. In fact, it's generally been either ignored or lumped under the category of small business.

But consider this: the Small Business Administration defines a small business as any organization with 100 to 1,500 employees. In all but the most abstract terms, the approach needed to operate a one-or two-person venture must of necessity be substantially different from what's required to run a company with even ten employees. Yet unfortunately, many of the recommended courses, books, and other resources available to people who are going out on their own are actually scaled-down versions of what's known about running the traditionally *large* small business.

We believe that's like trying to dress a monkey in a costume made for an elephant. And if you ever had to wear hand-me-down clothes, you know how difficult that can be. Perhaps that's exactly how you feel now that you're out on your own—like someone who's outgrown last year's clothes but isn't ready, or even interested, in stepping into the clothes of giants.

And you don't have to. You don't have to become like the large bureaucratic businesses you're trying to escape, nor do you have to go back to another constrictive job. It's a matter of tailoring this hybrid of self-employment to your own goals and talents. Fortunately there is lots of flexibility, and there are almost unlimited possibilities.

The Classical Entrepreneur versus Today's New Propreneur

In writing our best-selling book *Working from Home: Everything You Need to Know about Living and Working under the Same Roof* we discovered that most of the people going out on their own today are, like us, a new breed of entrepreneurs who are faced with making up their own rules and discovering their own new and different ways of earning a living.

In the early 1970s, when we began feeling the pressures of being a two-career family, we had no intention of becoming entrepreneurs or starting a business. We simply wanted a better way of life. I, Sarah, was working for the federal Head Start program. It was an exciting job, but in trying to juggle my career with the demands of being a wife and mother I developed a life-threatening stress-related illness. My doctor said I would have to change my lifestyle.

I knew I needed to make a change. But I wasn't willing to settle for less than what I wanted from life. I wanted a meaningful, challenging career, and I wanted a chance to enjoy my family and raise my son. I had no idea how I could do all that without the stress, which was making me ill. Then one day I went to a meeting with Richard Nadeau, one of our free-lance consultants. To my surprise his office was in his home, and the moment I walked through the door I knew working from home as my own boss was the solution I'd been looking for. I decided to go back to school, get a master's degree, and open a private counseling practice in my home.

Two years later I opened my practice and began working from home. At that time Paul was serving as CEO for a research-and-development corporation. His job was challenging to be sure, but he found himself wanting greater freedom to get things done and make things happen. Inside the corporation, everything new took a long time to develop, and met with resistance of one sort or another. He wanted to see his ideas take form quickly.

So as I was beginning my private practice, Paul opened his own political consulting firm in a downtown office. He soon found, however, that he was getting most of his work done at home. He was driving downtown later and later each day just to deliver dictation tapes and sign checks, and so shortly thereafter he moved his office home, too—secretary and all. Says Paul of those times, "I was one of those people who dutifully brought a briefcase home every evening and opened it maybe twice a year, so I didn't trust myself to work from home. I was surprised to find I was getting my most productive work done at home. And best of all, Sarah and I got to see each other every day."

We were amazed at how dramatically our lifestyle improved once we were out on our own. Suddenly we had time for each other, for our son, and even for regular exercise. Our stress-level went down immediately. Simultaneously, however, we realized that in our search for a better life we had unwittingly become *entrepreneurs*—people who, as the dictionary reminds us, have created a commercial endeavor that requires considerable initiative and risk.

We knew, however, that we were not what you think of as classical entrepreneurs, turn-of-the-century capitalists like Henry Ford and John D. Rockefeller. We weren't even like today's high-profile entrepreneurs such as Steven Jobs, Bill Gates, Donald Trump, and Harvey MacKay. We weren't captains of industry seeking to build a financial empire.

Later, in interviewing people for *Working from Home,* we met thousands of others like ourselves who are self-employed but do not fit the classical entrepreneurial profile. Like us, these new entrepreneurs are highly motivated to be their own boss. They have good ideas and valuable skills and talents, and are willing to work hard. But they're not prepared to run a business, nor are they particularly interested in running a business.

Today's new entrepreneurs are professionals, artists, and service providers—from accountants to video producers, from computer consultants to public-relations specialists, from caterers to designers and writers, from plumbers to publishers, from word processors to inventors and toymakers. Most of us have wondered at times if we were suited to be on our own. We don't always do well on the many self-scoring quizzes you find in popular books and magazines that tell you whether you're entrepreneurial material. Nonetheless we're making it by the thousands. Personally, we've been self-employed for sixteen years, and we're pleased to say you don't need to be an entrepreneur in the classical sense to survive and thrive on your own.

The New Breed of Entrepreneur

The classical entrepreneur loves the business of business. He or she probably had a lemonade stand and paper route as a child and by high school or college was running one or more sideline businesses to help pay expenses. For this classical entrepreneur, business is like a game; money is the scorecard. Making deals and living with the uncertainty and experimental nature of business are exciting. The classical entrepreneur moves eagerly from venture to venture, loving the business of doing business.

Chances are if you're reading this book you don't fit that profile. Most of the people who are venturing out on their own today don't, either. Instead, you are probably one of the emerging new breed of entrepreneurs who like us are setting out on their own in order to have greater control over their lives, to work on their own terms in their own way. Many of this new breed are women or men who wish to earn enough to have a good standard of living and still be at home to raise their children.

For the new breed of entrepreneurs being in business is more a means to an end than an end in itself. And for this reason we call them *propreneurs*—individuals engaged in business enterprise not for it's own sake, or even for the profits per se, but *for* a purpose beyond the enterprise. Propreneurs want to create a livelihood for themselves that enables them to do more meaningful work, enjoy life more while doing what they know how to do best, and doing it the way they want to do it. They're more interested in doing the work of their business than in running a business.

For example, Chellie Campbell is a classical entrepreneur. She took a job as a bookkeeper and, seeing the potential for bookkeeping services, proceeded within two years to buy out the owners of the business. She wasn't particularly interested in doing bookkeeping herself. In fact, she immediately hired other bookkeepers to do the bookkeeping so she could go out and get more business. Soon she had sales personnel to do that as well so she could spend her time overseeing the business. She plans to expand her company to several locations throughout her local metropolitan area and perhaps someday across the country.

Georgia Graves, on the other hand, is a propreneur. When her daughter was born she didn't want to place her baby in day care and resume commuting each day to the downtown accounting firm where she worked as a bookkeeper. She loves doing bookkeeping, especially helping people manage their money. So she had no intention of giving up her career. In fact, with the new baby she and her husband needed her income more than ever because they had just moved from their rented apartment to a house. Georgia believed her chances for any substantial salary increase on her job were small. Opening a bookkeeping service of her own was a way for Georgia to do what she loves without having to leave her young daughter, and still make more money than she did on salary. "I work when I want, as much as I want, and I love what I do," she says. "I have the best of both worlds."

When she gets more business than she can handle herself, she farms it out to other free-lancers in the area. As soon as possible she plans to hire an administrative assistant to help her manage the business side of her work. "The better known I become for doing a good job for my clients, the higher the fees I can command. And that's the way my business will grow."

Ron Andrews is a classical entrepreneur. He always wanted to run his own business, and after many years as a corporate executive he decided to search the marketplace to identify a good business opportunity. Based on his research, he decided to buy a dry-cleaning company. By hiring the right people, he got his first location running well and decided to open a restaurant. We asked him why he chose dry cleaning and he said, "Why not? The cash flow's great and it's all a game. It doesn't matter to me what the business is as long as it's legal and profitable."

For the propreneur, however, the nature of the business is often the main motivation. For example, Dr. Nancy Bonus teaches people how to lose weight permanently without dieting or exercise. She spreads the word of her work through seminars, audiotapes, a radio program, and speeches. As her business has grown she has hired more people to help her run the business so she can continue to devote her time to teaching her methods.

Ed Crystal is also a propreneur. After thirty years of doing other work, he decided to do what he'd always wanted to do—pursue a career as an artist. He was able to do this after all those years because he and his wife opened a picture-framing business. The flexibility and profits of running this business have provided him with the opportunity and the economic security to begin painting and to open a gallery of his own.

Donald Marrs is a propreneur. Donald was working as the creative director at one of the country's largest advertising agencies when he realized he was writing ads for cigarettes, junk food, gas-guzzling cars, and other products he not only didn't use, but didn't believe in. After considerable soul-searching, he left the agency and opened his own company, working with clients whose products he believes are making a positive contribution to life. He's written about this decision in his book *Executive in Passage.*

Callan Pinckney is also a propreneur. She began teaching classes to show people how to exercise safely, spurred on by her anger at the many exercise programs on the market that she believes can actually hurt people. From this passion have come three best-selling books and three megahit videotapes on her exercise methods.

Kathryn Dager is another propreneur. A manager for a large retail chain, she became disheartened by what she saw as a declining level of customer service. She was encountering an entire generation of young people who, having grown up in a self-serve society, had never actually experienced service. So she opened a customer-service training firm, helping retail stores to recruit and train service-oriented personnel. Her company is growing by leaps and bounds, and she offers her programs nationwide.

Like Nancy, Ed, Donald, Callan, and Kathryn, many of today's new propreneurs would continue doing the type of work they do even if they won the Publishers Sweepstakes. Sometimes they can't imagine ever retiring from their work. They may foresee the themes of their work changing, but the work they do is for life. It's almost like a mission or a calling.

In other cases propreneurs see business as a means to truly excel in the career they love. Mike Greer, an instructional designer, was frustrated by the bureaucratic inefficiencies of the educational-design companies he worked for. He felt like he was getting in only five good hours of work a day; the rest of the day was spent hassling with office politics. He also knew his employers were billing his time out at nine times his hourly rate. He was confident he could do a better job on his own and charge substantially less. And he was right. After creating I.D. Network he tripled his income, although he was charging his clients substantially less. He was still working only five hours a day, but the rest of the day was his own.

Chris Shalby, a marketing consultant, who created Bottom Line Communications, puts it this way: "If you work for a corporation, your idea may never get heard, or will be so watered down by the time you get approval to do it that it's not your idea anymore. My employers' attitudes were that if their PR personnel were really that good, why would they be here?" So now he's not. "In your own business," he says, "you can actually see your ideas come to life."

As you can see from these examples, the classical entrepreneur—the one for whom most business courses and books are written—wants to work *on* the business; the propreneur wants to work *in* the business. Which are you? Take the simple quiz on the following page and find out.

One of the best tests of whether you're an entrepreneur or a propreneur at heart comes at the time when your business grows to the point where you must decide whether to expand or consolidate. For example, as Howard Shenson grew increasingly successful with his seminars and books on how to become a consultant, he moved his office away from his home and began adding staff and acquiring more and more office space. A true entrepreneur would be riding high on such growth; each expansion would be more invigorating. But for Howard, the larger he grew, the less rewarding his work became. By the time he reached nine employees, he told us, "I found I was spending my time managing and not creating. And that wasn't enjoyable to me." He decided to pull back on the growth of his business and returned to being essentially a sole practitioner. His business continues to prosper, and he's much happier.

Propreneurs often respond to growth in this way. They like success, but they don't want hassles and complications. They don't like the pressures of management and weighty payroll responsibilities. They like making money, but once they're making enough to lead a comfortable life, enjoying their work and their life is more important than acquiring more money.

Patricia Lineman felt that way. Eight years ago she lost her job when the company she was working for closed down. Having worked her way to the top in that company, she didn't think another company would give her the same authority, money, and responsibility she had grown accustomed to, so

---

Are You an Entrepreneur or a Propreneur?

Circle the choice that best describes you.

1. a. I always wanted to run my own business.
   b. I never actually wanted to run a business, but I want to be on my own.
2. a. I set up lots of little businesses to earn money when I was young.
   b. As a young person, I had an allowance or took various jobs.
3. In going out on my own,
   a. Any business venture would be just as good as another so long as it was legal and profitable.
   b. I would only start a business that involves something I like doing and find meaningful.
4. My primary work identity is:
   a. A businessperson.
   b. Someone who does the type of work I do (for example, an artist, accountant, typist, doctor, consultant, editor and so on).
5. If I could hire someone to help me with my business, the first person I would hire would be:
   a. Someone to help me provide the product or service itself so I could spend more time developing the business.
   b. Someone to help me run the business so I would spend more time providing my product or service.

The more a's you chose, the more like a classical entrepreneur you are. If you chose more b's, you're more like a propreneur.

---

she decided she would have a better chance on her own. She found a need and filled it. She founded Patricia Lineman and Associates, consulting with apparel-manufacturing firms on negotiating collections. Within the first month she had five clients, and her business grew rapidly from there.

Soon she had gone from running a one-person home business to managing a ten-employee office. Although she says she had to try growing a big company, now she's back to working by herself from home. "This is where I make the most money and this is where I'm happiest," she told us. "I also serve my clients better. I can say that unequivocally, and they feel that way, too. I serve fewer, but I serve them better.

Eleanor Dugan, a market researcher, also feels this way. She says, "I tried to expand to accept all the jobs that were coming my way, but now I'm going back to being a one-person business. I found out I was the product. My goals for the company have narrowed, shifting to quality of life. Maybe I won't earn $600,000 this year; but if I earn a third of that, I'm still in a good spot."

Howard, Patricia, and Eleanor are proof that you can succeed gloriously on your own without becoming a slave to your business. If you're like most propreneurs, chances are you went into business so you could take charge of your life and you want to keep it that way. Fortunately you can. You don't have to choose between being on your own and having a life of your own. But you will need to take a different approach to earning a living than you would as either an employee or a traditional business.

Propreneuring Requires a Different Approach

Since a propreneur is more interested in and better prepared for working *in* the business than *on* it, some aspects of doing business that the classical entrepreneur finds exciting and enjoyable can be uncomfortable and even intimidating for today's propreneur. Notable among these are selling, negotiating a deal, projecting profits and losses, managing cash flow, financial planning, and marketing. Yet without these functions there is no work. So the propreneur is faced wth learning as much about running a business as he or she can. Unfortunately, however, much of the available information about becoming your own boss is geared to classical entrepreneurs; it advocates that you get even more involved in the business side of doing business.

Ellie Kahn, who created Living Legacies, found herself in this position. She doesn't really enjoy the business side of her work. She's on her own because she wants to use her talents to write and produce biographies and video documentaries, and she knows that no one will employ her to do that. So she's struggling to learn how to handle the business aspects in order to keep her dream alive.

Another case in point is a man who came to us for a consultation. An excellent management trainer, he had become frustrated with having to spend 50 to 60 percent of his time on the job dealing with administrative trivia and office politics. He wanted to spend his time training and making a positive difference in people's lives. After much inner conflict, he decided to leave his job to establish a training and consulting firm of his own. One year later, however, he was despondent. He was having to spend 50 to 60 percent of every week finding, negotiating, and administrating opportunities to do a day or two of training here and there. He never had enough business and was on the verge of giving up the idea of being on his own and taking another job.

To make matters worse, the business books and courses he turned to for help focused on how he could master the intricacies and complexities of marketing, negotiating, and other business strategies so he could grow into an even larger, more profitable business. For him, however, learning and implementing these strategies just meant more time away from doing what he wanted to do—management training.

What he needed, like most propreneurs, was not more business textbooks, but practical ways to streamline the business-side of self-employment so he could profitably pursue his work. Fortunately, with growing numbers of propreneurs venturing out on their own, we're evolving such streamlined approaches—ways of taking care of business so there's plenty of time to do what you do best.

In short, propreneuring involves leaving behind both the payroll mentality and the classical approach to doing business. It means operating with a new approach. While most good employees have learned to operate effectively within a system of rules, most entrepreneurial profiles suggest that successful entrepreneurs traditionally had a propensity to operate outside the rules—to be mavericks. They identify themselves as having rebelled against the rules even as children, taking delight in standing out as different from the crowd. Frequently they did poorly in school and ran into conflicts on the job. One middle-aged entrepreneur, for example, told us she'd held only one job in her life, and it lasted eighteen months. She couldn't get to work on time.

At a recent seminar for classical entrepreneurs, the instructor asked members of the group to raise their hands if they'd made poor grades in school, gotten lots of traffic tickets over their lifetimes, or had a history of business failures. Most of the people in the room raised their hands on each point.

If this describes you, you may actually be having an easier time adjusting to being on your own than your propreneurial counterparts, because you've been operating outside the paycheck mentality all along. Your chore will be to learn how to master the self-discipline that's required to pursue your goals and satisfy your customers. This could be a challenge because up to this point it's something no one else has been able to get you to do.

Today's new entrepreneurs, the propreneurs, however, don't meet that maverick profile. They usually did their best in school and have been good employees. Sometimes they were even the cream of the crop, the people who made the honor role or became employee of the month. Many get as near to the top as they can before hitting a plateau. They go out on their own to achieve even more. Today's propreneurs are highly achievement oriented and strive for excellence in their work.

If this describes you, you are actually well prepared to excel in serving your clients and customers. Your challenge will be in learning to break out of the limitations of payroll thinking so you can survive in the creative, free-form world of self-employment. Rest assured you will not need to develop a devil-may-care attitude, nor will you need to start getting speeding tickets. But it's a world without fixed rules, a world in which very little comes to those who wait and where quality and performance are a given, not a determiner of success. Once you become familiar with its nuances, however, you'll find it to be a world of unlimited possibilities, with no plateaus, dead ends, or glass ceilings, a world you can shape to your liking.

CHAPTER
TWO

■ ■

Thinking Like Today's Successful Propreneurs

*It often happens that I wake at night and
begin to think about a serious problem and
decide I must tell the Pope about it. Then I
wake up completely and remember that I
am the Pope.*

POPE JOHN XXIII

Have you ever noticed how eagerly we
seek the thrill of the new and the novel while tenaciously clinging to the
familiar. We seek freedom. We want to be in charge. Like a small child who
begs to take the wheel of the family car, we yearn to be in the driver's seat.
And the moment we go out on our own, we've done it. We're behind the
wheel. But are we in command, or will we career wildly into oblivion?

That's the fear most people have when they say good-bye to the security of
a paycheck. Often we feel little more prepared to assume full responsibility for
our destinies than a small child would be to take the wheel of a moving car.
All the thousands of self-employed individuals we've talked with found being
on their own to be filled with surprises—some big, some little; some delightful, others dreadful. Confronted with such unfamiliar circumstances, most
people try to turn the novel into the known so it's only natural for us to want
to operate from the paycheck mentality, which has been so familiar to us for
so long.

Once we have the chance to be on our own, we try very hard to run our
lives in much the same way we did when we were on the job. But that's like

trying to drive a car from the passenger's seat. From over there it looks easy, its hard to imagine all the complications that can arise once you take the road.

I know I, Sarah, certainly experienced this. When I went out on my own I was at once confident and uncertain. I boldly declared what I was going to do. I read everything I could, talked to everyone I knew, took several classes. I was sure of myself . . . until things didn't go according to plan. I'd been told to develop a business plan. This plan was my security. It showed me exactly how many clients I would need each week and told me exactly how much I needed to charge per hour. I established my business name, obtained my business license, set up my bank account, printed my cards and letterhead, and even prepared my first brochure. I had been told how to announce the opening of my practice, and I followed the guidance I'd received and my plan to the letter.

Then I waited for the phone to ring. It didn't. The only business call I got those first two weeks was a wrong number. That was when I realized there was more to this than anyone had mentioned. The next few years were not pleasant ones. The shift from having a position of influence where I wielded the power and authority of the federal government to being a sole practitioner on my own was a jolt. I went from feeling powerful to feeling powerless. The logical and dependable world I knew had given way. I was no longer being controlled, but I was not yet in control.

Not everyone faces such a crisis of expectations so immediately. But once we leave the familiar world of having a job, at some point we are usually confronted with having to make an adjustment in how we approach earning a living. For Charles Cannon the crisis came after what looked like a great start. Charles's medical-billing business took off quickly. He was a stunning success within a year. He, too, did everything he was told. He, too, thought he had done it right. Then his major client suddenly decided to go elsewhere. He came close to bankruptcy.

William Sayer's computer-consulting business took off right away, too. He had two major clients lined up even before he left his job. He, too, thought he'd done it right, so much so that he took out a handsome profit the end of his first year and went on a long-earned vacation. When he returned, however, he discovered that in having completed his major projects, he was out of work. It took him over three months to secure his next project.

These setbacks were unnecessarily devastating to the three of us, and probably occurred in the first place only because we were each still viewing the world from a *paycheck mentality*. We expected life to work the way it had when we were employed. We thought if we followed directions carefully, we would succeed. But sooner or later, operating from a paycheck mentality makes being self-employed a confusing, frightening, and pressure-filled experience. And business decisions based on fear and doubt made under the pressure of imminent failure only make matters worse.

Fortunately, when things got bad enough each of us finally concluded we had to approach earning a living on our own in a fundamentally different way. The challenges we faced had pushed us, so to speak, into a new reality. And when viewed from this new profit-oriented perspective, what had been confusing became clear, what had been dreaded became welcome, and what had seemed impossible became manageable.

We each were able to emerge, like a champion, with a new ability to take whatever came along in stride, to apply it to our advantage, and to make the difficult look easy. We were no longer employees trying to be on our own. We had made the mental shift you see reflected in the champion's face, gait, and demeanor. We had shifted permanently from a *paycheck* to a *profit* mentality, and we were empowered.

If you doggedly continue pursuing your goals you, too, will make the inevitable mental shifts from living on a paycheck to living on your profits. Whatever painful lessons you learn will make you stronger, as they did us. But you can avoid many of the most painful adjustments. You can begin right now to think like the people who work successfully for themselves. By making the following twelve mental shifts, you can begin today to ease your transition from payroll to profit.

Twelve Mental Shifts from Paycheck Thinking to Profit Thinking

1. The Odds Are Changing in Your Favor: Shifting From Pipe Dreams to Practicalities.
2. Ambiguity Means Opportunity: Shifting from Certainties to Possibilities.
3. Security Lies Within: Shifting from Waiting for a Break to Making Your Breaks.
4. Success Is an Experiment: Shifting from Following Rules to Following Results.
5. Being Good Is Not Enough: Shifting from Mastery to Marketing.
6. Failure Is a Stepping-Stone: Shifting from Dreading Mistakes to Building on Them.
7. Excess Is Essential: Shifting from Playing It Safe to Keeping Your Options Open.
8. It Gets Better and Better: Shifting from Boundaries to Breakthroughs.
9. Money Is a Multiplier: Shifting from Earning-to-Spend to Spending-to-Earn.
10. The Only Authority You Have Is What You Can Command: Shifting from Position Power to Personal Power.
11. Success Is a Joint Venture: Shifting from Help Me! to How Can I Help?
12. You Can't Afford the Luxury of Bad Morale: Shifting from Employee to Coach, Colleague, and Cheerleader.

---

that 10 percent of all work done in the United States is done at home. And these numbers are growing at a rate of over 20 percent a year! Even the number of people earning a living on their own in the arts is growing. The futurist John Naisbitt forecasts that independent artists—actors, directors, authors, dancers, choreographers, designers, musicians, composers, painters, photographers, and so on—will become one of the nation's megatrends.

And while the number of people going out on their own is going up, according to the Small Business Administration the rate of small-business failure is going down. In the mid 1980s, when we began teaching courses on starting a business, the statistics were not particularly encouraging. Four out of five small businesses were gone within the first five years. The most recent figures published by the SBA, however, show that number has dropped by 25 percent. A more recent study by American Express and the National Federation of Independent Business is even more encouraging. They surveyed about three thousand new businesses and found that 70 percent succeeded.

We think that an even higher success rate is inevitable. As major changes in our society line up to support those who venture out on their own and as more people learn how to do it successfully, increasing numbers of ventures will survive and thrive. In fact, we think it's time at least as far as self-employment is concerned, for what has been called the business *failure rate* to be called the business *success rate.*

You Have Profit Potential

In the industrial age, money was the most important resource needed to succeed in a business of your own. Large amounts of money were required to set up and operate large facilities and meet large payrolls. A business might have to operate for years before the owner made a return on the investment needed just to open the doors that first day.

In this information age, however, you are your most important resource. You are selling your time, your skills, your knowledge. You can open your doors to do business each day with little or no added costs. By working from your home you can keep your costs down to little more than your basic living expenses. Like so many self-employed individuals we meet, with the right know-how you can turn a profit quickly and more easily than your larger competition. And because you are working alone on your own, or with a small number of employees, you have the flexibility to respond quickly to fluctuations in your market and redirect your efforts in more profitable directions when needed.

As an employee, every hour you work, you're earning money for someone else. You are an expense. Obviously every employer wants to keep expenses down. That means keeping your salary down. The day you went out on your own, however, you instantly became an asset—the principal asset of your business. As long as you keep your costs down, everything else you earn is yours to keep and there is no arbitrary ceiling. The sky is the limit. You are

1. The Odds Have Changed in Your Favor: Shifting from Pipe Dreams to Practicalities

We were wild with joy because tomorrow we would leave the known world behind. What a wonderful feeling . . . to be able to decide your own life and destiny, obeying without limitations your own mysterious calls, and dreams and passions.

DOUCHAN GERSI

In the past, aspiring to go it on your own wasn't usually considered to be economically viable. As recently as twenty years ago, most people were forced by financial realities to forgo any ideas of pursuing their own business. The practical concerns of supporting themselves and their families dictated that they go to work for someone else, doing something that was more "realistic." Only a very few very talented, very determined, well-placed individuals could make it on their own.

But times have changed. Now the practical concerns of supporting ourselves and our families are shifting. Economic, technological, and cultural forces are converging not only to support and encourage you to take your economic future into your own hands, but in some cases to demand that you rise to the challenge to get out on your own and assert your independence by doing something you're good at and care passionately about. So in deciding to venture out on your own, you are no longer going against the tide. You are riding on the forefront of an entrepreneurial wave of unprecedented proportions.

The Force Is With You

To borrow a famous line from the classic movie *Star Wars,* the force is with you now as you set out on your own. What we're doing today will be commonplace in the future. As many as half of all individuals will be self-employed. So although you are on your own, you are not alone in your endeavors. You are taking part in epochal changes that are altering forever the way we live and work. You are in the right place at the right time, and you're better positioned to succeed as your own boss today than at any other time in history.

Self-employment began to rise in the 1970s and has taken a sharp turn upward since 1987. Today a new business begins every twenty-four seconds. An estimated 1,600 new home-based businesses start every day. At that rate, a new home business began somewhere in America just since you started reading this chapter!

According to the research firm BIS CAP International, 16 million people are making it on their own from home. In fact, the *Wall Street Journal* reported limited only by your own time, energy, creativity, know-how, and willingness to do what it takes. Properly positioned, you can certainly make more than you would ever be able to make as an employee doing the same work.

Eleanor Duggan is a good example of what's possible. She was making $32,000 working for a market-research firm. When she asked for a raise, the president told her she was making enough money for a woman her age. At the suggestion of her accountant, she decided to go out on her own. From her very first year, she was working to her full capacity. Seven years later she was making $700,000 a year.

Even two generations ago, success was highly dependent upon such factors as where you went to school and who your parents were. Most of what you knew was learned either at home or in school. Whatever you got there usually set the course for what you could achieve over the remainder of your life. Today, however, virtually anything you need to know in order to do virtually anything you want to undertake is available to you through an ever-growing wealth of books, tapes, workshops, seminars, public education programs, consultants, and training programs. And all this information is available anytime you need it.

So should discouraging events cloud your perspective at times, should you begin to wonder if you can make it, remember you are no longer pursuing pipe dreams. The tide is turning. Instead of pushing against you, it is carrying you forward. Today making it on your own is a practical and possible reality.

2. Ambiguity Means Opportunity: Shifting from Certainties to Possibilities

The best way to predict the future is to invent it.

ALAN KAY

When you're an employee you *receive* a paycheck. As long as you show up and do what you're told, it *arrives* automatically. It's a certainty you come to rely upon. But when you're on your own your profit is *created,* not received. On your own, nothing arrives except the bills. You have to create any money you receive. You don't even get a chance to work unless you generate the opportunity to do so. But as we said, the possibilities for what you can generate are unlimited.

This shift from the certainty of a paycheck to the ambiguity of the opportunities for possible profits is probably the most difficult mental shift people have to make when venturing out on their own. It stops more people from following their dreams and sends more people back to a job than any other aspect of being on your own. After all, receiving a paycheck is a culturally ingrained symbol of security; the entire nation trembles when our major corporations undergo layoffs. A shiver goes down the spine of the entire community when a major employer relocates. Perhaps, other than the fear of death, there is no greater fear than that of losing one's paycheck. Yet to enjoy being out on your own, you must cast off this deep-seated fear and replace it with anticipation of all the possibilities of self-generated gain. Making the following shift in perspective can help you do this.

Security Is an Illusion

Increasing numbers of people who have been merged, purged, laid off, and otherwise downsized are beginning to realize that a paycheck no longer necessarily provides security. When translator Jim Waldron started out on his own he realized that when you're employed, your fate is in the hands of one person—your boss. He told us, "A decision by one person can put you on the street. But in your own business, every one of your customers has to fire you before you're out of business." This one shift in the way he thought about his work gave him the sense of security he needed to make friends with the ambiguity of being on his own.

Karen Rubin had held more than 120 jobs during her thirty-five years, but she had never been fired for poor performance. She decided that working for herself couldn't possibly be any less secure than her own job history. She created Organizers Extraordinaire and helps her clients organize their lives and offices. She has been in business three years now, making over $40,000 a year.

As Jim, Karen, and thousands of others are finding, perhaps the sense of security we feel with a paycheck is more illusion than reality, more historical than actual.

Ambiguity Is Our Only Hope

On the other hand, consider this. Ambiguity—the sense of not knowing what lies ahead—is actually the only context in which we can create a future different from our past. When everything is certain, there can be only what has been. But ambiguity by definition means that anything is possible.

A beleaguered but undaunted actor once wrote a telling dramatic scene that captures the sense of hope and anticipation many feel in deciding to choose the ambiguity of making it on their own. In this scene, a young actor is living in near poverty, waiting tables and going out for auditions every day, trying to break into show business. His brother drops by to invite him to a family gathering. The brother, who drives up in a Mercedes and is dressed in expensive clothes, begins chiding the actor for living such a meager existence. "Why don't you stop all this and come work with me at the used-car lot?" he asks. "How can you live like this?" The actor replies, "Look, things may not be so great for me right now, but I know that any day can be my big break and all this will change."

Few people who work a job can say that. On a job, you pretty much know what the next day will be like, and the next day, and the day after that. Years after leaving your job, you could go back to visit your former employer—as I, Sarah, did—and feel like you walked back into a time warp. Everything was exactly the same. Although it was five years later, it was as if I had just walked out of a staff meeting for a brief break. The same people were in the same kind of meeting talking about the same kind of issues.

On your own, if you keep working toward your goals, you always have the possibility of creating a new future, one that is more satisfying and rewarding than the present. Chellie Campbell, head of Cameron Diversified Management, puts it this way: "When you're out on your own, you're making stuff up. Nothing happens unless you create it."

And isn't that what we really want, the opportunity to create what we desire? So often that's at least part of why we go out on our own in the first place. Being on your own is the ultimate act of creativity. As Chellie says, "I was an actress, a singer, and a dancer before I started my business, and I've never had to be so creative in my life as in running my business. It has called upon every ounce of creativity I possess. Every day I know I can create the day the way I want it. I am totally the master of my own fate. I can look at the success I've created and say, 'I did that!'"

Many self-employed individuals talk about the surprising sense of control that comes from knowing that you can use your raw talents, ideas, and concepts to create a product or service or experience that others find so valuable that you can support yourself comfortably.

Being on Your Own Is Perhaps the Ultimate Security

There's nothing more rewarding or more empowering than knowing that you can support yourself by creating something valuable from nothing. Miss America of 1985, Debra Sue Maffit, captured the sense of power that making it on your own can provide when she told us, "If I lost everything today I wouldn't be afraid, because, having [been successful] once, I know I could do it again."

But when you look at the calendar and don't see any appointments for the next month, or you see the balance of your checkbook dropping and there are no checks in the mail, or you notice that the phone hasn't rung all day—that's when the ambiguity of being on your own can be disconcerting. But it's only so if you're looking at these events from the old paycheck mentality, which says you have to know in advance exactly how much is coming in when.

When we first began working on our own, I, Sarah, remember how I would look at my appointment calendar and see all the blank spaces for the next week and a sense of terror would strike me. How were we going to make it through the month? This sense of terror lived in the corners of my mind for years. Sometimes it would become almost paralyzing. But I kept doing everything I knew how to do to build my practice. Finally, I realized that I had been looking ahead at blank weeks for years. Yet when each week arrived I had clients. Week after week, month after month, year after year, I was still in business. I decided it was time to relax and trust in myself and my business. The uncertainty I saw through the eyes of paycheck thinking was an illusion.

Michael Russo, an accountant, had to summon all the courage he could muster to take the step out on his own. He had already lined up business before he left his job, but would it work out? He said about the transition, "You are always breaking through your comfort zones, and there's always a piece of you that wants to stop. But you have to push through the comfort zone. You have to keep jumping and taking the risks. Each jump has the 'Oh, my God' stage. The more you jump, however, the easier it gets and you realize you can handle anything that occurs." Russo did 240 percent more business in his first year than he projected.

Trust Is a Decision; You Can Put It Where You Want

The decision to trust yourself and your ability to support yourself is exactly that, a decision. As the weeks and months go by, if you refuse to be immobilized by fear and doubt and continue doing everything you know how to do to succeed even though you may be afraid and have many doubts, you will discover *the ultimate security*—the knowledge that you can and will make it on your own. And once you've shifted to knowing that you will profit from continuing a quality effort, ambiguity becomes a comfortable and loyal companion, reassuring you each and every day that anything can happen.

3. Your Security Lies Within: Shifting from Waiting for a Break to Making Your Breaks

> *Destiny is not a matter of chance, it is a matter of choice; it is not a thing to be waited for, it is a thing to be achieved.*
>
> WILLIAM JENNINGS BRYAN

Being able to relax into the ambiguity of not knowing when, or how, or if you will have a profit from your efforts requires finding a new locus for your trust. To the extent that we've learned to trust that a paycheck will arrive, we've learned to look outward for our direction and sense of security. We've come to put our trust in the system, in the powers that be. And, of course, the reverse is true as well. We put the blame on external factors when things go wrong. We find fault in others and expect them to make it right.

Looking outward for our source of direction and support goes back to trusting our parents to protect us—or at least believing that they should protect us. We transfer this expectation to our employers, believing that they should provide for and guide us, that we're entitled to a job and a paycheck or some other source of income.

But making it on your own means leaving that mindset behind forever. Ultimately the power to determine the future of our lives always rests with us. As George Bernard Shaw observed, while people are always blaming circumstance for their lives, "the people who get on in this world are the people who get up and look for the circumstances they want, and, if they can't find them, make them." Nowhere is this more true than when you're working for yourself.

When you're on your own, no one owes you anything, no matter how nice you are or how good you are at what you do. No one is there to rescue you. Whereas a boss might take pity on you, customers won't. People don't buy products or services from a sense of pity or guilt, or even fairness. They buy based on competence and the results they receive. No one is looking to give you a break. Your raise becomes effective when you do.

Succeeding on your own means learning to trust yourself to be able to respond effectively to real needs that people have. It's learning to trust that you will come through for them and for yourself.

There's No One to Blame

In other words, the source of power in your life must shift from an external source to an internal one. One woman told us how she ultimately made this shift: "I didn't go out on my own by choice. I got laid off and couldn't find a job, so I thought, Why not start my own business? But whenever business was slow, I got scared. I wanted to blame someone for it. I wanted to blame the economy, I wanted to blame my competition. I even tried to blame my customers. I felt like they weren't appreciative enough of all the work I was doing or they would send me more business. I felt *so* angry at them that I finally recognized how ridiculous I was being. Of course it wasn't their job to keep me in business. It was my job to make my business work. From that point on, when I got scared I stopped fretting. Instead I'd roll up my sleeves and start working on getting some businesss. After a while I could see how my own efforts paid off and I knew that I was truly the source of my own security."

Developing Your Self-Management Muscle

Once on their own, some people simply try to enforce the rules, habits, and expectations their previous employers had for them. They set up the same rigid hours and demands as were made of them on a job. Sometimes this works. More often than not, however, we tend to rebel against such arbitrary expectations, and without an outside force to keep us in line it becomes necessary instead to learn what we can actually expect of ourselves and plan accordingly. We have to learn to tune in to our own desires, interests, patterns, and preferences and literally manage ourselves. We call this developing your *self-management muscle.* That's the one that's located somewhere between your brain and your bottom.

As the free-lance photographer Charles Berhman found, this shift can actually be freeing. Charles worked full-time as an engineer for fifteen years while he built his business as a photographer. He told us, "Your paycheck is tied to what someone else wants you to do. Your success is being rated by someone who doesn't even know what you can do. On my own, I have the satisfaction of knowing that any progress I make in the business is because of what I do."

Trust Comes from Experience

In essence, making the switch from *being bossed* to *being the boss* forces us to stop dreaming and waiting for what we want, or blaming others for the fact that we don't have it. It forces us to start actively creating and initiating what we want. Haven't most of us been dreaming and waiting for a long time? Hasn't it been a world of *someday it will be great*? Being on your own is your chance to turn someday into today.

But you may say, "How do I know I can count on myself? How do I know I'll come through?" And the answer is that you don't. Like building any other muscle, your self-management muscle takes time to develop. You have to give yourself time to learn how to manage yourself, and you have to believe that ultimately you and yourself will make a great team.

Anytime you find that things are not going as you would have them, consider this not as a time to despair or give up, but as a time to roll up your sleeves and make some magic. And every time you put your trust in yourself to do that, you become just that much more worthy of your own trust. We *learn* to count on ourselves. It doesn't happen automatically.

Parents might think either children are trustworthy or they're not. But that's not the case. Those who become trustworthy are those who are already trusted and called upon to live up to the trust others put in them. If you believe in yourself long enough and lovingly enough, you will become someone you know you can count on.

Succeeding on your own is somewhat like planting a garden. A farmer can dream of a great garden, but it will remain a dream until he or she gets out there and starts the backbreaking work of planting and tilling the soil. And despite all these efforts, for a long time there's no evidence that all the work is paying off. The ground looks as barren as ever. Then one day, green shoots break through the soil. But even then, the farmer cannot lean back and count the money. The tender shoots must be nurtured to maturity. Only later in the season does he or she get to harvest the crop.

So it is with your own ventures. You can't become impatient with either the farmer or the crop. You've got to give yourself and your crop a chance to grow. You've got to stay at it every day.

Give Yourself the Break You've Been Waiting For

On past jobs you may have had lots of leeway to goof off, take off, or knock off. Unless you really messed up, you'd probably still have had your job even if you gave less than 100 percent. With the recent shifts in our economy, however, that may no longer be true even on the job. It certainly isn't true when you're on your own.

Greg Blanchard, a singer and actor, is a great example of how you can, and indeed need to, make your own breaks. When Greg read that the producers of the musical *Les Misérables* were coming to Los Angeles to hold an open call for the upcoming production, he decided to try out even though he'd had very little professional musical experience. And of course he wasn't the only one to respond to the open call. In fact, by the time he got there the line of hopefuls was so long that officials had closed the line, feeling certain they had more prospective talent than they would ever need.

Not willing to leave his future to such happenstance, however, Greg struck up a conversation with the doorman and suggested that he create a backup list just in case there was a need for additional people at the end of the day. The guard agreed, and of course Greg's name was at the top of that list. When by 7:30 that evening everyone in the original line had been seen and there were still roles to fill, the producers turned to that backup list. Greg had his chance to sing for them and ultimately got a leading role.

Debbie Fields of Mrs. Fields' Cookies had to use a similar bit of initiative to get her cookie company off the ground. She was convinced her cookies would be a hit, despite others who bet she would never make it. So you can imagine her horror when halfway through the first day she opened her store no one had even come into the shop. But again she wasn't willing to let fate take it's own course. She loaded up a tray of cookies fresh from the oven and began walking up and down the sidewalk, giving out cookies to everyone she met. Before she knew it a trail of people were following her and the wonderful smell of her cookies back to the shop.

You Make the Magic

We've heard literally hundreds of such stories. After losing his job, the engineer Payne Harrison dug in and wrote an unsolicited novel, *Storming Intrepid*. Although Harrison had never written before, it became a best-seller. The comedian Michael Colyer performed on the street for five years before he won the 1990 *Star Search* Competition. The singer Terry Bradford tried out for *Star Search* five years in a row before he had a chance to appear. He went on to become the 1990 $100,000 Male Vocalist Champion. When Leroy LoPresti left his job as a corporate executive, he had to travel all over the country to find the financial backing he needed to do what he'd always wanted to do—build his own airplanes. But he found the money, and in 1989 the LoPresti

Swiftfury Piper made it to market. He sold over five-hundred planes in the first year! The playwright David Steen got so tired of waiting for someone to see the value of a play he had written that he produced it himself and received immediate critical acclaim.

All these people persevered. They kept putting in the time, doing what it took to do what they wanted to do. You never know how long it will take or which effort will be the one to do the trick, but as the singer Kenny James told us, "success is like a grocery line. If you stay in line long enough your turn will come."

4. Success Is an Experiment: Shifting from Following Rules to Following Results

You have to listen to your heart. Sometimes you'll be right. Sometimes you'll be wrong. You can't be perfect, but you can be and do whatever you want."

HEIDI MILLER OF HEIDI'S FROGEN YOZERT

Having read many business books, taken hundreds of hours of courses and seminars, and listened to a wide variety of audiotapes and consultants, we've discovered that, contrary to what most of these resources claim, there are no fixed rules for succeeding on your own. There is no right way. No one knows *the* answer.

The books, tapes, seminars, and consultants relate many dramatic success stories, but their most notable feature is how dramatically contradictory these stories are. Our own experience in interviewing hundreds of successfully self-employed individuals is equally spiced with glowing contradictory stories. Again and again we find there are many right ways to succeed. And many wrong ways. And the right way for one person is the wrong way for another.

For example, Paul Moreno, the founder of Los Angeles's first radio guide, told us, "Having a solid business plan was one of the keys to our success. We would recommend it as a must for any new business." On the other hand, Hal Schuster, who with his brother Jack founded Pioneer Press, a $5-million-a-year home-based publishing house, told us that one key aspect of his success has been that he's never limited himself by having written a business plan.

Both these entrepreneurs have been successful. Their way works for them. Take almost any aspect of business and you'll find many similar polarities. Some people have told us they were able to make it because they started on a shoestring and didn't waste any money up front. Others say their success was the result of investing everything they had up front, not skimping on anything. Some people tell us direct mail is a fabulous source of business, while others claim it is a waste of time. Some tell us pricing low is the best way to start. Others say the one thing they learned is never to price low. The contradictory advice is so abundant it could be enough to drive you nuts.

Making It on Your Own Is an Experiment

There is no predetermined right way to do it, but the process of *discovering* what works leads to otherwise unimagined success. This one fact is at the heart of every decision and every action you will take, from marketing your business to pricing your product or service. The key word is *experiment*—an act or operation for the purpose of discovering something unknown.

From this perspective, you need not become distressed about the array of conflicting business advice you encounter. Consider it to be a cafeteria of solutions others have found from which you can select various approaches to experiment with yourself. Try one thing and then another; follow your hunches, test, evaluate, and redirect until you find a way that works.

There Is No Right Answer Until You Find It!

In the book *Are You Happy?* the *Today Show* weatherman Willard Scott told Dennis Wholey that he had spent weeks agonizing over why a talk-show pilot he created didn't succeed. He kept asking himself, "What is wrong? What am I doing wrong?" Finally he concluded that the only thing he was doing wrong was trying to figure out why he had failed instead of moving on to something else.

Once you're on your own, you're in that same boat every day. You have to just move on. It can be frustrating to have done everything that you've been told to do and tried everything everyone else you know has done and still not get the results you want. But it just means you need to do something else. Often the solution for you is something no one else has tried. And the only way to find it is to move on.

In moving on and trying another approach . . . and another and another . . . you'll ultimately find the answer. Sometimes years later you can look back and see what went wrong, but that's only because you found what went right.

The Lack of a Clear Path Is Never a Sign to Turn Back

Uncertainty is simply a signal to look with new eyes, to improvise, to double your determination, to find one more possible route. Often the reason you can't see where you're headed is because you haven't gotten to the corner yet. The best thing about the unknown is knowing that anything is possible. Any day could be *the* day. Any call could be *the* call.

In setting out on your own, you're like the pioneers who crossed the western United States in covered wagons. They had learned many things from life in the towns and villages from which they began their journeys. But the challenges of forging raging rivers and crossing barren deserts while avoiding hostile forces who could kill them on sight called on them to develop an entirely different set of skills. And they had to develop these skills quickly. Or they didn't survive. There were no handbooks to teach them what they needed to know. Many of the tools they brought along with them were useless in handling the unexpected obstacles they encountered. Their maps were crude, incomplete, and sometimes inaccurate.

And so it is with making it on your own. How often we or others have put every last dollar into one more promotional campaign, or made one more phone call, or sent out just one more proposal, all the while wondering if doing that was the right decision. Would these investments produce the needed result before the money ran out? Certainly the more you experiment, the more you generate the opportunity for results and the sooner you find out what works.

Succeeding on your own means being willing to let go of the idea that there is a set of rules or procedures you can follow. Because despite efforts by some to make it into a simple orderly process, going out on your own remains an experiment. The rule book, employee manual, and job description must become things of the past. In their place, you'll find the confusion and frustration that are always involved in experimenting. But you'll also have the joy and elation of discovering what combination of efforts will produce the profits that will support you from this point forward.

Confusion Is Normal

No matter how hopeless the search appears, you never need to give up the experiment you've begun, because each renewed effort brings you closer to finding the results you seek. If you feel like you don't know exactly what you're doing, that's normal. If you feel like you don't know which way to go, that's normal. If you are puzzled by the results you get at times, that's normal. That's what it feels like to experiment. It means you don't know. You're seeking to discover.

To make it on our own, we need to shake the expectation that we're supposed to know what we're doing each step of the way. People who fear taking a step until they're certain it's the right one are destined to step only where they've already been. When you're going along a new path with many corners, you never know what lies ahead until you get to the next corner.

As you've undoubtedly already discovered, there is no straight line to success. The path to making it on your own is filled with many twists and turns. But as long as you know where you're headed—that is, as long as you know what you want to accomplish—before long you'll know if you're still on course and can adjust accordingly.

No Results—No Reward

Unlike when you're on a paycheck, you can't just go through the motions. You've always got to be looking at the *results* you're getting and adjusting your behavior accordingly. Usually when you are on someone's payroll, you're not encouraged to experiment. You're supposed to do what you're supposed to do. If it doesn't work, you still get paid. You were just doing what you were told. Not so in venturing out on your own. On your own, you don't get paid until you deliver the results.

When Sarah was a little girl, one of her household jobs was to dry the dishes after dinner. Of course, as a ten-year-old she always had a hundred other things she would rather do. So she'd hurriedly wipe the towel over the dishes exactly as she'd been shown to do. When her father went to put them away, however, he'd say to her, "These dishes aren't dry." She would defiantly respond, "Well, I dried them!" So night after night he would remind her, "Sarah, you haven't dried the dishes until they're dry."

So it is with running your own business. Whatever you're trying to do, you haven't done it until the results are in. You need to experiment until you discover what particular combination of your skills and abilities, at what price, will be valuable to what group of people within the current economic realities.

Let the Results Be Your Guide

Since you can't be certain about your results, since you can't know for sure just what the winning combination will be, all you can do is keep moving in the direction you want to go and keep your eye on your results, trying out and testing first one thing and then another. Ultimately you'll find a combination that produces the desired results for both you and your clients or customers.

The speech coach Sandra McKnight is a good example. She had been advised that telemarketers would be the ideal market for her seminars. So she approached one telemarketing company after another. Yes, she discovered, they could benefit from her services, but their personnel were paid so little that simply replacing them was more cost-effective than training those who needed improvement. This approach simply wasn't getting results. So she tried another and another and finally found one that worked—helping people with foreign accents communicate more clearly.

Ellie Kahn had a similar experience. Initially she planned to do audio and video biographies with the elderly. Although families were enthusiastic about her service, too often they couldn't afford to hire her. Again, she just wasn't getting the results she needed. So she began to consider alternatives, trying first one thing and then another until she decided to focus on producing institutional biographies. Sure enough, that worked.

We're not saying you shouldn't plan. There's nothing wrong with having a plan. But first you must have a clear outcome. Your outcome serves as your compass. As the home-based publisher Hal Schuster told us, "I have a clear idea of where I want to go with my business and some ideas about how I'm going to get there. But I can't pin down exactly how I'll do it because the variables are always changing and I have to be flexible enough to respond."

A plan is simply one possible route for getting from where you are to where you want to be. It's only as good as the results it produces. So never think you need to stick to a plan if it isn't working. Try out the approaches and methods others have tried, but realize that you're experimenting. When one approach doesn't work, you haven't failed; you're just one step closer to knowing what will work.

Why do you think people who buy a franchise have a higher success rate than people who start up a new venture of their own? It's because the franchiser has found a formula that works. That's what the franchiser is selling—a successful formula. Perhaps when you find yours, you can franchise, too!

5. Being Good Is Not Enough: Shifting from Mastery to Marketing

Customers are your only source of funding.

TIM MULLEN, CATALOG PUBLISHER

Having enough people to buy what you have to offer week after week, month after month, and year after year is the only *essential* element for making it on your own. And the one magic word that can put you in charge of having all the work you need is *marketing. Marketing* refers to all the activities involved in making sure the people who need what you have to offer know about you and are motivated to choose to work with you.

It's an unfamiliar concept to most salaried individuals. Frankly I, Sarah, admit I didn't know what marketing meant when I went out on my own. On the job, doing a good job is what matters most. But on your own, while doing a good job is vital, unless people know what a good job you can do, you don't get the job.

But that does not mean that you have to develop a sales personality or learn how to hype yourself and your work. Quite the contrary. We find that many successfully self-employed individuals not only don't have a sales personality, but have little or no sales experience and may not even like selling in the way we commonly think of it. What they do have, though, is what we call a *marketing mindset.* They're eager and excited about finding ways to let others know about what they do and how they can help, serve, improve, or make life better for those they work with.

In other words, they think about what they're doing from the viewpoint of the people who need it. A marketing mindset means that you focus not only on making sure you have a quality product or service but also on how what you offer is unique, what benefits it provides, and how you can spread the word about these benefits to those who need them.

You Have to Toot Your Horn

In her book *Skills for Success* Adele Scheele writes about two kinds of people: *sustainers* and *achievers. Sustainers* are the people who do a good job and hope someone will notice. They tend to complain a lot about being passed over for promotions and other opportunities in favor of people who don't do as good a job as they do. *Achievers* do a good job, too, but they make sure people know about it. They call attention to their work because they believe they can make an important contribution. Adele claims that most people are sustainers. And that's not surprising. It's an integral part of the paycheck mentality we've grown up with. We learn not to brag, not to toot our own horn, not to call attention to ourselves. Our work is supposed to stand on it's own.

To make it on your own, however, as W. S. Gilbert of Gilbert and Sullivan said, you've got to "blow your own trumpet or, trust me, you haven't a chance!" You have to brag; you have to call attention to yourself, or at least to your product or service. No matter how good you are, if you don't market yourself, so few people will know about your work that it *will* stand on its own—alone. And what a waste! Here you are with all your talents, abilities, education, and experience. And there's a world of people and companies that need what you can do. You owe it to yourself and to the world around you to make sure people know what you can do to improve their lives and make a better world. That's what marketing will do for you.

And while marketing yourself does not mean you have to use a lot of hype or become a slick sales personality, it does mean you have to develop a high profile, and do it in a particular way.

Toot about What You Can Do, Not Who You Are

When people with a paycheck mentality attempt to promote themselves, they usually think *résumé* and talk about their credentials. They're used to having to prove to the powers that be that they have earned the proper credentials to be competent at what they do. When they go out on their own, they attempt to use this same approach to market their products and services. And then they wonder why others with less experience and less quality somehow manage to get more business.

Here's why. Once you're on your own, people are much more interested in what you can do for them than in the details of how and why you can do it. Just look at the descriptions on the following page and see which appeal most to you.

Mastery Mindset	*Marketing Mindset*
1. I'm a board-certified gynecologist. I studied at Yale University and did my internship at Cedars-Sinai. Now I'm in private practice in Beverly Hills.	1. I work with women who are suffering from severe PMS. I've found several medical approaches that can actually help them become symptom free. I'm a gynecologist.
2. I am a graphic artist. I work in all media. I can do line drawings, airbrush, computer-aided design, color separations, and advertising mechanicals.	2. I help small businesses make a Fortune 500 impression on a limited budget. I design brochures, flyers, logos, cards, and stationery that look expensive but aren't.
3. My company is Laser New. We restore laser-printer cartridges using a new patented process that seals in toner using an air-pressure system developed in Europe by a leading physicist.	3. Our company takes your used laser-printer cartridges and makes them as good as new within twenty-four hours for almost half the price of buying a new one. Our company is called Laser New.

As you can see, developing a marketing mindset is simply a matter of shifting your focus from *how* you do what you do to the *benefits* of what you do. Here are six key steps you can take today to make that shift:

1. Describe in fifteen words or less what you do and what makes it unique or special.
2. Identify who specifically needs what you offer. Make a list of several groups of individuals or types of companies.
3. Write down ten ways these people or companies will be better off as a result of what you do.
4. Make a list of ten ways you could let these people know about these benefits.
5. Read, look, and listen every day for any clue that someone needs any of the benefits you offer and follow-up on any sign of potential interest.
6. Read, look, and listen every day for any opportunity to let people or companies know about the benefits of what you offer.

Coleen Springer used a process similar to this when she decided to begin selling her artwork. Coleen works in soft pastels, and her pieces are very calming. The goal of her art is to bring a sense of peace and harmony to those who view it. So she asked herself, "Who especially needs the kind of work I do? What can I do for them? How can I let them know about my art?" Here's her list:

Who?	Benefits	How to Reach Them
Drug rehab centers	Calms and relaxes	Send mailing offering
Prisons	people	free trial exhibit
Tax offices	Creates a more	Speak to trade assoc.
Dental offices	pleasant atmosphere	on effects of art
Hospitals	Makes the office more	Donate an exhibit and
Therapists' offices	attractive	get press coverage
Pain centers	Can be customized to	Offer sales reps who
Doctors' offices	existing decor	call on these people
Beauty salons	Sends message that you	a referral fee
Legal offices	care how people feel	

Coleen was particularly intrigued with the idea of placing her art in dental offices, so she started with that market. She joined the local chamber of commerce and met several dentists. From them she learned that the local dental college was sponsoring a symposium on dental phobias. Her next step was to contact the person planning the symposium and offer to do a presentation on the use of art to reduce anxiety. She also offered to provide an exhibit of her art at the registration table.

At the symposium she met several dentists who were interested in her work, and followed up to offer them a trial exhibit. She also overheard someone talking about a chronic-pain center that was opening soon. She contacted the developer and offered to volunteer to work with the designer. Ultimately she was commissioned to do the art for the center. She also realized that perhaps she could help the designer get business with other health centers, and they soon agreed to refer business to one another.

Most of the other artists Coleen meets do not have a marketing mindset. They are amazed at how well she does. Most are still working at low-paying day jobs, creating their art in the wee hours of the night and trying to get a gallery exhibit. Very few people ever see their work. Some, however, seeing Coleen's success, are starting to think about who specifically would benefit from their work. They're beginning to shift to a marketing mindset.

For more information about marketing your business, see "The Critical Mass Marketing Alternative to Having to Constantly Sell Yourself" in chapter 4 and "Diagnosing What You Need to Do to Get More Business" in chapter 7.

6. Failure Is a Stepping-Stone:
Shifting from Dreading Mistakes to Building on Them

The way to succeed is to double your failure rate.

THOMAS WATSON, FOUNDER OF IBM

Remember when you were a little kid and you tried to cover up your mistakes so your parents and teachers wouldn't see them? Remember the little white lies you told so you wouldn't get caught for doing something you shouldn't have done? Most of us just love to hide our mistakes, and we love to hide from our mistakes.

Looking good and covering up mistakes becomes a habit many of those around us may conspire to help us maintain. Parents, teachers, and bosses hate mistakes, so they may look the other way. Our paycheck mentality reinforces this habit. It says you've always got to look good. You're supposed to have the right answers and do the right thing. Most people believe that's what they were hired for. They fear they'll get in trouble or even lose their jobs if they make a mistake. So they do whatever they can to cover up and play down their mistakes.

On your own, however, covering up your mistakes can get you into a lot more trouble than making them. While results are your guide, mistakes are your best friend. Mistakes are the only way you know you're off course, before it's too late. It's been reported that the way NASA mission control keeps its rockets on course as they travel through outer space is by noticing when they're off course. So it is when you're on your own: there's nothing wrong with being wrong unless you ignore it or stick to it. Mistakes simply tell you when you need to correct your course.

There's Nothing Wrong with You

After hearing us talk about this needed mental shift, a guidance counselor came up to tell us, "I wish someone had told me about the value of making mistakes when I first went out on my own. I know I'm good at what I do, but even though I've been doing everything I thought you're supposed to do as a free-lancer, it's just not working. I've been thinking there must be something wrong with me. I guess the only thing wrong is that I haven't been trying other ways to do it." He was quite relieved.

A husband and wife we'll call Jean and Shaun were not so fortunate. They started a business providing referrals to all types of independent maintenance personnel like carpenters, plumbers, rug cleaners, and so on. After considerable investigation and advice from several consultants on how to structure their business, they wrote a detailed business plan based on charging each free-lancer a moderate fee to be listed with the service and charging the person who called to get a referral a small fee as well. On paper it looked very profitable. Their advisers suggested they follow this plan for at least the first year.

They had no difficulty getting maintenance personnel to sign up and pay the fee, but most of the people calling for the service didn't want to pay for a referral. This became apparent within the first few weeks of doing business. But to restructure their business plan would have required a major hike in their listing fee. That would have involved changing all their promotional materials and telling everyone they'd already contacted about the new policy.

They didn't want to admit they'd made a serious and costly mistake. So they tried to keep up a front and look good—and didn't make it through the first year.

Success Is More Important Than Being Right

It's difficult to admit you're wrong, especially if you think it means you are less of a person or that you're a failure. But ask yourself this: would you rather be right or rich? Once you get on your own you need to develop an entirely new relationship with the idea of failure.

In past generations, people tended to think that if they failed in business, that was it. They often didn't try again. Today we've discovered that the most successful people have also made the most mistakes. In her study of the lives of successful people, for example, Adele Scheele the author of the book *Skills for Success,* observed that mistakes and even failures are characteristic of successful people. Many successful people, like the motivational speaker and author of *Dare to Win,* Mark Victor Hanson, claim that their biggest failure was the turning point for their ultimate success. Academy-Award-winning actor and director Kevin Costner claims, "I've always gotten fueled by my disasters." Thomas Edison had five-thousand failures before getting a working light bulb. That's one failure a day for over thirteen years! In this sense, it appears that failure is a prerequisite for success.

So whenever you make a mistake or suffer a setback that you're tempted to view as a failure, *make yourself* look at it in terms of how it can be a springboard to your success. Make a list of the benefits you can and will get from this experience. Of course, at first you won't feel like doing this because we have been conditioned since kindergarten to dread the thought of failure. When we were growing up it was called flunking. But to succeed, you can't let failure stop you. The only way you can flunk now is if you quit at something you still want to do. You need to think of failure as a friend that's showing you the way to success.

As the highly successful private-practice consultant Gene Call puts it, "I view what I do as practice. I'm always looking for a way to make it better. If I send out a mailing and it doesn't get a response, it's not a failure; it's a challenge to my creativity."

Make Your Mistakes Where They Won't Hurt

Since mistakes are inevitable, especially in the beginning, get the bugs out of your operation by doing trial runs. Then you can actually enjoy making mistakes, because you'll be able to find and correct them before they can do you any damage. For example, don't try out a new speech on a group that could make or break you. Volunteer to do it for a supportive group of friends or an appreciative community group.

Experience makes you effective, and experience is built on a history of

What to Do When You Make a Mistake

Do's	*Don'ts*
☐ Compliment yourself for your courage and ingenuity in trying what you did.	☐ Dismiss it as unimportant, unchangeable, or something you can't handle.
☐ Remain confident in your ability to excel.	☐ Berate yourself.
☐ Resolve not to repeat the same mistake.	☐ Blame anyone: yourself, someone else, or something else.
☐ Take responsibility for what you did. There's always another chance.	☐ Try to ignore or overlook it.
☐ Do any necessary damage control.	☐ Decide to give up.
☐ Do what you can to make it right.	☐ Expect sympathy.
☐ Apologize if others were involved.	☐ Make excuses.
☐ Learn everything you can from it.	☐ Repeat the same error.
☐ Try again immediately, but do it differently.	☐ Avoid trying again for fear of repeating the error.
☐ Celebrate the fact that you won't have to make that mistake ever again.	☐ Use it as evidence that you can't or won't succeed.
	☐ Worry endlessly about where you went wrong.

corrected mistakes. That's why it's said that practice makes perfect. You get perfect by making mistakes at times when it doesn't matter. You'll find further information about how to deal with the feelings arising from setbacks in chapters 5, 6, and 7.

7. Excess Is Essential: Shifting from Playing It Safe to Keeping Your Options Open

Stress comes from doing less than you can.

JIM ROHN

On the job, one of the things you learn fast, if you didn't already know it, is to never, never take on more work than you can deliver. When you agree to take on something for a boss, he or she expects you to do it, and you will be in hot water if you don't. On your own, however, the opposite is often true. you've got to generate two, three, four, or more times as many prospects for work as you could possibly handle, because only a small number of them will actually come about. You always have to generate more potential work than you can actually do.

When Jeannette Monroe opened her consulting business for dental offices, she was delighted at the response she got to her initial calls and mailings. Many dentists were interested in having her come in and set up a more efficient administrative office. After talking with three or four dentists who seemed particularly interested, she realized that if they each hired her, she wouldn't be able to serve them all, so she decided not to follow up with any others who had expressed interest.

One snag after another, however, delayed a final decision from these dentists. Weeks turned into months and she still had no contract to actually proceed. She was without a paying client. Only after this painful experience did Jeannette realize that her paycheck mentality was on the verge of putting her out of business. She quickly began contacting as many dentists as she could and eventually did get her first client. Of the first four dentists she spoke with who were *so* interested, only one ever actually hired her, and that was over a year later.

Francis Dole created a line of hand-crafted antique model cars. He thought they would make ideal gifts. But when we met him he was very discouraged. A manufacturer's representative he'd been talking to for some time was interested in his line of cars but kept dragging her feet about whether she would actually carry them. During this time, Francis hadn't contacted any other reps because he was still negotiating with her. So there he was, dead in the water as weeks turned into months. Essentially he had given up his power and put the fate of his business in her hands. Of course, we advised him to tell her that while he hoped she would decide to work with him, in the meantime he would be talking with other reps. Actually that speeded up her final answer, which turned out to be a no.

A Deal Isn't a Deal Until It's Done

Opportunities that don't materialize can be disappointing and discouraging—but only because our payroll mentality creates unrealistic expectations. When your boss tells you to do something, the decision is made, and even if it's delayed you're still paid. But not so on your own. Decisions can literally take from days to weeks to years. We've worked to get contracts that weren't signed until more than a year after the initial contact. We've also had companies change their mind on contracts that were all but signed after nine months of discussions.

In other words, when you're on your own, you need to say yes to every desirable possibility that comes along and continue generating as many such opportunities as you can until you have actual cash in hand or a contractual agreement signed on the dotted line. You always have to leave your options open.

Of course, it's important not to imply that you will be available when you know you won't or that you can do something you can't, but you can always let prospects know about your timetable as your situation changes. And keep in mind that if you do get more business than you can handle at one time, you can refer it out or bring on associates. In fact, it's a good idea to line up reliable high-quality backup in advance, because you never know when you'll suddenly have more than you can handle.

8. It Gets Better and Better: Shifting from Boundaries to Breakthroughs

Victory always starts in the head. It's a state of mind. It then spreads with such radiance and such affirmations that destiny can do nothing but obey.

DOUCHAN GERSI

Usually at first, making it on your own feels like you're pulling a very large wagon up a very long, very steep hill. Actually, however, it's like riding a bicycle. At first, you've got to exert considerable energy to get it going, but once you do, you can stop pumping and ride along with only occasional efforts to keep yourself moving.

Like riding a bicycle, the initial effort to get yourself under way on your own is usually considerable. It may consume you day in and day out for months or even years. It may seem that everything that could possibly go wrong does, along with a thousand other things you would have thought could not possibly happen. During the initial start-up period, people sometimes feel like this isn't what they bargained for. You may ask yourself, "Who needs this?" And the answer, of course, is no one . . . except those who want to succeed at what they've set out to do.

On a job, your job description limits your turf and defines what you can and cannot be called upon to do. When pressed to go beyond the limits of what you normally do, you can justifiably say, "That's not my job." Although people sometimes find these turf boundaries restrictive, such limits nonetheless help make a job more manageable. They also seem only fair because no matter how much harder you work, you still get paid the same. And once people see that you're a hard worker, they'll probably just give you more to do.

When you're on your own, of course, having people bring you more work to do is exactly what you want, but suddenly there's no job description to protect your sanity. Suddenly everything is your job. You may be called upon to do anything at any moment. There probably won't be any average day at first. As the free-lance publicist Kim Freilich points out, "You no longer have to just be good at what you do; you have to be good at everything."

Even if you do hire help, ultimately you're still responsible. Your client doesn't care if your supplier was late or your child was ill or your secretary made a mistake. You have to handle whatever comes up. As Cindy Butler, a professional shopper and fashion consultant, discovered in running her business, Gone Shopping, "If you don't do it; it won't get done." Even though the more you're able to do the more you get in return, this demand for versatility and unlimited accountability usually seems overwhelming at first.

But have you ever noticed that human beings are experts at turning the novel into the mundane? We're like vacuum sweepers; we devour experience. We take in and process everything new we come in contact with and quickly turn it into the ordinary. Remember, for example, how complex learning to drive seemed the first time you got behind the wheel? But after only a few months, what could have been more ordinary than driving somewhere? You didn't even think about it anymore. We talk, eat, put on makeup, plan the day, listen to the news . . . all while driving.

So it is with being on our own. When unfettered by the limitations of job descriptions and organizational rules and regulations, most people find they can gradually take on more and more with less and less stress. Because you work when you want, the way you want, most people find ways to become optimally efficient. What once took days eventually takes only hours. What was once difficult becomes easy.

Success Has a Momentum of Its Own

In other words, you won't have to continually put up with the incredible level of exertion that going out on your own requires at first. Success begets success. You'll discover that the more you do, the more you can do. The more you can do, the more you get to do. You'll surprise and delight yourself. It's a delicious circle: the more you do to get work, the more work you get; the more work you get, the better your work gets; the better your work gets, the more work you get—and so on and so on.

If you have something to offer that people need and you make sure they know about you, the day will come when suddenly, like magic, your business will click in and take on a life of its own. When that breakthrough comes, you will be able to catch your breath and your business will keep running. In fact, the more efficient you become, the less and less time you will spend to earn more and more. If you wish, you may even have the time and energy to take on and create other things with the funds generated from your business.

Earlier we mentioned how the artist Ed Crystal has been able to do that with the picture-framing business he started. Once he got the business going, he could afford to spend several days a week pursuing his life-long desire to be an artist. His framing business also financed his opening an art gallery of his own.

When we first went out on our own, we agonized through the tremendous amount of effort that went into submitting just one proposal or getting just one newspaper article written about us or stimulating even one person to take our calls or write just ten pages for an article. There were times we thought we must be crazy to think this business would work. It didn't seem cost-effective. It didn't seem practical. It didn't seem worth the effort. All that kept us going was how much we wanted to accomplsh our goals. There was certainly no indication we ever would.

But each year it became easier, and then one day we reached a turning point, a breakthrough. We noticed that our phone was ringing regularly through no direct effort of our own. People were eager to take our calls. We could prepare a proposal in no time flat. And while our first book took four years to write, we wrote three new books in one year. We had generated so much momentum from those years of effort that we were sailing along— riding the wind, so to speak. We had crested the hill, and it was smooth sailing on the other side.

On your own, you'll find that your rewards increase in direct proportion to your cumulative effort. It's just the reverse of being on a job. As an employee, you get a reward immediately whether you produce much or not. Your salary carries you through the learning curve. But then no matter how much you produce ultimately, you run into a limit on what you can get in return. On your own, while the initial efforts are great, the initial rewards are small. No one carries you through the rough times, but once you've made it, there's no limit to what you can reap from what you've produced. There is no glass ceiling, no plateau, no salary scale.

And ultimately, as a result of your sustained effort over time, your business will become what we call self-sustaining—operating under its own momentum. At that point, you'll be able to stop pumping so hard and go along for the ride. In "Does It Have to Take So Long and Be So Hard?" in chapter 7, we talk about what determines when you can anticipate this breakthrough to occur. Until then, give yourself a chance to get there.

Success Takes Time

It's amazing what we expect of ourselves. Most people who go out on their own expect to hit the pavement running. Often limited start-up funds demand that we start making a profit or at least breaking even almost immediately. But we forget that even large corporations must often run in the red for years before they become profitable. There is always a learning curve. That's why athletes go into training before competition. That's why stage productions rehearse. Since we're generally so poorly prepared to become our own boss, don't you think we, too, should plan for the inevitable learning curve of launching a new venture?

Sometimes what's called *undercapitalization* or *mismanagement* is actually the result of having too long a learning curve. On the payroll, you have the luxury of on-the-job training. If you don't know what to do, often someone will instruct you or provide training; at least you can earn a salary while you learn on the job. Not so in your own business. There's no profit until you produce it. Nobody else pays for you to learn.

On a salaried job, getting your paycheck is only indirectly related to whether any actual income comes in from what you do during that particular week. In other words, if you are doing a research study for your employer, any income generated from the results of that study may be years away. Or if you are conducting in-house training for a company, the income the training will ultimately produce for the company will depend on whether the participants use the skills you taught them to boost their performance at some unspecified time in the future. Even if your students never do increase their performance and thereby the company never does profit from that training session, you have still received your paycheck for having conducted it.

On your own, however, if you take six weeks to do a market-research study, there's no income. If you attend a training program to build your skills, you don't make any money that week. If you take off to learn a new software package, no one else pays the bills. Going out on your own can be very much like being the mother bird who must push her baby out of the nest so it can learn to fly. You've pushed yourself out of the secure nest of a paycheck. You've given yourself the opportunity to learn to fly. Just like the young bird, you have all the necessary equipment you need, but you've got to give yourself the time to learn to use it.

Fortunately, you can build a financial net for yourself so that, should you fall before you can get your wings under you, you can simply start again. You owe it to yourself to have a clear-cut source of income sufficient to survive on while you learn to fly. Such a cash cushion will make your inevitable learning curve less painful. We recommend a cushion of three to nine months of income.

At the same time, you can put yourself on a steady diet of consultants, tapes, books, workshops, and seminars in the particular areas of expertise you need. These will help shorten your learning curve. Ideally you will take advantage of as many of these resources as possible before going out on your own. But those who are most successful on their own always stay one step ahead of their next challenge by continuing to learn.

The Suffering Is Temporary

Rest assured that you won't have to keep pedaling madly year after year after year, although some people mistakenly do this. They think that since it took so much effort to get going, if they stop the business will stop, too. But once your business gets going, you can actually let up little by little and allow the business you've created to begin carrying you and itself.

You will need to pay attention to the momentum at all times, of course. Because, again, just as in riding a bicycle or driving a car, when the momentum begins to wane, or as you approach a hill, you'll have to start pedaling again. You'll have to put on the gas. Not doing this is another way people get

Finding a Cash Cushion

There are many sources for a cash security blanket. Here are just a few:

1. Start your business on the side while you still have a job. When it gets going, leave your job.
2. Take a part-time job that will cover your basic expenses while you get your business under way.
3. Do temporary work while getting your business under way.
4. If you're living with a partner, cut expenses and live off one salary while you start your business.
5. Use your savings or other sources of income, like retirement funds, a sabbatical, divorce settlements, or an inheritance, as a cushion.
6. Take out a second mortgage on your home or arrange to get a consumer line of credit such as some banks are now offering to very small businesses that enables you to borrow if, and only if, you need to. These loans are backed up with the equity in your home or other assets.

in trouble. They get used to things sailing along and forget that they're still the engine that drives the business. If you catch the slowdowns soon enough, however, you won't need to exhaust yourself to get things moving again. A little bit of effort will be all that's required to keep you going at a reasonably steady pace.

9. Money Is a Multiplier: Shifting from Earning-to-Spend to Spending-to-Earn

Throw your money in the direction you want to go and the rest will follow.

DAVID BEAIRD, FILM DIRECTOR

Here are several comments we frequently hear from people who call us for advice about going out on their own. They're a litany for a paycheck mentality.

"I lost my job two months ago and now I'm out of money, so I guess I should start a business."

"I don't have money for marketing, so how can I get business?"

"I don't have any money to do it the way I should, but will this do?"

"I've spent all my money on setting up my office. Now what do I do to get business?"

When you live on a paycheck, your income is fixed by what your job pays. Although you can hope for an annual salary increase or a promotion that keeps up with or ahead of inflation, the amount of money you receive each week is relatively set. Therefore you must try to live within your means. If you spend what you don't have, you go into debt. And most Americans do. They go into debt to purchase things they'll enjoy like furniture, clothing, travel, gifts, and so on. They hope to get out of debt by gradually paying off these purchases over time. This approach works reasonably well for most salaried individuals. Once you're on your own, however, if you operate on these pay-check principles, you will most likely run into financial problems for three reasons:

1. You Have to Support Your Business Before It Will Support You

Starting a business venture is like raising a child: you have to support it until it can support itself. There isn't usually an immediate source of a steady income; it's more likely to be an immediate source of steady expenses. Some-times the expenses are low and the financial investment you need to make may be small. Peggy Glenn, for example, started a typing service for only $65. But Peggy had just walked out on her job in frustration, and that $65 was a stretch for her. At other times the investment required is larger. Herb and Linda Schultz invested $5,000 to purchase a rug-cleaning franchise. Tina Linert invested $20,000 in a dedicated typesetting system.

So as a rule of thumb, if you're completely out of money, the best route to a full-time income fast is to get a job. In fact, the best time to go out on your own is from the security of a steady job. And if you have a job, the best advice is to keep it. Let the job finance your start-up investments and provide you with the time to begin laying a foundation for going out on your own. If you don't have a job and you don't have any money or any immediate business on hand, think about getting a job at least part-time or doing temporary work while you launch your business. There is nothing worse than having to start a business from scratch with the wolf breathing down your back.

2. You Have to Spend Money to Make Money

Susan McNeil is a good example of someone whose paycheck mentality pre-vented her from making it on her own. Susan was tutoring foreign executives in American customs. Most of her initial clients came to her from a company where she used to work. After a few months, however, all the foreign execu-tives from that company had completed her program and she realized she would have to start marketing to other companies.

Since she had started out on a shoestring, she didn't have $500 in the bank to have an attractive brochure printed and mailed to a select number of companies. She didn't have the $250 she needed to join a local business organization where she could make key contacts. She didn't have the money to buy a laser printer. She kept saying, "I'll do that as soon as I get the money." Instead she hand lettered some materials on cheap paper and delivered them in person to several companies. She didn't get any business.

Of course she didn't. No company would take someone seriously who solicits a $250 workshop with a twenty-five-cent flyer. She thought she couldn't afford to do it right. Actually, she couldn't afford to do it wrong. Her company was going down the drain and she believed it was because she didn't have enough money. In fact it was because she didn't realize you have to spend money to make money. She needed to borrow the money or barter to produce the brochure, buy the laser printer, and join the networking organization. She needed to invest in at least one of them.

Whenever you hear yourself say, "I need to do that, but I don't have the money" or "That's what I need to do, but I can't afford it," take note: *you are operating from a paycheck mentality!* To make money, you have to invest money, but there is usually a creative way to get the money you need, especially if you can show yourself and the source of potential funds how what you will do with the money will pay for itself in an immediate return.

For example, if you can make a sale and produce a purchase order for it, your suppliers often will extend you the credit you need to fulfill the order. To make it on your own you have to shift your thinking from *How can I get the money I need?* to *How can I produce the money I need?*

3. The Money You Spend Needs to Make Money

While Susan didn't have money to buy a laser printer or to produce a brochure, she did spend several hundred dollars on clothing her first year in business. She felt she needed to look the role of a professional. And indeed she did, but the attractive business suits she bought didn't make any money for her. A sales letter printed on a laser printer with an attractive brochure, sent to the proper places and followed up with phone calls, could have paid for themselves and the suits, too, from the business they would have generated.

Developing a profit mentality involves thinking about how you can invest whatever money you have in activities that will produce more money. Money spent wisely on marketing, for example, can multiply itself. Money spent on products that you can resell at a higher price can multiply itself. Money spent on producing a workbook with valuable information people will pay for can multiply itself.

When a couple we'll call Charles and Rose started their training firm they invested their personal savings and retirement funds in a luxurious office, elegant stationery, the most advanced equipment, and a lavish open house to announce their business. All these things were, although important, not in-

Credit Sources

Credit cards. One or two credit cards that you use exclusively for business purposes can provide you with the funds you need to do what you need to do to get more business coming in.

A secured credit card. If you have no credit and no credit cards, you can build a credit history by using a secured credit card like the one offered through the First National Bankcard Center [(800)552-9895].

A loan from friends or relatives. You can show friends and relatives exactly how the money you are borrowing will generate ample money to repay their loan.

A personal bank loan. Some banks are now making consumer loans available to small businesses.

A line of credit. Some banks are making consumer lines of credit available to small businesses. A line of credit enables you to borrow only what you need up to a specified limit.

come generators. As a result they were out of money the day they started, and unfortunately it took too long to get business without any marketing budget. Their business closed before their first anniversary. Had they started their business from their home, however, and invested their savings in simple but attractive stationery and more basic equipment, they could have used the bulk of their funds to live on while they marketed their business.

When the film director David Beaird moved from Shreveport, Louisiana, to Los Angeles to make movies, everyone told him he was wasting his time and the little money he had. They said he wouldn't even get a foot in the door. And sure enough, when he began approaching studios, all the doors were closed. His strategy, however, was to take the little money he had and rent a theater where he could put on a play he'd written. Not only did the play provide a limited source of income; the theater also served as a place he could teach acting classes, from which he could earn some money and draw talent for the play. The play also served as a magnet to draw agents, backers, studio executives, publicity, and exposure.

And sure enough, he secured a backer to finance his first movie and then a second one, and finally he was placed on the directors' list of a major studio. This all came from investing the money he had in something that would produce the results he wanted.

So before you spend a cent, ask yourself, "How will what I'm doing with this money bring money back to me multiplied?" For additional ideas on how to generate more business and more money when you need it, see "What to Do When You Don't Have Enough Money" in chapter 7.

10. The Only Authority You Have Is What You Can Command: Shifting from Position Power to Personal Power

I don't like work—no one does—but I like what is in work—the chance to find yourself.

JOSEPH CONRAD

Going out on your own is incredibly empowering, because suddenly you are totally in charge of your life. No one can tell you what to do or how to do it. And that usually feels great. But consider this: while no one can tell you what to do, you can't tell anyone else what to do, either.

A job gives you a certain degree of authority—perhaps not a lot, but within the purview of your job description and your position within the organization you can get people to do what you want them to do because of the authority your job carries with it. The company you work for also provides you with a certain amount of authority. People may take your calls, answer your letters, agree to meet with you, or involve you in various activities because of the *position* you hold. This authority is what Dr. Eric Berne, the developer of the psychological theory Transactional Analysis, called *position power.* And to the extent that you have it, you can open doors and get things done.

The moment you go out on your own, however, the only authority you have is whatever authority you can command through your own personal power. This sudden loss of automatic authority can be an incredible shock to anyone who has had even a small degree of position power. It can be especially disorienting to someone who's had considerable authority within an organization.

Paul had been the chief executive officer of a research-and-development foundation affiliated with the famed Menninger Clinic. Before he left to go out on his own, he had two full-time administrative assistants and a staff of professionals working under him. Sarah was an administrator for a federal agency, personally responsible for a six-figure budget and overseeing hundreds of thousands of dollars in federal grants. Needless to say, we both commanded a comfortable degree of authority because of our positions.

The day we said good-bye to our paychecks, we also said good-bye to all that authority. We no longer had the power of the United States government or a research organization behind us. We had no secretary to screen calls, no administrative assistant to handle details, no one to get paper clips or even to clean up the office. But even more disheartening, when we placed calls people didn't necessarily know who we were anymore. When the secretary heard our name, we'd be asked, "Who? Will he know what you're calling about?" You undoubtedly know what that feels like. Suddenly we were nobody—or anybody.

What were we to do? The same thing we each must do on our own—reach down deep within ourselves and call forth the *personal power* we each have within us. *Personal power* is a source of power that comes from knowing who you are as a person, not as a job title or a role. It's the power that comes from believing in yourself and your talents. It's the power that comes from knowing that you are *somebody* in and of yourself.

You can hear it in people's voices. You can see it in the way they walk and carry themselves. You can see it in the way they dress. It is not based on age, although the older you are the more opportunity you've had to recognize and develop it in yourself. It is not just based on how much money or education you have. Money and education are other sources of power we tend to rely upon, and certainly personal power can be used to make money and is enhanced through the knowledge we acquire.

Personal power arises from the confidence and assurance that, despite any difficulties, life will work and respond to us. It is also called *charisma*, a personal quality that gives an individual a commanding influence or authority. And it's actually more powerful than any other source of power. It's a kind of presence that people stop and take note of. Once you own your personal power, you carry with you all the authority you need, regardless of your position or worldly circumstances.

Most of us are never called upon to develop this quality within ourselves because we can lean upon other sources of power provided to us through our roles and job descriptions, but also because working within an organization doesn't usually encourage the development of personal power. In fact, organizations usually have room at the top for only a few individuals with personal power.

Feeling powerless and having no other form of power to grab onto, however, is one of the best and surest ways to bring out one's personal power. In this sense, one of the greatest benefits of being self-employed is that it calls upon us to tap into and develop this inner source of strength. After having to start his business from scratch twice, wellness-research consultant Dean Allen would agree. He told us, "For anyone who wants to truly fulfill their potential, being on your own is the only way to go." Whereas it took Dean three years to turn a profit the first time around, he was booked to capacity within four months when he started over in a brand-new community following a coast-to-coast move. His growing sense of personal power made the difference.

The surest route to developing your personal power quickly is to identify clearly the type of person you want to be and start thinking and acting as if you were that person. Start being someone you like, someone you respect, someone you know you can count on. Of course, becoming that person may take some time.

You can begin, however, at any time, by asking yourself, "What would someone I most respect and admire do in this situation?" "How would such a person deal with these circumstances?" Then do that. If you can't pull it off at first, that's all right. Who can do something perfectly the first time? No one expects a new employee to perform like an old-timer. If you keep aiming toward becoming the confident and effective person you want to be, however, you'll bring that person out in yourself. And you'll feel, if you already don't, something like this:

"When I was a young person I used to look at all the beautiful people who were so successful and happy. Life seemed to work for them so effortlessly. Not that they didn't have any problems, but their problems didn't seem to interfere with their ability to live with gusto. I, on the other hand, was miserable. Even if things were going well I was too busy dreading the doom the next moment might bring. I felt like someone who was dealt an adequate hand in life but didn't know how to play the game.

"When I first went out on my own, it was worse than ever. At least on my job I was somebody. It said so right on my name badge. Now all I saw were closed doors that I'd have to open somehow. I felt like a teenager again, sitting on the sidelines feeling like a total klutz, wishing I could be part of the 'in' crowd. But this time I wasn't a teenager. I decided to go after those doors, and one by one I found a way to open them and my business started to grow. The more it grew, the better I felt about myself. I was pleased to discover what I could do!

"One day I was sitting in a business meeting across from a large plate-glass panel, and reflected there in the glass was a roomful of successful, competent people, the kind of people I'd always looked up to and admired—the beautiful people. All at once I realized that one of those people was me. I had become the person I wanted to be."

For more information on how to develop your personal power, see "Getting the World to Take You Seriously" in chapter 7.

11. Success Is a Joint Venture: Shifting from Help Me to How Can I Help?

There are no passengers on spaceship Earth. Only crew.

BUCKMINSTER FULLER

We believe that success is always a joint venture. You can't do it alone. And you don't need to. Seeking out and asking for help when you need it are basic to success at anything you do. Research shows that those who are most successful on their own make heavy use of consultants, mentors, and experts. They are willing to pay for the information and expertise they need. They also hire people to help them carry out aspects of their business they know little about or are too busy to handle.

Sandra McKnight is an excellent example of how successfully self-employed individuals network to surround themselves with the expertise and support they need. When Sandra decided to work for herself as a speech and diction coach she realized she didn't know a thing about business. So she began taking classes and talking with other professionals who were in private practice.

"I don't feel like I'm in business by myself," she told us. "Although I started out alone, I now have a marketing expert to guide me, whose courses I've taken and who I can call whenever an emergency arises. I have a sales trainer, a lawyer, an accountant, and a lot of friends who are self-employed. I'm an expert at what I do and that's my part, but I feel like this is their business, too. I'm on my own but I'm not alone. My success is their success."

Sandra's attitude illustrates a significant mental shift you need to make in building alliances and gaining support once you get out on your own. It's a shift many people miss as a result of their paycheck mentality. In many ways the payroll system resembles the family structure in which siblings compete for favors and attention from their parents. On the payroll, employees often compete with one another in a similar fashion, trying to impress their boss and win his or her favor and support. On your own, however, building alliances and contacts is not usually a matter of winning someone's favor. It's more a matter of doing someone a favor.

Sandra, for example, did not approach her mentors and advisers with her hand out. In some cases, she came to them with cash in hand, willing to pay for their expertise. At other times she exchanged services or otherwise discovered how she could help them succeed as well. And in all cases she came across as a competent professional, someone who had a great deal to offer.

A marriage and family counselor we'll call Mark also needed help to get his private practice under way. But his payroll mentality prevented him from getting the support he needed. He was hoping to get referrals from pediatricians. He had contacted several, telling them about his special methods for helping children deal with the traumas of divorce. "I tried to impress them with what I could do," he told us. But in each case he got a cold shoulder, even though he was certain many of their patients would benefit from his services.

Since we knew a pediatrician, we suggested he contact her. Several weeks later we ran into that pediatrician and asked if Mark had contacted her. "Oh yes," she said in an exasperated tone. "I get one of those calls almost every day." Curious, we asked what type of calls she meant. "Oh," she explained, "someone who calls to tell me what a great job they could do for my patients. I guess they see my practice as a happy hunting ground."

We asked her if she ever needed to refer a child out for counseling. She told us, "I refer out a lot. But I'm not a referral agency. I refer to my colleagues, other professionals who consider me to be part of their team. We refer to each other."

Over the years we've heard many similar stories. But here's something you can do to make sure you don't inadvertently fall into this version of paycheck thinking. The moment you think about something you need that someone else could provide, immediately ask yourself, "What can I do for them? How can I help them?" You may argue, "Oh, I'm just a . . . How could I help them?" But don't believe it! You have something valuable to offer. That's why you're on your own.

Let's take Mark as an example. Yes, he was just starting his practice, so he didn't have a lot of patients yet whom he could refer to a pediatrician, although he will when he's successful. But he does need to have pediatric backup in case of any emergencies. And he does have a special approach to helping children deal effectively with divorce. So he could print up a small booklet for divorcing parents on how to help their children accept the changes of divorce and provide these booklets free of charge to pediatricians for their waiting rooms.

In fact, before doing the booklets Mark could call pediatricians and tell them about his plans for the booklet and ask what information their clients would most like to have. Or he could print up a booklet for his future clients on what to ask their pediatrician when their child has physical symptoms during the process of divorce. Again he could quote or feature local pediatricians in his booklet.

Mark could also interview pediatricians for an article he would write about the role of the pediatrician in helping families handle divorce. The article could feature and quote leading pediatricians in the community. Or he could pull together a panel of pediatricians to speak about the health implications of divorce to the local chapter of marriage and family counselors. The possibilities are endless, once he shifts his thinking from "How can I get them to help me?" to "How can I help them?" This one shift transforms you from a beggar, supplicant, indigent, or struggling newcomer into a professional who has a lot to offer.

The more you get going for yourself, the more people want to be part of what you've got going. As we said before, business is not charity. Doing business is about benefiting from helping others benefit. So ask for help by finding ways to help. For additional information about getting help when you need it, see chapter 4.

12. You Can't Afford the Luxury of Bad Morale: Shifting from Employee to Coach, Colleague, and Cheerleader

I have never seen anyone in a good state of belly laugh-ter who was also panicky.

NORMAN COUSINS

On a job you get sick leave, vacation time, coffee breaks, quarterly performance evaluations, pep talks, and lots of down time. The average worker spends almost four and a half hours a week just socializing and addressing personal issues with fellow workers. And, of course, the boss is always there to keep you on your toes . . . be it with a word of advice, a pat on the shoulder, or a look that sets you straight. Although these incentives don't always do the job, they are designed to keep workers on their toes and raring to go. And, of course, the better management does this, the better the morale.

On your own, you don't get any of these perks . . . unless you give them to yourself. Without these built-in supports, keeping your morale up becomes more vital than ever. You literally have to become your own boss—your daily cheerleader, colleague, disciplinarian, mentor, coach, best friend, and trainer.

Twelve Ways To Keep Yourself Charged Up

1. Surround yourself with positive, successful colleagues, clients, and friends. Their attitudes and energy will rub off on you.
2. Join or create a weekly networking group with whom you can get support and share successes.
3. Take periodic electronic coffee breaks with friends and colleagues on the telephone or through a computer bulletin board.
4. Give yourself a break . . . in fact, several breaks. Research shows that a short break every forty-five minutes increases productivity.
5. Take a vacation . . . or several mini vacations . . . once a year, even if you don't feel like it, especially if you don't feel like it. Set aside funds to cover the costs of these breaks.
6. Give yourself an office with a window, or as close to it as you can get. Set up a nourishing home/office environment with good light, positive colors, relaxing and upbeat background music, comfortable and functional furniture, and appealing artwork or scenic views from your windows.
7. Set goals, and be clear about what you expect of yourself. Expect the best.
8. Compliment yourself liberally whenever you do things, even little things, that make you the kind of person you want to be.
9. Do regular performance reviews. Does your performance match your goals?
10. Notice immediately when you don't live up to your expectations, but don't berate yourself or dwell on it. Simply remind yourself of what you expect and affirm that you know you can and will improve.
11. Greet your negative feelings as valuable messengers, bringing you clues as to the actions you need to take. If you're overwhelmed, recognize that you need to get help or take on smaller tasks one step at a time. If you're anxious, identify what you need to do to reassure yourself.
12. Follow the advice of the psychologist Shad Helmstetter: to get in a good mood fast—smile. Or as Famous Wally Amos says, "Find the humor in every day. If you're getting ready for bed and you haven't laughed yet, just start laughing."

You have to charge yourself up and keep yourself motivated. You've got to reward yourself, reprimand yourself, and promote yourself regularly.

And while this is an unfamiliar role for most of us at first, you are none-theless in the ideal position to keep your morale and your energy at their peak, because you get to set up your own working conditions. When you work, where you work, and how you work can all be exactly the way you need them to be to perform at your very best.

How satisfied are you, however, with the working conditions you've set up for yourself? Do you like the boss you've become? Are you pleased with the perks you're providing for yourself? Do you give yourself enough time off? Do you let yourself get away with too much? Have you set up enough contact with others?

Take a moment to list the qualities of the kind of boss you'd like to work for and make note of the type of working conditions such a boss would provide. Then list the qualities of the kind of boss you'd most dread working for and the working environment that kind of boss would provide. How do you stack up? Give yourself a report card as your own boss.

For more information on making the switch from employee to self-employer, see Part 3, How to Become the Boss You've Always Wanted to Have.

Once you've made the mental shifts from paycheck mentality to profit mentality, you'll find that making it on your own is no longer an illusive glimmer to long for or struggle through. It's a reality to enjoy now—for you and for millions of others. You can breathe easy. From this perspective, you can see where you're going. You're ready to take charge with confidence and move forward step-by-step in the direction you want to go.

PART 2

· ·

Managing Everything That Needs to Be Done

> We are told that talent creates its own op-
> portunities. But it sometimes seems that
> intense desire creates not only its own op-
> portunities, but its own talents.
>
> ERIC HOFFER

As your own boss you no longer have a job: you've got three jobs. You've got to *get* the business, *do* the business and *run* the business. And heaven help the person who tries to do each one as the full-time job it could easily become. To survive and thrive on your own, you've got to make magic. You've got to make time for everything that needs to be done and still have some left over for yourself.

Is it any wonder that half the individuals we interviewed for this book list managing everything they need to do as one of their three major problems? Their concerns range from making sure they get to work and stick to business amid all the demands of both home and work to being able to stop working at a reasonable hour when their work is always beckoning to be done.

Nonetheless, while doing it all may seem impossible, it can be done. Thousands of successfully self-employed individuals are not only finding the time and energy to do it, but enjoying themselves in the process. In fact, some are even working fewer hours than when they were on a paycheck. Judy Wunderlich, for example, wanted to stay home to raise her two small children. She now makes $200,000 a year working twenty-five hours a week in her home-based employment agency for graphic designers. And you may recall that the instructional designer Mike Greer ended up making three times the money he earned working for someone else while working three fewer hours a day.

How is that possible? That's what this section is about. You'll discover you can have the time of your life and to some extent even get your business to run itself.

CHAPTER
THREE

■■■■■■■■■■■■■■■■■■■■■

Having the Time of Your Life

*Never before have we had so little time in
which to do so much.*
FRANKLIN D. ROOSEVELT

To have *the time of your life.* Isn't that
what we all want . . . to feel like we own the time that constitutes our lives?
In many ways, your time *is* your life. What you do with your time is what you
do with your life. In this sense, being on your own is the greatest gift you can
give yourself. The moment you step into the world of self-employment you
own your time. What you do with every minute of your day is up to you. Of
course, strictly speaking that's always true. But having a job is like putting a
long-term mortgage on your time, and thereby on your life.

With a job, you've agreed to be some specific place doing some specific
thing for the bulk of your waking day, five or more days a week. While you
might think financial gain is the primary reason people choose to become
their own boss, research shows that the majority of people don't go out on
their own for the money. According to a poll by United Group Information
Services, only 3 percent of small-business owners do what they do for financial gain. The other 97 percent say they are on their own because they want
to be in charge. In other words, it's more freedom, not more money, that lures
us away from the paycheck.

Our research shows that *freedom* is the number-one reason people decide
to go out on their own and is what they enjoy most about being their own
boss. And it's no wonder freedom plays such a role in why we want to be on
our own. Louis Harris Associates reports that leisure time in America shrank
from 26.2 hours a week in 1973 to 16.2 hours in 1989. Almost a third of
people feel rushed on a daily basis while two-thirds feel rushed at times. Even

weekends are no longer our own. An R. H. Bruskin survey of 1,008 people found that the typical adult spends fourteen weekend hours on chores. And, according to Bruskin, nine out of ten people feel no more energetic on Sunday evening than they did on Friday evening.

One result of these time pressures is that increasing numbers of Americans are stressed out. *Prevention Magazine's* "Prevention Index" claims that 63 percent of Americans suffer from frequent stress—up from 55 percent in 1983.

But you may be wondering whether it's *really* any better for most people who are self-employed. After all, there's more to do than ever. Not only do you need to do the work for which you get paid; you also have to market yourself so you will have work to do, plus you have to administer the business aspects of being on your own.

Our research shows that the average home-based self-employed individual works sixty-one hours per week. That's about the equivalent of a top corporate executive. But does this mean that we're simply trading one set of time pressures for another? Have we simply escaped from one taskmaster to become indentured to another—our own work?

The good news is that for most people the answer is *no*! Self-employed individuals who work from home free up at least four weeks a year that they once spent stuck going to and from work in rush-hour traffic. This extra time acts like a cushion. Even though many self-employed individuals continue to grapple with managing their time, they tell us they are still less stressed than they were when they were employed. They claim, and research confirms, that the more control you have over what you do and how you do it, the less stress you experience. So even though their days may be as high-pressure and full as ever, because what they do with their life each day is now up to them their situation no longer feels hopeless. Time pressures have become a problem to solve, not a burden to bear.

And that's what this chapter is about. It's about claiming your time and taking charge of what you do with your life. It's about knowing what you're doing so you can direct yourself competently and thereby use the precious hours of each day in the ways you wish. It's about acquiring a new attitude toward time, an attitude you couldn't have when your time was mortgaged to someone else. It's about approaching time as a resource you can draw upon and spend as you choose, not as a constraint you have to live with or an enemy you must struggle against. This chapter is about learning to enjoy the newfound freedom of being on your own.

Making Time for It All

> *The happy person is one who sees all things as possibilities.*
>
> LEO BUSCAGLIA

"I just don't have the time!" How often do you say that, even now—or especially now—that you're on your own? In the fast-paced high-pressure world of supporting ourselves, even though we are now free to use our time as we wish, it's still hard to find time to be with the ones we love, to create the true masterpieces that live in our hearts, or to pursue the dreams that hide deep in our souls. After all, now we have to do it all, even down to getting the paper clips and dusting the filing cabinets. It's easy to simply impose the same inflexible deadlines and rigid time pressures upon ourselves that were once imposed upon us by our employers. Why do we do that?

Often it's simply a matter of conditioning. It's the same reason that seven-ton eleven-foot-tall circus elephants sit passively chained to a small metal stake in the ground. Although these powerful creatures weigh about the same as a Greyhound bus and most certainly could easily pull up the stake, they don't even try to do so. They learned at a very early age, while they were much smaller, that no matter how hard they tugged and pulled on the chain, they weren't strong enough to get away. So eventually they stop trying to free themselves . . . forever.

An experiment with a fish known for its aggressiveness further illustrates how early conditioning can bind us with needless limitations. This fish, a pike, starved to death even though enough minnows were swimming around it to make a tasty meal. Initially when the pike was placed in the fish tank it was separated from the minnows by a glass bell jar so no matter how hard it tried, it couldn't get through to the minnows. By the time the bell jar was lifted and the pike was given free rein, it had long stopped trying to get to the minnows. The minnows actually swam right through the pike's mouth without risk!

This is the same conditioning process that limits the way we spend our time once we finally get out on our own. Many people become so accustomed to believing that they have to let their work and other obligations run their lives that even when they are free to run things any way they want, they continue to let force of habit call the shots.

Another reason we don't take charge of our time is that on our own, we may be even harder on ourselves than any boss would be. Driven by fear of failure or blind ambition you may find yourself enslaved to the tyranny of the clock, working into the wee hours of the night and right on through the weekend. I know that I, Sarah, certainly did. I was terrified that I wouldn't have enough clients, so to quell my fears I just kept working. I thought somehow if I worked unceasingly I'd have to succeed. It was actually years before I realized—thanks to a dear friend and colleague named Richard Nadeau—that I would be just as successful working more reasonable hours.

When Richard went into private practice as a psychotherapist, he, too, worked madly to assure his success, cramming his days with clients, his nights with groups, and his weekends with workshops. But eventually he began talking about his growing unwillingness to work morning, noon, and night. He began setting limits on the number of hours and days he would work. He told me he wasn't willing to give up his life for success.

"When I first went out on my own," he recalls, "I had a feast-or-famine attitude. I think we're like petrified little children. There's this fear that if we say no we'll be out of business the next day. My great terror was that all my clients would conspire to cancel their appointments at one time. I feared that somehow these thirty unrelated individuals who didn't even know one another would all decide to cancel. It was ridiculous, of course. But I used to have to take out my appointment calendar regularly just to check out the objective reality and assure myself that I wasn't going into Chapter 11."

I had the good fortune to watch Richard summon the courage to cut back his time and see him become even more in demand. I watched him raise his fees so he could work fewer hours. I watched him pass up lucrative opportunities to do workshops so he could enjoy some free time. And I liked what I saw. While he was working less, he was earning more. I became committed to doing the same. And while it was frightening at first, I gradually developed an entirely new outlook on time that has truly put me in charge of my life.

A New Outlook on Time

Instead of thinking of time in terms of twenty-four-hour blocks into which we can never quite fit everything that needs to be done, what if we approached it as an endless, flowing supply that never runs out? Actually, there's always plenty of time. Time is a bountiful resource! We have all the time in the world. In fact, as long as we live, all we have is time. Every day, every minute, we get more of it . . . no matter what we did with our previous allocation. Time is totally democratic. Every day everyone gets a fresh supply. Whether we waste it, savor it, manage it, or invest it, we still get a steady flow of time.

And once you're on your own, your time is like a brand-new shopping bag you receive every morning. As you shop your way through the day, you can fill your bag with all the good things you like, taking some of this and some of that, sampling whatever seems most valuable or most enjoyable to you.

But, you may say, that's *not* how my day goes! It's true that sometimes you get up in the morning only to discover that your bag is already filled with the leftovers from yesterday. Or perhaps you awaken to find that someone else has filled your bag with things they want you to do. Or maybe you've accepted a standing order, so you wake up to the same dull routines every day.

If you approach time like a cafeteria line and take some of everything, you'll undoubtedly live with a chronically overstuffed day. And if you're willing to take potluck, you can end up not liking a lot of what is dumped into your life. But now that you're on your own, you're in the position to be the one who decides how your day goes. You, and only you, decide who puts what into your day. If you don't like what gets in, you can dump it out and say, "No more!" You can take charge and put first things first.

It's as simple and as difficult as that. While there's an endless supply of time, it can't be preserved. You can't make more. You can't buy more. What you waste or invest poorly is lost forever. As the teacher Marva Collins tells her students, "This day has been given to you fresh and clear to either use or throw away."

For Naomi Stephan, a career counselor, this discovery came early one morning: "When I first went out on my own, I used to answer the telephone at every hour of the day and night. Then one morning I woke up and realized I don't have to answer the phone whenever it rings! I went out and bought a two-line phone, and now I put on the answering machine when I don't want to be interrupted!" You can do the same with any aspect of your work and your life.

Putting First Things First

Decide what you want, decide what you are willing to exchange for it. Establish your priorities and get to work.

H. L. HUNT

If life is a vast ocean and time is the vessel in which we journey through life, how would you describe your journey now that you're on your own—or about to be? Are you traveling at the helm of an ocean liner in command of the seas on a clearly charted course? Or are you on a sailboat drifting about on the winds of life—as the wind blows, so your day goes?

We've found that the more successful you become, the more challenging managing the varied aspects of your journey through time becomes. At times we've felt like we were traveling in a leaky rowboat, pushing and pulling, struggling and fighting against the seemingly impossible demands of time. Sometimes we've felt like we weren't even in the boat anymore, but were hanging onto the sides trying to ride out each day's storm.

Perhaps you've felt like that at times, too. Because everything is up to you, it feels like everything needs to be done right now. This is especially true when you're first getting started or when things are more difficult to get under way than you anticipated. But it's also true no matter how successful you become. How do you put first things first when everything seems to need to come first? Where do you begin? What can be done later? And what doesn't need to be done at all?

"Sometimes there's so much to be done that I just don't do anything!" one person told us. We know that feeling. But there is one overriding principle that can get you out of this dilemma again and again. This one principle puts you in charge. When we follow this principle, things work. When we don't, life gets out of hand again.

The first person to uncover this principle was the nineteenth-century economist Vilfredo Pareto. Pareto found that a small proportion of any activity produces the majority of the results. His discovery is now called the 80/20 Rule or the Pareto Principle, and if you apply this rule to your life, you will have much more of everything you want and much less of everything you don't. Examples of the 80/20 Rule abound in every aspect of life. Think about this. Don't you wear 20 percent of your clothes 80 percent of the time? Don't

20 percent of the people in your life create 80 percent of your problems? Don't 20 percent of your calls or letters or projects produce 80 percent of the results? Don't you use 20 percent of your files 80 percent of the time? That's the 80/20 Rule at work, and it applies to virtually everything you do.

In other words, about one-fifth of everything in your life produces about four-fifths of the results. That means a lot of what we think we need to do doesn't need to be done. It means that if we can identify what works in our lives, what produces the results we want, we can let the rest go. We can get more of what we want and less of what we don't for much less time, money, and energy.

Do you find that hard to believe? We did. But two things happened in our lives that convinced us it just might be true. First, when we decided to go out on our own, we wanted to work from home instead of renting office space for our respective businesses. At the time, however, we were living in a 750-square-foot apartment. So working from home meant we'd have to move into larger quarters. We bought a new house and began packing. Our son's room was filled with toys, most of which he no longer played with, so we planned to give away many of his older toys. But he threw a fit over each toy we planned to discard. Each one was a special treasure he *had* to keep.

So we devised a plan. We packed all the older toys into a very large box, and when we moved we left that box in the basement of our new home, assuring him that any time he wanted those toys, he could always go down and get them. Guess what? Two years later that box had yet to be opened.

We thought, as perhaps you are thinking, "Well, that's just kids, right? Adults have surely outgrown something like that!" But we couldn't overlook this as a childish phenomenon. It was too similar to something that had happened to me, Sarah, two years before we moved. I was working as a specialist for a federal child-care program when our agency was moved from one office building to another. I carefully boxed up all the outstanding stacks of material on my desk: correspondence, in-house memos, phone messages, projects I was working on, and so forth. These papers were so important to me at the time that I decided to transport this box to the new office building in my own car.

As in any office move, things became pretty hectic, so when I got to my new office, I set the box in the corner while I addressed the urgencies of the moment. I told myself I would get to them as soon as possible. Two years later, when I was clearing out my office to go out on my own, I found that box, packing tape still carefully sealed. Over that time, no one had called or written or dropped by to ask me about any of the *important* matters addressed in those materials.

Interesting, isn't it? In reality, we simply don't need to attend to much of what comes into our lives. Of course, there are many things that we do need to attend to, but they are the few—the vital few—among the trivial many. As self-employed individuals we truly don't have the luxury of relating to the trivial many. We can't earn a living and succumb to bureaucratic inefficiency.

In fact, our ability to streamline and do things efficiently is what enables us to survive and thrive. It gives us the edge to get things done more quickly and proficiently than the larger bureaucratic organization.

Following the 80/20 Rule to Quadruple Your Results

Just imagine your life without the 80 percent of things that are bogging you down and leading you nowhere. Just imagine what it would be like if you could identify the 20 percent of things in your life that provide you with 80 percent of your satisfaction and results. What would happen if you were doing *those things* 80 percent of your time? It would be like finding six extra hours a day! Three extra file drawers! And perhaps a 25 percent increase in your income!

That's exactly what happened to us when we decided several years ago to *80/20* our life. We sat down and asked ourselves, "Which of our efforts provide us with 80 percent of our enjoyment in life? Which efforts produce 80 percent of our profits?" Slowly, piece by piece, we began eliminating the unrewarding 80 percent of hassles and trivia that used to fill our lives.

We had a gigantic garage sale to free our home from the many things we owned but rarely used. We emptied our closets of clothes we rarely wore. We cleared out our overstuffed file cabinets. We reorganized our business to focus only on those aspects we find rewarding and profitable. We began spending more time with the people who support and nurture us.

We began to truly put first things first in our lives, and in so doing we traded in the leaky rowboat we'd been clinging to for a gleaming ocean liner, and we took the helm. Subsequently, we've discovered that most of the successful propreneurs we interview have also learned to apply the 80/20 Rule, although they don't always call it that.

For example, the career counselor Naomi Stephan told us she found being on her own a real juggling act until she started to ask herself, "What is the core of my business? What am I in business to do? What has always brought me the most business?" She decided that was what she needed to concentrate on. Wellness researcher Dean Allen finds that things work best when he follows one simple rule: "I don't plan anything I don't want to do, and I don't do anything I don't want to plan."

Chellie Campbell, owner of Cameron Diversified Management, told us, "I've gotten to the point now that I only do those things that are income producing or fun—preferably both. For example, I don't have time for negative, difficult clients. I only work with positive, bright people who also want to be successful and therefore don't have time for hassles."

Perhaps when you were working for a paycheck you couldn't run your life like that. Your job was to handle whatever came across your desk. But now that you're on your own, you can absolutely make room for those things that work and drop out those things that don't. The three things we did to 80/20 our lives are listed on the following page. Since we've taken these steps, our

---

How to 80/20 Your Life

Work on purpose. What motivated you to go out on your own? What do you want to accomplish? Why are you doing all this? Whether it's to be with your children, become a millionaire, or express your creative talents, your reasons give purpose to your day, and this sense of purpose enables you to know where you're going and to put that first in your life.

Clear out your backlog. If your desk, files, cabinets, and calendar are filled with things that don't relate to your purpose, you won't have the time or the space to put first things first. Therefore, once you know your purpose, and before you take another step, you must clear the other things out of your life to make room for what matters most.

Schedule for results. Once you know where you're going and you've cleared the way, setting goals will take you where you want to go, but only if you bring them down to the minute. Leaving your goals on a notepad in a drawer somewhere puts them out of sight and out of mind. You've got to get them onto your calendar and let them become the focus of what you do every day.

---

business and our income have increased, yet we have more free time and we're certainly enjoying our lives more.

Working on Purpose

Nothing can resist a human will that stakes its heart upon a purpose.

BENJAMIN DISRAELI

If there's no one expecting you to get to work, if there's no job description or company policy prescribing what you're to do and when, if there's no guarantee of a paycheck—then why get up and get to work on any particular day? Why today? Why not some other day? Or sometime later today? How do you decide what to do when you can do anything you want, and when do you start when there's no particular time to start? When do you quit if you can quit anytime you want to, especially if you're the only person who'll know when you're goofing off.

Clearly, when you're on your own, if you want to get any work done, you've got to *want* to do it. You have to *want* to do it badly enough that you actually will, because no one else is going to make you do it. In other words, you've got to have a compelling *reason* to do it. There has to be some *purpose* for doing it. Otherwise you probably won't get around to it.

I (Sarah) remember when I was working for the government, that I used to wake up in the morning and begin mentally planning my day while I was getting ready for work. Usually I looked forward to getting a lot done. Anticipating all the things I would accomplish felt good. But before I knew it, the day was over and I was wondering where it had gone. Somehow I never got around to most of the things I planned to do—the things I most wanted to do. I was always getting sidetracked by other people's demands and expectations. And that didn't feel good. My life was moving, but not in the direction I wanted it to. Weeks melted into months, months into years. And although I'd done many things, I hadn't done what I wanted to do.

When I went out on my own I thought things would be different. After all, now I was my own boss. I could call the shots! I was surprised that somehow I still found myself at the end of the day not having done most of the things I'd intended to do. I still wasn't directing my life toward what I wanted to accomplish. I was still responding to the events of the day, and those events were determining the course of my life. I was disappointed and frustrated because my own agendas still seemed to end up on the back burner. I wasn't working on purpose.

The Power of Knowing Why You're Doing What You're Doing

Until recently it made little sense for most people to spend much time dwelling on the inner purpose for their life. Their options were more limited by the circumstances of their birth and upbringing. In fact, having deep personal desires often simply led to a life of frustration and disappointment because most people were bound to choose a so-called more realistic life. Today, however, that has changed. Now we have the opportunity to pursue our inner callings. In fact, if we listen carefully, we each have something we're working toward in this life, some reason for our being here, something that calls upon us to use our unique talents and skills to the fullest. We call this reason for being our *life purpose.*

Having a chance to pursue your life purpose may be the reason you decided to go out on your own in the first place. In talking with other propreneurs and entrepreneurs, we find that often their decisions to go out on their own arose from an inner sense of needing to make a change so that their lives would be more fulfilling and rewarding. Usually it's this sense of purpose that propels them to work long enough, hard enough, and eagerly enough to make it. Just knowing what you want to get away from is not usually enough; you have to know what you're working toward.

And even then, once you get out on your own the pressures of self-employment can divert you once again from doing what you intend to do with your life. Surprisingly, however, getting clear about your purpose is the most powerful self-management tool available to you.

Knowing what you want to do and how you want to do it need not lead to frustration, as it did in the days when someone else was directing you. In fact, now that you're on your own, in order to put first things first in your life, *you* have to know what *you* want to come first. You have to commit yourself to putting it there. Defining what you intend to do in your life and how you want it to be is no longer a luxury. It's a survival tool.

Without such clarity, on your own you'll probably always have a hard time with time. You'll have a hard time with choices. You won't know what needs to be done today and what can wait until tomorrow. You'll agonize over what to keep and what to throw away. You'll be confused about which advice to follow, whose demands to respond to, which role to play, what direction to take.

When you're living your life in accord with a sense of inner purpose, however, not only will you find making decisions much easier; you'll also feel a greater sense of gratification and fulfillment from everything you do, even the more unpleasant aspects of being on your own. You'll feel like you are making a difference, a contribution.

Without a sense of purpose, you may feel like you're spinning your wheels, going nowhere. You have nothing to aim for. And when you aim at nothing, you hit it every time. Keeping your purpose clearly in mind, however, gives you something to get out of bed for. It keeps you going when things get rough. As the philosopher Friedrich Nietzsche said, "He who has a why can bear almost any how." Working on purpose also provides the foundation for setting goals and priorities and for making critical choices throughout the day. You'll be astounded at what you'll be able to do and how quickly it will get done. We certainly were.

Up until the time we clarified and committed ourselves to our purpose, we had been going in many directions, searching for what would pay off. We'd try first one thing and then another. We kept thinking that if we could just get something profitable under way we'd be able to pursue what we *really* wanted to do. Once we got clear, however, on what we really wanted to do—that is, once we knew our purpose—that's when our efforts really began to pay off. The results were dramatic. Suddenly we knew which projects to pursue and which to pass by. We knew which expenses would be worthwhile and which would not. We knew what needed to take priority in any given day.

Within one year we accomplished more than we had in the previous seven years we'd been out on our own. In a year of working on purpose, we completed three books, designed three seminars, and produced a line of audiotapes. Today our message is heard on radio and television across the country and there is much more to come—all because we began working on purpose. Now at the end of each day, we usually have the wonderful feeling of knowing that we like where we are, that we're getting where we want to go, and that we'll love it when we get there.

Three Steps to Getting on Purpose

If you don't feel like you're working on purpose, you can start today. You can start working *with intention,* with a desired end result in mind. You can begin to live your life by design as opposed to by accident, deliberately as opposed to by happenstance, with determination and resolve instead of from circumstance. Doing so will give new meaning and significance to what you do and to those things you must endure along the way.

Commit, or recommit, yourself to finding and relentlessly pursuing your life with purpose in mind. Chances are you already know what the greater purpose of your effort is. It may be something you've been wanting to do since your childhood. Perhaps it's what you've always been good at or what you've done in whatever spare moments you've had. It's probably related closely to the reason you've decided to go out on your own.

If you don't immediately know what will give purpose to your work, all you need to do is listen closely to your inner desires and dreams. They are like a beacon leading you directly to what you need to be doing not only to find fulfillment in your work but also to guarantee your financial success. Ask yourself the following three questions and listen patiently and quietly for the answers.

1. What would you be doing if you could do anything you wanted without concern for the money it would produce? At the heart of this question lies the secret to your ultimate success. At first it may appear that your answer has nothing to do with your work. Like Bill Jack you may say, "I'd just like to play tennis all day." Or like Rita Tateel you might say, "I'd love to watch TV, go to the movies, and give parties." Or perhaps like Geneen Gardner you'd say, "I'd travel throughout the world." Or, as Janet Belinkoff might say, "I'd just spend my time playing with animals."

But think about this. When Bill Jack asked himself this question, he was suffering from cancer. He didn't know how much more time he had to live. He decided he was going to do only work he found gratifying, so he quit his management position and began teaching tennis. Fortunately, he recovered from his illness, and his purpose became to teach others to enjoy the sport he finds so fulfilling.

When Rita Tateel asked herself what she would do if she could to whatever she wanted, she decided to open *Celebrity Source,* a company providing celebrities for fund-raising events. She now finds that "90 percent of what I enjoy outside of work is now part of my work, even watching TV and going to parties." And yet her work is important. She helps many worthwhile charities obtain hundreds of thousands of dollars each year.

When Geneen Gardener asked herself what she loved doing most she shifted the nature of her business to organizing and conducting educational travel tours. She took groups to the Soviet Union before *glasnost* and continues to conduct tours that bring people from foreign cultures closer together. When social worker Janet Belinkoff began feeling burned out on her job, all she wanted to do was play with animals. Now she and her husband own and operate a successful pet-sitting service.

These propreneurs are but a few of the many who have discovered that maximum performance comes from maximum enjoyment. So if you're in a business that doesn't relate to what you most want to do, begin rethinking and refocusing your business to be more in line with what will give meaning and purpose to your work. You'll be surprised at how much more easily you'll be able to motivate yourself and how quickly your success rate will rise.

And that's not all. Once you're working on purpose and you're doing what you really want to do, anytime you don't know what to do, anytime you feel like quitting, anytime you're tired and discouraged, anytime you wish there was someone to tell you what to do—all you need to do is remind yourself of why you're doing all this and you'll find the inner wisdom, resolve, and desire you need to continue.

In his book *Creative Work* Edmond Bordeaux Szekely quotes Patanjali, the founder of the ancient Indian practice of Yoga, as saying, "When you are inspired by some great purpose, some extraordinary project, all your thoughts break their bonds: your mind transcends limitations, your consciousness expands in every direction, and you find yourself in a new, great, and wonderful world. Dormant forces, faculties, and talents become alive, and you discover yourself to be a greater person by far than you ever dreamed yourself to be."

2. What's the point of what you're doing?   Why does what you do for a living matter? This is certainly a good question to ask in order to successfully market your business. But it's also at the heart of knowing the purpose of your work. If your work doesn't matter, why should you get up and do it? Why should you undertake all the challenges involved? Whatever your reason for being in business, it needs to matter—to you—and to your clients or customers. It needs to make a positive difference both to you and to others.

At first you might think, "Oh, I *just* do . . ." But if you have any clients and customers now, or if someone has ever paid you to do what you do, it means that what you're doing does matter to someone. It's important to them or they wouldn't be paying you their hard-earned money. Your work doesn't need to be glamorous or extravagant to be important. Peggy Glen *just* did typing for her customers. But they were so pleased with her work that they brought her flowers and candy for doing a good job for them on time. Chellie Campbell *just* does bookkeeping, but her service gives the business owners she works with a restful night's sleep knowing their finances are in order. She's even rescued some clients from the brink of financial disaster. James McCallister *just* cleans carpets, but the carpets he cleans not only make a difference in the quality of life for his customers, they also affect the bottom line of these business establishments by making them more presentable.

Think about how what you do impacts the lives of those you work with and how those results impact the world. Don't be concerned about becoming too grandiose in understanding your purpose. Although what you do may seem small at first, as you think more about it, never forget it's all the little things that collectively shape life's ultimate reality.

3. Why is it important that **you're** *the one who's doing what you do?* Why should someone turn to you instead of to someone else who does something similar? This is another important question to ask in order to market yourself successfully. But it's also an important question for clarifying your purpose. Your background, skills, talents, aptitudes, and personality are unique. No one else has exactly what you have to offer. In an industrial society, manufacturing processes were built around being able to stick some *body* at any given work station. But even in industry today, management has discovered, sometimes painfully, that one *body* cannot necessarily be replaced by another. The skill, experience, knowhow, and makeup of each human being is unique; each individual can contribute something that no one else can in quite the same way.

There is no future in any *job*. The future is in the *person* who holds it. This is particularly true in today's information and service society, where what you're most likely selling is your unique expertise. For example, one of Sarah's unique gifts is her enthusiasm. She has the ability to see the big picture of what could be and to get people excited enough about what's possible to get busy creating it. Paul has an ability to analyze and make sense out of complex and apparently contradictory information. He can make useful what might otherwise be intimidating.

Bill Jack knows how to make learning tennis fun. Rita Tateel is an expert at linking up people who need help with one another. Geneen Gardner can make the foreign and unfamiliar seem both exciting and safe. Janet Belinkoff can make friends with animals and put them at ease. Chellie Campbell can take the stress out of financial management.

Knowing what makes what you do unique clarifies and validates your role on this journey called life. So think of your work as the role you're uniquely qualified to fill on this voyage. With that in mind, you'll be prepared to make clear goals, set priorities, reach decisions, and design strategies with greater ease. You'll be able to fill your day with those things that will help you accomplish your dreams.

Using a Purpose Poster to Stay on Track

> *Examine yourself; discover where your true chance of greatness lies. Seize that chance and let no power or persuasion deter you from your task.*
>
> SCHOOLMASTER IN *CHARIOTS OF FIRE*

Okay! You know what you want. You know where you're going. But it's still easy to get off track, isn't it? Some days make your head spin so fast you can't even remember your Social Security number, let alone the reasons you're doing what you do.

So how do you keep on track when all around you is going haywire? We had to face that question when we were writing our first book, *Working from Home*. Like so many people, we had to sandwich the dream for our book between the many other things we were doing to earn a living. There were interruptions galore. At times we began to fear the book would never be finished.

To help myself stick to business, I, Sarah, hung a sketch of the book jacket behind my computer, so I was looking straight at it while I worked. As interruptions and distractions arose, I would see that book cover and know that I had to continue writing no matter what was going on around me or that jacket would never be filled with pages.

That cover kept us on track. And sure enough, as you might imagine, once we completed the book and Sarah took down the book cover, the distractions of the day took charge once again.

That's when we realized the value of having a Purpose Poster, a picture you can hang behind your desk that displays your goals and dreams in living color. And that's just what we decided to create for ourselves. We had an artist design a poster that reminds us moment by moment of where we're headed. At that time, we'd recently moved from Kansas City to the southern California megalopolis. We were strangers in a strange land. But we wanted to live by the ocean and find friends in Los Angeles with whom we could share our work and our lives. We'd written one book, but we wanted to write others. And we wanted to speak on radio and television and before large groups of people to spread the word about becoming your own boss and taking charge of your life from the comfort of your own home.

We had no idea how these things would come to pass. And they certainly didn't occur overnight. There were even times when we wondered if they would ever happen. But now as we look at that poster, most of the things on it are a regular part of our lives. We live two blocks from the ocean; we can see it from our balcony.

Think about what you're working toward. What does success look like for you? See it right now in your mind's eye. Imagine it in full detail. What does it sound like? What does it feel like? How would you describe it to someone? Keep that image in mind and write it out or sketch it on a sheet of paper you can hang above your desk. Or clip pictures from magazines that capture the essence of your image and create a montage.

Whatever you're seeking to accomplish by being on your own, your mind will go toward whatever's in front of you. So create your own Purpose Poster to remind yourself of what you're doing all this for.

Clearing Out the Backlog

It's easier to win than to worry. The mind is like a calculator; it has to be cleared of all previous problems before you can solve a problem with it. Worry jams up the mechanism. We can't solve our problems unless we clear our minds.

EARL NIGHTINGALE

Before you can get to work on your purpose, you need to make ample time, space, and energy for those things that will produce the results you want. Too often our file cabinets, appointment calendars, desk space, and even our minds are littered with so many competing and trivial concerns that we end up operating on the *Hope System*—that is, "I hope I get to that," "I hope I get that done," "I hope I can find that," and so forth.

Isn't that too often the way we run our day, juggling many little but seemingly important balls and dropping a few along the way—a call that doesn't get returned, a letter that isn't sent, a missed meeting, a misplaced file, to-do and must-do lists scattered here and there?

Our experience is that worrying about all the things you have to do and whether you'll get them done is one of people's biggest time wasters.

All the incomplete minutiae that clog up our time is what we call the *backlog*. It's the backlog of life that keeps us from getting where we want to go. Yet it's this backlog that never seems to be addressed in most time-management courses and books. Time-management resources are usually full of helpful ideas, but until you can clear out the backlog you're juggling, how can you possibly get around to using even the most basic time-management principles? To clear out your backlog here and now, take these three steps:

1. *Clear your mind with an Everything List.* There is no way you can concentrate on what you need to do at any given moment if you're simultaneously trying to keep track of all the other things you *could, should, and ought* to be doing. To literally clear your mind, sit down and make up a list of everything you think you need to do—*everything*, from sending a birthday card to your aunt to calling your lawyer to cleaning out your file cabinets to sending a thank-you note for a recent referral.

The purpose of this list is not to overwhelm you. The purpose of this list is to give you a place where you can store all the things you're trying to keep track of. We suggest keeping it in a daily planner or personal organizer, either in paper or electronic form. (See "Use a personal organizer to make time" on the following page.) At least once daily, while you're making plans for the day, review your Everything List. Cross off or delete items that have been completed, and put the important or urgent tasks from your list onto your schedule for the day. Should you feel overwhelmed by looking at your Everything List, don't panic. Just remember: *there will never be time for everything on your list, but there will always be time for the most important things.*

2. *Throw out everything you don't need.* Clearing out the backlog also means throwing out everything you no longer need. And the time to do that is right this minute, right now, today. Begin with your Everything List. Cross off or delete those things you don't really need to do—those things that make no contribution to what you want to create in your life. Ask yourself, "What benefits will doing this provide me or my clients? What will happen if I don't do this?" If there's no gain from doing it and no major loss from not doing it, forget it. If, however, you still want to do it, you can. You're the boss. So leave it on your list.

Then move to your closets, desktop, drawers, and filing cabinets. If you don't use it and won't use it, lose it. Again, ask yourself how the contents contribute to what you want to accomplish in life. What benefits will keeping this provide; what will happen if you don't keep it? Be ruthless. You owe it to yourself! This is your life. It should be filled with those things that nurture, assist, support, reward, and fulfill you and that make a positive contribution to your life.

If you can't stand to throw away some things you no longer want or need—or if you don't have the time to go through all the piles and files you've accumulated—you can still clear out your life. You can do as we did for our son: put these things—whatever they might be—in one or more large boxes in the attic, garage, or basement. After several years, discard the contents of any boxes you haven't opened. We've often done this ourselves with books we were afraid to part with.

3. Start afresh with a time and place for everything. Once you've cleared your mind, calendar, closets, file cabinets, drawers, and desk of the backlog, you'll have more room for the important things in your life. If you designate a specific time or place for each of these things, you'll find managing your work much easier. There will be no need for stacks and piles to build up. You'll be able to put your finger on everything you need to locate. Things will get done routinely in a timely manner.

You may even see your profits go up. That's exactly what happened when an advertising executive came to Sarah for a consultation on how to boost his sales. He came in feeling frustrated by how he never seemed to be able to get the solid base of sixteen accounts that he needed to make his income goals. He had a good marketing plan and was good at sales, so Sarah decided to ask him about his accounting system. She wanted to know if he had a ledger for his accounts. He didn't. He just kept track of each account individually. She suggested that he set up a ledger with eighteen rows and bill, record transactions, and track the status of each account weekly.

To his amazement, within no time he routinely had eighteen accounts. "When I made a physical space for the accounts I wanted," he recalls, "and then had to look at them weekly, the missing ones were constantly staring me in the face. I began talking with others about having openings for another client. Actually, I don't know exactly what happened; I just know that now I keep steady at eighteen accounts. Maybe I should set up a ledger for twenty and see what happens."

Here are several ways you can make sure you have a time and place for everything that matters most to you.

Use a personal organizer to make time. Using a personal organizer or time planner is an invaluable way to make sure you have a time for everything you want to do in your life. Paper organizers come in various sizes: pocket, purse or notebook. We recommend one with a loose-leaf binder like *DayRunner, Harvard Planner* or *Filofax* so you can remove and add pages as needed. We also recommend selecting one you can conveniently carry with you to meetings and appointments. Available in office-supply and stationery stores, such planners have customized pages you can mix and match to meet your needs: month-at-a-glance, week-at-a-glance, and daily calendars; addresses and phone numbers; goals sheets; project sheets; and notes. If you prefer to organize your day electronically, you can do so with your personal computer using software like *Sidekick* and *PC Tools.* You can carry your schedule and plans with you by using one of the pocket-sized electronic organizers like the Sharp *Wizard,* Casio *Boss,* or Atari *Portfolio.*

Place all important tasks, appointments, meetings, events, and activities on one master calendar in your personal organizer, including those related to your personal and social time. People often reserve their calendars for business-related activities only and wonder why their private life suffers.

For example, if you want to exercise daily or every other day, reserve time on your calendar for it. If you want to spend time with your children each day, reserve time for it. If you want to pay bills, catch up on filing, learn a new software package, or read a book, don't leave these to chance: put them on your calendar. Of course, you can always move them if necessary. But make sure you do *move* them, not cancel them. In other words, place them on your calendar for another time, and be careful about making too many exceptions.

Set aside a time each day to plan your day in your personal organizer. Either first thing in the morning or last thing in the evening, plan how you will allocate your time for the upcoming day. You'll notice that those things that you make room for in your day are the things that will get done. You'll get results in those areas of your life that you invest time and energy in. The areas of your life you don't invest in will usually deteriorate.

For example, if you don't have enough business, review your calendar. Notice how much time you've invested in the past month in getting new business. If your relationships aren't working, review your calendar. Look to see how much time and energy you've invested in building the relationships you want. If you have trouble with cash flow, look at your calendar. How much time have you invested in billing, managing, and tracking your funds? If your health is suffering, review your calendar. How much time have you spent relaxing and taking care of yourself?

If you make room for these activities on your calendar and invest concentrated time and energy in them, you will see them grow and develop in direct proportion to the investment you make. You will get the results you want!

Establish an activity center for key tasks, and keep everything related to these tasks in that place. Did you know corporate executives waste an average of forty-five minutes every day looking for things they can't find? It's true, and *they* usually have secretaries to help them keep track of things! Self-employed individuals, who usually must organize and keep track of everything themselves, can't afford to spend time like this each day trying to find things.

There's nothing more frustrating than trying to find something you need and know that you have . . . *somewhere.* But the primary reason desks, floors, closets, counter tops, tables, and drawers get buried in piles of random stuff that you can't find when you need it is because there's not a *place* to put these things when they come into your office or your life. When you don't have a place for things, you don't know what to do with them when they arrive. And too often you don't have time to figure out what to do with them. And when you don't know where something belongs, no matter where you put it, out of sight will be out of mind. As one person told us, "Once I put something in a file, it's lost forever."

If, however, you have one, and only one, place for everything you need to keep track of, and that one place is where all the other things like it are located, then putting things away and getting them back out when you need them becomes quick and easy.

The Four Essential Activity Centers

To establish a place for everything so you can keep it in its place, think of the primary activities you carry out each week and create a *center* or work space where you carry out that activity. Then keep all materials and supplies related to that activity in that same work area. Such a center need be nothing more than a particular drawer or shelf. Or, depending on how much material and activity is involved, it could be an entire table, separate desk, or even portion of a room. Here are examples of several key *centers* most self-employed individuals need in order to make sure everything has a place.

1. A telephone work center. Have a place near your work phone where you keep your card file of names and addresses, answering machine, and all phone messages. You might locate this area on your desk or next to your computer. We have an *answering pad* by the phone on which we record all phone messages. This pad is invaluable for making sure we don't misplace calls to be made, dates, addresses, and other data people give us over the phone.

2. A mail center. Have a place where you process all your mail. Here you can have a bin or box to place incoming and outgoing mail. Here you can keep stationery, envelopes, stamps, cards, publicity materials, and anything you need to mail out regularly. This area might be on a work table, on top of a cabinet near your desk, or in a desk drawer. We have our mail center on a work table in a walk-in-closet-sized storage room off the loft where we have our desks. There, in addition to the things already mentioned, we also keep items like a postage meter, mailing and shipping envelopes, overnight-delivery materials, and a paper cutter.

3. A money-processing center. If you want to make sure you have enough money, you have to mind your money. That means having a time and space for processing your financial transactions such as banking, record keeping, invoicing, and bill paying. We have set aside a drawer in our office for all our bank records and a file drawer for all current tax records. There we keep deposit materials, checks, receipts, bills to be paid, and bills that have been paid.

We also recommend computerizing your financial records. In chapter 4 we list software that can help you streamline financial-management tasks like billing, inventory, cash flow, accounting, and so forth.

4. Filing centers. If you have a place for each file and a file for each type of written material you need to keep, you'll have no need for piles. Actually, *filing cabinets* should be called *retrieval cabinets,* because the goal of filing is to put something where you can find it when you need it. To keep your desk and other surfaces clear and still have quick access to what you need, create three filing areas:

Immediate files. Keep files you refer to daily or which you are working on currently within arm's reach—in a file drawer in your desk, a movable filing cart placed beside your desk, stack trays on your desk, or a nearby bookcase or credenza.

Current files. Files that you use on a weekly or monthly basis can be kept in a filing cabinet in a closet or nearby storage area. These include your current client files, financial records, and relevant subject-area files.

Archives. Materials that you are keeping for reference or for purposes of documentation can be kept in remote locations out of your immediate office area such as a basement, attic, or garage. We call this filing area *deep storage.* Financial and tax records from previous years, completed projects, and other materials you are either required to keep or might otherwise have to reconstruct should be kept there.

We've found that clearing out the backlog of your concerns, files, and piles to make time and space for more of what you want in life works miracles. Actually it's in accord with a major law of physics: nature abhors a vacuum. If you continue holding open time and space for the most important things in your life, there will be less and less room for those things you don't find rewarding because you'll attract more and more of the things you've made room for. You'll have made room to expand and grow in the directions you desire.

Scheduling for Results

If you don't know where you're going, you'll probably end up someplace else.

YOGI BERRA

Nothing happens until you create a space for it, and that's what a schedule is for. Your schedule, if you make and follow one, carves out time for the things you want in your life. You can think about your schedule for the day as a table with a limited number of chairs. Each chair can either be reserved for an honored and cherished guest or be left open, to be filled on a first-come, first-serve basis. Of course, as with any dinner party, the guests at the table determine how much you enjoy the meal. So although in business there will always be periodic surprise guests, you want to make sure that for the most part the party goes according to your invitation list.

Undoubtedly you've already heard about the importance of setting goals if you want to succeed. Brian Tracy, motivational speaker and author of *The Psychology of Success,* says, "Goals are dreams with a deadline." Goals bring your intentions to life. In fact, a University of San Francisco study has clearly demonstrated that the highest indicator of success is the passion to pursue well-defined goals. But just setting goals is not enough. A study on goal setting sponsored by the Ford Foundation showed that:

- Twenty-three percent of the population has no idea what they want from life and as a result they don't have much.
- Sixty-seven percent of the population has a general idea of what they want but they don't have any plans for how to get it.
- Only 10 percent of the population has specific, well-defined goals, but even then, seven out of ten of those people reach their goals only half of the time.
- The top 3 percent, however, achieved their goals 89 percent of the time. That's an .890 batting average. What any baseball player wouldn't give to hit that well!

Like us, the researchers wanted to know what accounted for the dramatic difference between that top 3 percent and the others. They found that of all the possible variables, the only difference between the top performers and the rest was that the top 3 percent *wrote down their goals.*

Operating from Goals

If you want to increase your chances for success and up your batting average, you have to do more than just *set* goals. You need to write them down and then bring them to life. Making up a list at New Year's and then forgetting about it won't get you nearly as far as incorporating your goals into each and every week. If you can see them on your calendar and make room for them on your schedule, you'll get where you want to be much more quickly. Here are six steps for turning goals into reality.

1. Define specific goals. Goals are a target for you to shoot at. They enable you to know where you're going, how you'll get there, and when you'll arrive. The more specific you can be and the more urgency you give them, the better. Set goals in terms of measurable results you're committed to achieving. For example, don't set a general goal like "I'll have a successful desktop publishing business" or "This week I'll get more clients." Be specific.

- "By December 31, I will have produced $65,000 in income from my desktop publishing service."
- "By next month, I will have two new contracts of more than $4,000 each."
- "This month I will interview five product reps and select one to represent me."
- "This week I will make twenty sales calls and sell $2,000 worth of products."
- "I'll finish thirty pages of the report this week."
- "I'll have my newsletter in print by April 1."

Such specific goals enable you to know what you have to accomplish by what date. If you miss the target, however, don't despair. You haven't failed; you just haven't succeeded yet. Simply aim again until you hit the bull's-eye.

2. Write your goals down. Create a separate file on your computer or electronic organizer for listing your goals. Or list them on a separate page in your personal organizer. Or write them on three-by-five index cards you can carry in your calendar or wallet. Under each goal, list all the tasks you will need to do to reach that goal, and cross off these tasks as you achieve them.

3. Keep your goals in your line of sight. Remember, the mind goes toward what's in front of it. So don't bury your goals somewhere and look at them once a year. Carry them with you. Post them above your computer. Hang them on the wall behind your desk. Have them printed on your calendar.

4. Review your goals daily. Refer to your goals when planning your schedule and constructing your daily to-do list. Don't let a day go by without taking some step toward your goals. In fact, make sure you take several steps toward your goals *every* day by putting key tasks on the calendar. I, Sarah, like to write my goals on my weekly calendar. I find that even though I'm often just rewriting the same goals each week, the process of writing them out makes sure they stay in the forefront of my attention.

5. Do a daily goal check. At the end of each day, ask yourself, "What have I done today to achieve my goals?" Don't be satisfied with excuses and rationalizations. Even if it means staying up late or missing out on an evening of TV, agree not to go to bed without having taken at least one step in the direction you're headed. This will be a real motivation for making sure you take steps toward your goals during the workday.

6. Create goals for all aspects of your life and career. One common way to sabotage goals is to set them for only one aspect of your business or your life. For example, as self-employed individuals we not only have to do the business; we also have to get the business and run the business. If we concentrate on only one of these vital aspects, the business will ultimately become lopsided and suffer. Therefore, set goals each week or month for the following.

- *What business you will actually do*—how many clients, projects, or portions of projects you will complete.
- *What marketing efforts you will undertake*—how many networking meetings, sales calls, thank-you notes, ad campaigns, or mailings you will attend to.
- *What administrative tasks you will complete*—when you will do the filing, bookkeeping, purchasing, and invoicing.

Don't forget to include your personal, social, and financial goals. If the only goals you make are work related, don't be surprised if your health, relationships, and personal well-being suffer. We get results in those areas of our life that we invest time, energy, and money on. Spending time with friends and family, relaxing, meditating, learning, and nurturing and entertaining ourselves are equally important to our success. Your goals could include:

- Meditating daily
- Going to the gym three times a week
- Enjoying a family outing each week
- A romantic evening on Friday nights
- Dinner with friends twice a month

Bringing Goals into the Moment

> *Even if you're on the right track, you'll get run over if you just sit there.*
>
> WILL ROGERS

Having a clear purpose for your work, setting specific goals, and having good ideas for what you want to accomplish will get you on track, but ultimately the best measure of your effectiveness is how quickly you can turn your ideas, goals, and dreams into reality. And that's a matter of what actually makes it off your schedule and into the events of your day.

Here are three ways to make sure you bring your goals into the moment.

1. Prioritize your daily to-do list. Based on your goals, as you list the things you need to do each day, put them through the 80/20 Test. Mark each item *A* or *B. A* is for the items that produce 80 percent of our results—the truly essential, important or urgent activities. *B* is for everything else—the trivial, insignificant, and extraneous.

Screen your *A* list again. Are there some items on this list you can do without? Are they truly essential, or do you only think they are? Post your *A* list on your desk, phone, drafting table, or computer while you work. Resolve to work until you do as many *A* tasks as possible. We like to use Post-it notes to list the *A* tasks for the day. Sometimes there's only one big item. Usually there are one big one and four or five little ones. Some days we have to keep a Post-it hanging around for a few days before all the items are done, but it sure feels great when you get to throw it out and start a new one.

2. Stick to your priorities. The most common time wasters are procrastination, interruptions, emergencies, not being able to find the information you need, mismanaged meetings, unnecessary phone calls, trying to do everything yourself, and overworking. As you've undoubtedly discovered, if you allow them to, these activities can eat up 80 percent of your time while producing only 20 percent of your results. To make sure this doesn't happen, identify which activities are your biggest time wasters. What sabotages your plans? What gets you off course? For a week, keep a log of the activities that get you off course, and pinpoint the 20 percent that cause 80 percent of your problems. Then take action. Once you recognize the culprits, you're halfway to eliminating them.

For example, if you have a client who calls you endlessly with one headache after another, maybe you need to summon up the courage to refer this client elsewhere. If you find yourself driving an hour each way to an office, maybe you should move your office home. If your kids intrude too often into your workday, maybe you need to arrange for child care for part of each day. If the paperwork involved in being a corporation or having an employee is taking up too much of your time, maybe you need to operate as a sole proprietor or subcontract your work.

Do whatever it takes to stick to those things that produce your best results. Schedule the *A* events of your day during your high-energy peaks. Reserve more taxing activities for time blocks when you're fresh. Leave less demanding tasks for off hours. Set up a system to touch any piece of incoming paper only once. Screen your calls, and return them during a specified time block. Put up a DO NOT DISTURB sign. Say no politely but firmly. And build in time for the few but unavoidable emergencies that will still arise. Then, when the time comes, close the door on work.

3. Focus your efforts. Since you undoubtedly will have multiple *A* items on your list, focus your energy by grouping the things you need to do into effective time blocks. Put similar tasks together and schedule these blocks rather than putting random activities on your calendar throughout the day. For example, you might set aside a time when you make all your phone calls. Or do your paperwork in one block. Cluster meetings and appointments back-to-back. Run all errands on one trip.

Scheduling your day with activity blocks instead of sprinkling various types of activities throughout the day saves you time in getting out and putting away materials. It cuts down on interruptions and helps people know when it's best to reach you. And best of all, because each type of activity demands its own mindset, working in activity blocks helps you concentrate and stay focused. And be sure to remember to include a block of time each day for your personal life.

Making Time for Your Personal Life

Down time can be very uplifting.

DR. CLIFF MANGAN, PH.D.

If you tend to overwork and therefore have difficulty making time for the personal aspects of life, treat your personal time with the same discipline and dedication with which you approach your work. For example, develop the habit of putting personal and social free time on your calendar just as you would an important work activity. When business-related tasks are proposed for those times, you can then rightly say you're already booked for that time—because you are.

You are as important as your work. In fact, as the source of your work, you're the most valuable asset of your business. As such, your well-being is vital to your success. You need to be healthy, happy, rested, and nourished. What kind of breeder would run a prized racehorse day in and day out without rest? What race driver would allow his or her multi-million-dollar car to go without regular maintenance? What kind of boss works his or her employees morning, noon, and night? Would you want to work for someone who has no respect for your personal life? Isn't that part of why you wanted to work for yourself? Would you drive someone who was working for you that hard? Why do it to yourself?

Of course, there are exceptions. There are times when you must put in long hours. But unless that's the way you honestly want to live your life, don't let fear or drive make you into the kind of management that incites a strike. Ultimately that's what our bodies do for us when we overwork. They get sick. Often illness is the body's way of going on strike.

That's what happened to a very successful independent insurance broker who came to consult with Sarah. He was one of those people who, obsessed with work, drive themselves fourteen hours a day for weeks on end. Periodically he would collapse in exhaustion, unable to work at all for days or even weeks. During that time he'd lie in bed weak and drained, chiding himself for leaving his clients and projects hanging in the air. Finally he'd recover enough to get back to work and start the cycle over again. His periodic illnesses forced him to cancel important appointments and miss many deadlines, and he would feel compelled to make up for these inconveniences to his clients by working even harder, which would ultimately put him back in bed again. In his desire to do the superhuman, he had actually become unreliable.

When he came to talk with Sarah his hope was that she would help him to work harder so he could be more reliable. Instead, she helped him recognize the overwork/collapse pattern he was living out again and again. Once he realized that if he had a boss who drove him that hard he'd certainly quit (and probably file a workmen's-compensation claim, too), he applied the same remarkable determination that had driven him to overwork to maintaining a more realistic work schedule. To his surprise, he got just as much done over a six-month period and still had time to fall in love, enjoy weekends and evenings with his lover, and even take regular three-day weekend trips.

Needless to say, this is an extreme example. But it illustrates how we can in fact have it all, but only if we make room for it all. Once we're on our own, it's actually our own excesses that create the illusion that there isn't enough time to balance our lives.

Why wait until you get sick to make sure you have time each day to relax and enjoy the personal aspects of your life? Pretend you are your own labor union. What bargain can you strike with yourself? When the time comes to close the door on work, you must simply stop wherever you are. Isn't that what you would do if you'd scheduled an appointment with a VIP client? Would you stand that client up? Would you keep him or her waiting? Of course not. Well, don't put your life on hold, either. Don't stand yourself up.

Making Time to Work As Much As You Want

> I regard myself as . . . one of the happiest men on
> earth because I've been doing what I like all my life.
>
> ASHLEY MONTAGU

But what if you're one of those people who *want* to work all the time? Many people who go out on their own love what they do so much that they *want* to do it morning, noon, and night. They eat, sleep, drink, and breathe their work. Left on their own, their life would become their work and often does. If this describes you, you probably feel energized by your work and have little interest in finding free time. Instead you probably feel pressured and beleaguered by the demands of others in your life who are always trying to pry you away from your work. Perhaps you feel guilty for not spending more time with your family and friends.

But remember this: *on your own, you are in charge of your life.* Don't turn your family and friends into the thorn in your side that your boss once was. You get to decide who sits at your dinner table, so to speak, and what goes onto your plate each day. If you want to work morning, noon, and night, it's truly your choice. Is that really what you want? And is it actually working for you? Are you healthy? Are you producing the quality of work you want to be producing? Are you enjoying it? Or are you driving yourself from fear, anxiety, obsession, or to escape other things in your life that aren't working? If so, an honest assessment of your situation will probably show that the quality of your work and the quality of your life would be far higher were you to relax a little.

If, however, you are in fact enjoying your work and you find it rewarding, fulfilling, and energizing to work constantly, then the truth is there's room for little else in your life. You will do yourself a favor by taking the time to explain this honestly to the others around you. Tell them about what your work means to you and how you feel about it. Often when people know what they can expect and understand the significance of it, they are willing to support you, even if they would prefer to spend more time with you.

A child, for example, whose single parent must work two jobs to support the family may not like having so little time with his parent, but he will probably understand that the lack of attention he gets is actually coming from love and is not a sign that he is unimportant, unworthy or unlovable. A child whose parent could easily spend more time with him, however, might feel like he's not loved. From his perspective what else could it mean? He may think there must be something wrong with him—or with you, the parent. But once the child understands why what you do is so important to you, he may feel proud of your work and of you, even though he sees you very little. This can also be true of spouses and friends.

If you are *fully* present for children or loved ones at those times when you are available, this will help, too. If by the time you get to them you're exhausted and grumpy, that will only compound the problem and increase their disappointment and dissatisfaction. Of course, simply taking them for granted when you are free will, too. But if they know you are delighted and pleased to be with them in the time you do have, everyone will be more supportive. This means you have to free yourself from any guilt you may be feeling about working so much, because feeling guilty about not being more available will only put further distance between you and the others in your life when you are together.

You will certainly enjoy life more if your partner and friends are supportive and excited about your work. But they will be able to do this only if you help them understand what your work means to you and to those you serve. If, having done this, they still don't and won't support you, perhaps you will be better off parting ways and developing other relationships that are more compatible with each of your goals and life purposes. In building new relationships, be sure to let others know from the start what they can expect from you in terms of time.

Interruption Busters

1. Put on the answering machine or engage an answering service or voice mail so you can devote large periods of uninterrupted time to your work. Set up a time later in the day to return phone calls and deal with other matters that arose during these periods.

2. Free the majority of your week for uninterrupted work by setting aside a day or half day to handle all the administrative aspects of your business. Set up a file or in box for all the matters you must address that day.

3. Hire a full- or part-time assistant or outside business services to do whatever aspects of your work you can afford to delegate to them.

4. Set up your office and the business side of your work so that they will run themselves as much as possible. Chapter 4 outlines how you can use routines, technology, and creative approaches to free yourself to do what you do best and enjoy most.

Sometimes it's not just friends and family who try to take us from our sacred work. Often it's the *administrivia* of being on our own that prevents us from getting anything done. We resent the constant intrusions of phone calls, piles of mail, urgent letters from the IRS, bank statements that need justifying, and on and on. Isn't it amazing how such minutiae can devour your day? Above are several things you can do to protect and preserve your ability to work with uninterrupted abandon.

As you can see, you can learn how to get done what needs to be done and still enjoy your life. The world desperately needs your very best, and you've got what it takes to succeed. Use it to have the time of your life.

Resources

Embracing Each Other. Hal Stone and Sidra Winkelman. San Rafael, CA: New World Library, 1989. The best book we've found on understanding and healing relationships.

Executive in Passage. Donald Marrs. Los Angeles: Barrington Sky Publishing, 1990. The autobiography of a highly paid advertising executive who encounters a crisis of consciousness when he discovered that his job is at odds with his personal values and ethics. It outlines how he came to establish and operate a business that integrated his values and his career.

Finding Your Life Mission. Naomi Stephan. Walpole, NH: Stillpoint Publishing, 1989. A guide for finding rewarding and meaningful work.

How to Stay Up No Matter What Goes Down. Sarah Edwards. Here's How, (Box 5172, Santa Monica, CA 90409), 1988. This audiocassette album provides practical daily messages for getting organized, sticking to business, and living your life on purpose.

Live Your Vision. Joyce Chapman. North Hollywood, CA: Newcastle Books, 1990. A book about discovering what you really want and how to make it happen.

Love Is the Answer: Creating Positive Relationships. Gerald Jampolsky and Diane Cirincione. New York: Bantam, 1990. Seven steps to creating positive relationships and fifteen lessons for transforming fear into love.

The Path of Least Resistance. Robert Fritz. New York: Fawcett Columbine, 1989. The underlying thesis of this book is that we have the capacity to create new structures in our lives that will take us precisely where we want to go.

The Psychology of Success. Brian Tracy. Chicago: Nightingale Conant, 1986. A six-cassette audiotape program.

Working from Home. Paul and Sarah Edwards. Los Angeles: Jeremy P. Tarcher, 1990. See especially Part 4 and Part 5.

CHAPTER
FOUR

■■■■■■■■■■■■■■■■■■■■■■■

Getting the Business to Run Itself So You Can Do What You Do Best

The last thing I get to do is sing.
LOU RAWLS

How much of your time do you actually spend doing the parts of your work that you enjoy and find rewarding? Like the singer Lou Rawls, do you find that your work is the last thing you get to do? If so, you are paying a high price for the privilege and freedom of being your own boss. Instead of having the time to enjoy the work you do, you may feel more like you're struggling to hold down several part-time jobs— spending hours as a receptionist answering the phones and responding to mail; hours as a salesperson finding leads, making presentations, and closing sales; hours as a file clerk and administrator keeping records, filing, billing, collecting, and getting in supplies; even hours as a housekeeper or janitor keeping the home and office presentable.

And, worst of all, you don't even get paid for doing these jobs—they're your overhead! Unfortunately, such administrative aspects of being on your own can easily consume a disproportionate amount of your energy and eat into your actual billable time. Often self-employed individuals spend up to 40 percent of their time marketing or selling themselves and 25 percent of their time administering their business. That leaves only about a third of your time to actually do what you went on your own to do. It also means you have to either charge more or earn less, because you've got to live off what you make in that vital third of your time.

But what if you could reduce the time you need to spend marketing and running your business? What if you could set up the business side of what you do so that it essentially runs itself? That's what this chapter is about. There are actually many simple things you can do to shrink the most time-consuming, non-income-producing aspects of being on your own. In this chapter we'll address how you can position yourself so that instead of having to go out and get business, ample business will come to you in the course of the work you do. We'll show you how technology can streamline otherwise tedious and time-consuming administrative tasks; how you can create routines that will take care of details automatically; and ways to avoid unnecessary make-work and to double up what you're doing to more than double your results. We'll provide guidelines for how to decide when it's time to call in or send out for additional help.

Of course, if you're a one-person operation, chances are you can't literally get your business to run itself entirely on its own. In other words, you probably won't be able to become an absentee business owner. But most likely that's not why you went out on your own anyway. What you can most certainly do is create a momentum that will enable your business to become self-generating and self-sustaining. You can literally get the world around you—your daily operations, your industry, your clients and customers—working for you.

Nine Principles for Getting Everything Working for You

Imagine this. You're working on a rewarding project. It keeps you busy, and it pays well. Throughout the project you get frequent requests to work on other projects. You consult your timetable and begin filling in your calendar. Before you know it, you're booked for the next few months and then for the next year. Invoices go out; checks come in.

Or perhaps you're selling a product and you get your first large order. Soon more orders are coming in and your accounts begin renewing their orders automatically. Whereas you once had to make several phone calls, meet with buyers, and send volumes of follow-up correspondence to get an order, now buyers are calling you for information. Purchase orders come in; products go out; checks come back.

That's what we call *momentum*—that is, an impetus or directed movement that accelerates seemingly under its own power. The more momentum your business generates, the less effort you need to expend to keep things going and the more the details and administrivia of doing business become automatic and routine, freeing you to enjoy the excitement, drama, and challenge of doing rewarding work. That's the way it's supposed to work. If you liked grappling with administrative hassles you would probably have kept your job. So don't re-create these hassles on your own. Develop enough momentum around your work that it will support you in an easy and orderly fashion.

Think of yourself as training for a long-distance race. At first your steps are labored and you're short of breath. But as you continue to work out, your stride becomes steadier and your pace picks up. You go longer and farther with less effort; no more straining, huffing, and puffing. Going the distance becomes second nature. That's the way you want your business to develop. You want to reach a stride that will carry you through the race and over the finish line.

If you're continually struggling and suffering on your own, that is not normal. That's not par for the course. It's not all you can expect! If you're just beginning, then yes, as with the new long-distance runner, some degree of struggling and suffering could be considered par for the course—but only at first. For heaven's sake do not think that's what being on your own has to be. That's only what it's like when you're starting out or if you're doing it the hard way. Here are nine key principles for building ample momentum to keep you going with less effort.

1. Commit to having things work smoothly and easily. Don't settle for a difficult, time-consuming, cumbersome life. No matter how long it takes, don't accept difficulty as your way of life. Identify the administrative things that take up inordinate time and energy and resolve to find ways to streamline them. Don't assume overwork and struggle are just the price you have to pay for being on your own. Although sometimes you may have to pay a stiff price at first, if you demand more of life, you're much more likely to find a way to make it work the way you want it to.

2. Adopt technology that will help you do it quicker or easier. We're in the midst of an unprecedented technological revolution. There is more technology available to improve our lives today than any of us can absorb. If you're a technophobe, give it up. Embrace new technologies that will make your life work better. Many courses and consultants are available to help you learn how to use them.

Later in this chapter we'll introduce you to what we consider to be the ideal technology for someone who's self-employed. But we can't begin to mention all the specialized technology that's available for your particular field. You'll find news about these technologies in trade journals from your field and by talking with colleagues and friends. When you see or hear about innovative new technology, keep an open mind. Say yes to it mentally. Avoid the temptation many of us have to immediately think, "Oh, I don't need that" or "That wouldn't work for me" or "I can't afford that." Usually we can find a way to do whatever we decide we need to do.

Often equipment will actually pay for itself directly in increased savings or sales. Operating your own copy machine, for example, can cost less in a few months than driving to and from a copy store and paying print-shop prices for each copy. A laser printer can pay for itself in what you save on the cost of typesetting your newsletter. A fax can pay for itself in overnight-delivery fees and speed all forms of communication with clients and suppliers, including billing. A computer and printer can enable you to do your own direct-mail campaign in half the time and can pay for itself in increased sales from the additional mailings you do. If you receive a lot of mail, an electronic letter opener can free your time for billable activity. And if you send out a lot of mail, a postage meter can more than pay for itself.

Sometimes technology will pay for itself indirectly, by increasing the value of your product or service sufficiently that your sales or prices can go up, or by giving you a professional image that gets you in the door so you can get more business. An ergonomically designed chair, for example, can save you discomfort, lost productivity, and physical-therapy bills.

Such cost savings and increased sales make strategic equipment an investment you can't afford not to make, and well worth buying on credit if you don't have funds to pay in full up front. And of course the cost of your business equipment is tax deductible, and you can amortize the cost over time.

3. Get help.   Although you're on your own, you don't have to do everything yourself, even if you can't afford to hire full- or part-time employees. Many of your biggest time-consuming tasks can be done by contracting for outside help on a project-by-project basis. Bookkeeping, public relations, filing, mailing-list management, newsletter preparation, house-cleaning, and even sales are all functions that many people find can be cost-effectively done by hiring someone else on an as-needed basis.

People frequently tell us they can't afford to hire outside help. But sometimes you will actually save money by hiring someone else. On the following page are some rules of thumb for deciding when and if it's time to hire out.

Whenever you identify something that is taking up time you could be spending more profitably and pleasantly, think about how you can find someone else to do it for you quicker and more cost-effectively. Ask yourself if there's a service that could do this more cheaply. Then think of how to make sure the work you pay others to do can directly or indirectly pay for itself in increased income. In other words, amortize the cost of hiring staff or services just as you would your equipment.

4. Use OPE—Other People's Energy.   Hiring help is not the only way to get others to work for you. There are many creative and mutually beneficial ways to get customers, clients, colleagues, suppliers, gatekeepers, and mentors to work for you as well. Why not do joint mailings with others whose products or services are compatible with yours? Or arrange to slip your materials in with someone else's mailings? With the proper incentives and information, a few highly satisfied clients can become an extension of your sales effort. You can offer discounts, free services, or even finder's fees to people who bring business to you.

When to Hire Help

1. When the time you could spend marketing or earning income instead of doing the tasks involved covers or exceeds the cost of the help. For example:
   - Hiring someone to design and send out a direct-mail piece that will generate more business for you than the cost of the help to produce it
   - Hiring a publicist to do public relations so you can take on an added project that will more than cover the fee of the publicist
   - Hiring a computer consultant to set up and install your computer when trying to learn it yourself will eat away hours of billable time.
2. When the cost of hiring the staff would be self-liquidating. In other words, when the person's activity would generate as much income as, or more income than, you would have to pay them. For example:
   - Hiring someone to sell your services
   - Hiring a service to take your calls when losing one call because no one was there to answer a potential customer's questions would more than pay for the service.
   - Hiring someone to publish a newsletter for you that will draw in more business per issue than it costs to produce the publication.
3. When paying someone else would cost you less than doing it yourself. For example:
   - Contracting out to print one hundred copies of a ten-page project report instead of printing them out on your laser printer.
   - Hiring someone to oversee the production of a brochure that would cost you more to sub-contract to multiple individuals.
4. When you are bringing in enough income that you can cover the costs of hiring help to increase the quality of your life. For example:
   - Hiring someone to clean your home/office
   - Hiring someone to do your filing

Cross-referring clients with other professionals can also be a low-cost, time-saving marketing method. For example, if you do accounting, your clients may need legal services at times and you can arrange to cross-refer your clients to an attorney, who will in turn send you his or her clients who need an accountant. You can do the same with your suppliers.

The speech and diction coach Sandy McKnight made creative use of OPE when she arranged with a temporary-help service to offer a free introductory seminar on accent reduction. Since the seminar would attract new personnel to the service, the service owners agreed to provide the space and pay for an ad promoting the seminar. They also agreed to mail a flyer to all their existing temporary staff. At the free seminar, Sandy enrolled those who wished more assistance in an ongoing seminar for which she split the profits with the agency.

In such an arrangement, everyone wins. By offering something its competitors don't offer, the agency gains a competitive edge and attracts new personnel. The participants get good information, and Sandy gets to fill her seminars without any out-of-pocket advertising costs. She calls this arrangement value-added marketing and plans to make as many such arrangements as possible.

Often, even when speaking for free before a professional or community group, you can get the organization to publicize you and your appearance by sending a news release to the local media. You can also request that the organization enclose some of your materials with its meeting announcements. Or you can volunteer to do work for a trade association in your field in exchange for piggybacking on association mailings and being featured in a special article in the association's newsletter.

Also, building a relationship with one or two well-placed *gatekeepers* (people who can unlock opportunities for you), can save you hours of mar-

---

Ask Your Way to Success

Success is clearly a joint venture, a team effort. You can't do it alone. But sometimes it feels lonely along the road to your goals. How would you like to have a team of experts, mentors, guides, and well-wishers to assist you along the way? Sound good? Well, you may be surprised to discover that there are plenty of such supporters who could be at your beck and call.

In fact, as author and motivational speaker Brian Tracy says, you can *ask* your way to success. There are always people who are complimented by your asking for their help. There are, however, certain rules for attracting benefactors into your life. Here are a few we've learned.

- **Admit you don't know.** Too often we think we have to put on the appearance that we know it all. And even worse, sometimes we even fool ourselves into thinking it's true. In reality there's always something new to learn from life and from others. The pace of change is accelerating rapidly, and there are more scientists and specialists breaking new ground than at any other time in history. It's not a sign of weakness to admit you don't know. It's a sign of strength to approach life as a lifelong learner, curious and eager to know more. So routinely take note of areas of your work or business that you would like to learn more about.

- **Go to the source.** Once you identify something you need to know more about, go to those people who are clearly the authorities in that area. Identify who has the talents, expertise, and knowhow you need. Start there. If they can't help you, they'll probably know someone who can.

---

keting. For example, an interior designer might get most of his business from one prominent architect. A commercial real-estate agent can be a source of business for a cleaning service. So identify who comes into regular contact with people who need your service and see how you can work cooperatively to save each other time and money.

5. Use experts. The British prime minister Benjamin Disraeli once said that, all other things being equal, the person who succeeds will be the person with the best information. Just one key piece of information can save you hundreds to thousands of dollars and hours, months, or even years of time, not to mention safeguarding you from the agony of painful mistakes. In fact, a Dunn and Bradstreet study found that 92 percent of business failures could be traced to the lack of some type of knowledge or how to apply that knowledge.

When any aspect of your endeavors isn't working for you as well as you'd like, don't accept defeat. Nothing is inevitable. Don't accept even marginal results. Seek out the specialized information you need to get the results you

---

- **Be specific.** Gatekeepers and mentors are eager to help, but they can help you only if they know what you need. So do your homework before you ask for help. Such people are intrigued and challenged by intelligent and well-thought-out questions. And when you don't know what you need, ask about that: Where should I go to find out what I need to know to do this successfully?

- **Be willing to pay.** People are flattered when you ask for their help, but if what you need requires more than a phone conversation or guest lunch, offer to pay for the expertise. If you have the right person, it's worth every penny. Most certainly plan to pay whenever the help you need is what the person does for a living.

- **Accept the help you're offered.** One of Sarah's mentors told her recently that he was glad to see she was using his advice. He said he often hesitates to take the time to share his expertise with others because while many people seek his advice, few actually use it. Is it any wonder that 20 percent of all medical prescriptions are never filled? If you respect someone enough to ask for their help, at least give their advice a try. Most certainly don't take up their time telling all the reasons their advice won't work for you.

- **Express appreciation.** For heaven's sake, make it a point to thank the people who help you. Isn't that one of the major reasons people help each other? Everyone likes to be appreciated. We all want to know we've made a difference.

- **Pass it on.** Circulate what you learn. When you learn something that could be helpful to others, pass it on. We all grow from what we know. As Jesse Jackson said, "You aren't known for what you know; you're known for what you teach."

Your Personal Information Network

- Accountant or tax adviser
- Computer consultant
- Information researcher
- Insurance agent
- Investment counselor

- Lawyer
- Marketing and advertising specialist
- Public-relations specialist
- Professional organizer

---

want. This is the information age. Information is available on almost any subject you need. Read, attend seminars, identify consultants who specialize in helping people accomplish what you need to do. Someone, somewhere, knows about something that can help you.

The owner of a gift-basket business knew that being able to take Master-Card and Visa would increase her sales, but every bank she approached turned down her request for merchant status because she ran her business from home. Through the Working from Home Forum on CompuServe Information Service, however, she discovered a list of companies that broker merchant status for home-based businesses. And sure enough, now that she can offer credit her business has increased without her having to spend any additional time or money.

A graphic designer used to spend hours trying to balance her bank account. She felt stupid and incompetent. Finally she overcame her embarrassment and told a colleague about the problem. The colleague recommended a software package called Quicken that keeps her balance automatically.

These are just two examples of how the right information can free you from business tasks. Actively seeking out the key information and expertise you need can make your life simpler. The reference librarian at your local library may be able to direct you to the information you need as well as sources of information for finding books, tapes, and seminars. Professional associations are often a rich source of information. They are a particularly valuable source for finding reliable consultants. Information brokers are another resource you can turn to for strategic information. They specialize in finding difficult-to-locate information for a fee.

We urge you to build a personal information network of experts whom you can call upon when you need assistance. Consider building relationships with reliable individuals from the lists on these facing pages.

6. Find the little things that make a big difference. Often in working successfully on your own, it's the small things that make the biggest difference. Little things that don't cost much and aren't terribly glamorous or exciting can often simplify your day and make your life a lot easier. Many of

---

Valuable Sources of Expert Help

The Small Business Network, 1341 Ancona Drive, La Verne, CA 91750; (800) 825-8286. A knowledge network of professionals that's designed to help people obtain the information they need to start, develop, and maintain a successful small business. Each chapter has a panel of professionals available to all members.

American Business Management Association, Box 111, West Hyannis Port, MA 02672. Business, tax, and financial-planning services for small and home-based businesses. When you join this association you have access to a network of business consultants from your community who specialize in helping people start and organize small businesses. Currently in Los Angeles, San Diego, Boston, New York, Phoenix, and San Francisco.

Small Business Administration Mentor Program. The Small Business Administration's Office of Women's Business Ownership offers a mentoring program for women business owners who are ready for business expansion. For information contact the nearest Small Business Administration office.

CompuServe Information Service. CompuServe is an on-line videotext service that you access through your telephone via a personal computer and modem. There you will find a wealth of expert help. The Computer Consultants Forum is a good way to meet computer consultants in your community. The Computer Training Forum is a place to get advice and information about learning to use a computer. Also, major manufacturers of hardware and software have staff on-line who will help with problems and answer questions. The Disabilities Forum is a source of support and information on resources and opportunities for individuals with various disabilities. The Working Home Forum offers business expertise and networking with professionals and successful home-based businesses from coast to coast; we founded and run this forum, where you'll find access to highly practical marketing, tax, legal, public-relations, and business advice. In addition, many professional groups have on-line forums.

The National Association of Professional Organizers, 3824 Ocean View Boulevard, Montrose, CA 91020.

Association of Independent Information Professionals, c/o Brody Information Services, 9 Hillcrest Road, Port Washington, NY 11050.

Independent Computer Consultants Association, Box 27412, St. Louis, MO 63141.

---

these lifesavers don't make it onto the list of must-haves in setting up an office. In fact, they're easily overlooked. They may be things you never think of or just never get around to shopping for.

Little Things That Make a Big Difference

A cordless phone. Have you ever noticed that whatever document you need to refer to while you're on the phone always seems to be in another location? A cordless phone frees you from the ball-and-chain effect of a standard phone. You can go to and from files and bookcases and from one room to another while talking on the phone. You can continue your phone conversation while you answer the door as clients or deliveries arrive. And of course if you're working on tasks in an area away from your desk, you can take the phone with you and answer incoming calls without having to drop what you're doing. They're also great for those moments when the dog is scratching noisily to be let out while you're talking to a key client. A mute button that cuts off unwanted noise helps at moments like those as well.

A telephone headset. If you spend much time talking on the phone, a headset is a lifesaver, and specifically a neck saver! Rather than trying to cradle the phone on your shoulder while you take notes or enter text, you can have both hands free to write or do other tasks while you talk. This is particularly handy when you've been put on hold. Instead of getting aggravated about the delay, you can go on about your work while you wait. We find Plantronics headsets to be comfortable and to provide satisfactory incoming and outgoing voice quality. Headsets come in both corded and cordless models.

A copy holder. What contortions we go through to enter text or numbers from a paper copy into a computer! We crook our necks. We prop up the paper on the monitor—but, of course, it falls over and we lose our place. A copyholder ends all this needless frustation. They come in many styles, from freestanding magnetic or clip-on desktop models to flexible arms that attach to your monitor. Legal-sized and extra-wide holders for spreadsheets are available, too. Copyholders range in price from under $3 to $150 for an electric model that advances your copy as you work. A new version, the Copy Hinge from West Manufacturing, holds paper with a roller grip rather than a clip hinge, making it possible to insert and remove pages with only one hand and to display more than one page at a time.

A good way to identify the little things that will make a big difference in your day is to notice the repetitive tasks you find most frustrating. Undoubtedly, tasks that frustrate you over and over again are irritating to others, too, so chances are someone has created something to help. Why suffer? Visit office-supply stores and browse through mail-order catalogues such as those from Reliable and Quill. You'll be surprised at the little things that have been developed to make your working life easier, more convenient, and more comfortable. A few of our favorites are listed on these facing pages.

Grammar checking software. Certainly nothing makes a worse impression in business correspondence than poor grammar. But bad grammar is like bad breath: you don't know you have it until someone points it out—and usually no one does. Fortunately, grammar-checking software can save you the embarrassment. You can quickly and routinely run your documents through a grammar checker right along with your spell checker. We use Reference Software's *Grammatik IV,* which lists for $99 but can be bought by mail order for as little as $47.

A digital postage scale. How much time do you waste waiting in line at the post office? Somehow the lines are always longest just when you're most pressed for time. A digital postage scale makes meeting the pickup deadlines easy and saves you hours every month by enabling you to weigh and stamp all your outgoing mail yourself. There's no more waiting in line. To determine the correct amount of postage, request a booklet on rates and fees from the U.S. Postal Service, and keep a supply of stamps in many denominations on hand. And don't forget to keep a supply of overnight-mail envelopes and stamps handy, as well as forms for certified and registered mail. Having to go to the back of the line to fill out a form can be double punishment. Costs for digital postage scales begin about $100.

Preinked and customized stamps. Customized preinked stamps are neat and make a more reliable impression than the old ink pads. We have ones reading *First Class, Priority, and Fourth Class Mail.* You can also get them made for your return address, your signature, and to designate particular actions taken.

Plastic silverware trays. Usually desk drawers are better suited for sweaters and underwear than for the many little things we need to keep in them. More likely than not, when you open your desk drawer it's all there in a hodge-podge—pens, pencils, Post-it pads, paper clips, rubber bands, scissors, stapler, and so on—that you have to rummage through every time you need something. Happily, plastic silverware trays fit perfectly in desk drawers and provide an excellent place for keeping everything neatly in sight and at your fingertips.

Plastic stacking trays. If you can't find the top of your desk, plastic stacking trays can clean up desktop clutter in a snap, and they're only two to three dollars a piece. They're also ideal for storing documents you use too frequently to be constantly filing. Unless you are diligent about weekly filing, however, we advise against using them as to-file piles. They work best as handy receptacles for work in progress.

---

7. Work smarter, not harder.   Hard work is often due to the piling up of the easy things you neglect to do. So don't make extra work for yourself. In other words, running an office is like cleaning up the dishes: what you put off doing gets hard, and you can't get it off without a lot of elbow grease. Consider the following ways we make extra work for ourselves.

- If you don't create a pile, it doesn't have to be filed.
- If you don't accumulate a bunch of receipts, they don't need to be sorted.
- If you charge when you deliver your service, you don't have to bill or invoice.
- If you get timely payments, you don't have to spend time collecting.
- If you handle a complaint now, you won't have to call back later.
- If you order enough, soon enough, you won't run out in the middle of a project and have to rush around to order again.

As a general rule, when it comes to handling the details of being on your own, what you can do in a minute now can take you an hour later. It's easier to handle something once than to do something with it that will require you to handle it again later.

8. Set up routines to take care of details automatically. Whenever something needs to be done routinely or repetitively, the first thing to ask yourself is how you can get it to happen automatically. This applies to most aspects of business: marketing, billing, inventory, filing, cleaning, ordering, and so on. There's nothing like a routine to make things happen automatically. Routines enable you to make a habit of taking care of minutiae in the quickest and least intrusive way. Once established, they enable you to take care of many details without even thinking about them.

Essentially, having a routine means having a regular time, space, and manner for handling something. Here are several routines that most self-employed individuals will find helpful. Have a standard time, place, and procedure for:

- Processing the mail
- Filing receipts
- Balancing the checkbook
- Taking orders and/or phone calls
- Making follow-up marketing calls
- Sending out thank-you notes
- Reading newspapers, journals, and newsletters
- Filing and cleaning up work in progress
- Ordering supplies
- Running business errands

Each of these activities is easier to put off until tomorrow. They're easy to forget about and lose track of. They require much less time to do in a timely manner than once they've accumulated. And usually if you have no routine for these activities, you fall behind in doing them. Then they back up and ultimately bury you.

Although routines are often considered to be restrictive and dull, they actually free us to attend to more important matters. Routines are like the boiler room of your office. You want them to remain in the background and just keep chugging away while you go about your business. To create useful routines, identify the details you need to handle regularly and assign a convenient time and place to do them. Then commit to following your routines diligently for at least six weeks. If you find yourself avoiding or resenting your routines, it's sign that either the ones you've established aren't functional or you need additional help in managing them because they're taking up too much of your day.

9. Piggyback activities.   The more business activities you bundle into any one effort the better. For example, you can avoid doing a special mailing if you put sales promotional materials and reorder forms in every product order or invoice you send out. You can avoid extra phone calls if you keep a list by your telephone of things you want to pass on to people who call you.

With every business activity you undertake, get in the habit of asking yourself how many uses you can make out of it. If you're traveling to Houston for a conference, for example, think of the networking contacts, sales calls, or media appearances you can make while you're there. If you're speaking before a trade group, what materials can you distribute to those in attendance? Which key individuals can you invite to hear your presentation. What media coverage can you get? If you have a meeting in a particular area of the city, what other errands could you run in that vicinity while you're there?

Sarah has become adept at piggybacking activities. If she's making a speech, for example, she might have it taped to use as a demo for getting future speeches; she'll have the tape transcribed and then edit it into an article or handout; she'll collect names from the audience to call for future interviews; she'll conduct on-the-spot market research by asking key questions of the audience. Everything you do holds a wealth of potential piggybacking opportunities. If you're going to do something, why not make the most of it?

Making Light Work of the Most Time-Consuming Tasks

It will probably take you some time and energy to set these principles in motion in your work, but once they're operating, the momentum they create will free you to do more of what you want to do. You'll be able to make more money doing it. And you'll have more time to enjoy yourself in the process. So begin with the one idea from this chapter that could save you the most time, money, and energy. Implement that idea, and then with the extra time you save, do the next one and the next, until things are running themselves with just a little help from you.

When you start to apply these principles, you'll find they can help you make light work of the two most time-consuming and unpaid aspects of being on your own: marketing and administering your business. Let's take a further look at how.

The Critical Mass Marketing Alternative to Having to Constantly Sell Yourself

Marketing can make a small business large.

JAY CONRAD LEVINSON

Basically there are two ways to get work for yourself: go out and get it, or get it to come to you. The first is faster, but much more time-consuming and energy intensive. On your own, time is money and you're not getting paid while you're drumming up work. So if you want your time and energy free to earn money doing what you do, you're probably looking for methods that will bring work to you with the smallest investment of your time and energy.

In the book that we wrote with the marketing expert Laura Douglas, *Getting Business to Come To You,* we outlined thirty-five methods for attracting more business to you. You'll find them listed on the following page.

We now want to outline a particular marketing strategy for using these varied methods that can ultimately produce a steady stream of business with virtually no extra effort on your part. We call it *Critical Mass Marketing.* It's a method for those people who don't have the time or inclination to sell themselves in the traditional ways. It may initially be slower and more indirect than more traditional approaches to getting business such as advertising, telemarketing and cold-calling, but it does work.

Critical Mass Marketing is a strategy that involves giving yourself and your work a sufficiently high profile that your name becomes a powerful magnet that draws business opportunities to you. The goal is to create a situation whereby whenever someone needs what you offer, he or she will think about, hear about, read about, or otherwise be directed to *you*! Here's an example of how it works.

Helen Berman decided to become a consultant and sales trainer for the publishing industry, but the competition was tough. There were already a number of well-known consultants serving this industry. So how was she to break in? She knew that calling a list of the thousands of potential customers would be very costly both in time and in money. Because the people on that list didn't know about Helen Berman or her training programs, she would have to place many calls to make each sale. So instead, she set about building a high profile for herself and her programs that would cause interested, qualified individuals to identify themselves to her. Then when she contacted them, they would already know who she was and be motivated to talk with her; the same number of calls would lead to many times more sales.

Thirty-five Ways to Get Business to Come to You

Word-of-Mouth

1. Networking
2. Mentors and gatekeepers
3. Volunteerism
4. Sponsorships
5. Charitable donations
6. Referrals
7. Business name
8. Letterhead and business card
9. Product packaging
10. Point-of-sale display

Public Relations

11. Writing articles
12. Letters to the editor
13. News releases
14. Speeches and seminars
15. Publicity:
    Newspaper
    Magazine
    Radio and TV
    Business and trade publications

Direct Marketing

16. Sampling
17. Incentives
18. Discount pricing
19. Contests and giveaways
20. Newsletters
21. Circulars and flyers
22. Trade shows and exhibits
23. Sales seminars
24. Demonstrations
25. Direct mail

Inventive Advertising

26. Classified ads
27. Business directories
28. Yellow Pages advertising
29. Bulletin boards and tear pads
30. Your own radio show
31. Your own TV show
32. On-line networking
33. Fax
34. Direct-response ads
35. Card decks

Having researched what the hot sales topics would be, she contacted meeting planners for upcoming conferences in the publishing field and proposed that she provide seminars that addressed these topics using her sales methods. She got several bookings. Simultaneously she began calling the trade magazines in the field to explore writing a sales column for them. Soon she was writing a column for *Folio,* the publishing industry's leading trade magazine. From attendees at her workshops and contacts made as a result of her column, she identified potential clients who would immediately recognize her as a credible professional. She contacted them by phone and mail, and soon her training calendar begin filling up. By the following January, Helen was booked ahead for the entire year.

You've heard the saying "Success attracts success." Critical Mass Marketing operates on that principle. It assumes that if you create enough momentum around yourself and your work and then follow through by providing a top-quality service or product, your success will grow.

Boldly Standing Out from the Crowd

Another way of thinking about this approach to creating opportunities for yourself is to remember that people are attracted to bright, shiny, moving objects that stand out from the crowd. That was what Helen was able to make herself into. In a short period of time, she was able to catapult herself to a level of prominence that a traditional lower-profile approach would have taken years to achieve. She went from seeking business to being sought after.

Here's another example of Critical Mass Marketing. You may recall that when the aspiring movie director David Beaird came to Los Angeles, everyone told him Hollywood didn't need another director. And indeed he found the studio doors closed tight. Having taught acting and built a theater company in Chicago several years before, however, he decided to use that experience to get into film directing. He rented a theater and began teaching acting classes there on Monday evenings. Soon he put on a play he'd written, starring students from his classes. He then invited the press and industry representatives to see it. Many liked it. It received several drama awards from a local trade paper. The momentum was building. Based on the response to his play, he was able to attract backing for a low-budget film.

Although the film was never distributed, he did get to show it at the Cannes Film Festival and received some attention. That led to further backing. After his second low-budget film he reached his critical mass and was placed on the directors' list for a major studio. Three years later, as of this writing, he's finishing the film verion of the original play he put on at the threater. It's called *Scorchers,* and it stars Faye Dunaway. David was able to create the critical mass he needed to leap to a level of success that might have taken many years to accomplish via more traditional routes.

Becoming Self-Generating

One of the most rewarding aspects of using the Critical Mass Marketing approach is that it's like riding a bicycle: once you get the momentum going it enables you to go further faster with less and less effort. Activity you generate develops a life of its own, and you find that not only do you have to call fewer people, but a growing number of people are calling you. Efforts from months and years ago continue to bear fruit. We still get calls from articles that people clipped five years ago. That's why we use the term *critical mass.* Once you achieve it, the momentum will keep your business going.

Making Your Marketing Efforts Self-Liquidating

Critical Mass Marketing has other advantages as well. Most self-employed individuals have limited marketing funds. But they do have a strong need to generate income. Critical Mass Marketing not only enables you to produce revenue to pay for itself; it can also be a potential profit center.

Sometimes, for example, Helen is paid to make presentations at the trade-association meetings where she markets her programs. Or she may be offered a free booth at a convention. Even when she is simply reimbursed for her expenses, most of her marketing costs are being paid for. Sometimes she's paid to write for trade magazines and journals. But even if she contributes an article for free she can arrange to barter for ad space in exchange for her article.

By like token, David can charge for his acting classes, and thereby cover the cost of the theater through which he is able to promote his work. Charging admission to the play also helps offset his marketing costs.

Letting Your Work Market Itself

Another advantage of Critical Mass Marketing is that instead of spending your time selling and/or learning to master traditional marketing methods, you can market yourself by simply doing what you do. In both her articles and presentations Helen is providing concepts of her sales training program. At the theater David is demonstrating his writing and directing skills. And since that's what they love doing and they're good at it, marketing becomes fun as well as profitable.

To begin producing these dramatic results for yourself, here are several steps you can take to begin using Critical Mass Marketing as a springboard to a new level of success.

Four Steps to Building Your Critical Marketing Mass

1. Identify your unique advantage. To call attention to yourself and your work you have to distinguish yourself from the crowd. You need to find and highlight what makes you extra-special. And everyone *is* special in some way. For Helen, it was her proprietary sales methodology. For David, it was his ability to stun and startle an audience with a very low budget. Although there may be many others who provide a product or service similar to yours, no two businesses are the same. Each word-processing service has its own personality. Each PR firm has its unique advantages. What do you do that's unique to you?

A good way to identify your unique advantage is to research your competition. Read their literature, study their advertising. Ask your customers and clients about their previous service providers. Find out what they liked and didn't like about the service they received. You'll soon begin to recognize that indeed you do have your own modus operandi. And that's what you want to highlight. That's what makes you distinctive!

2. Find a platform to show off your unique advantage. Helen's platform was annual trade meetings and her column for *Folio.* David's was the small theater he rented. Teaching trade-school classes was the platform for the programmer James Milburn.

James began his career as an accountant, so he understood what small-business people needed in customized software. He spoke their language and could get the computer to speak it, too. But how was anyone else to know he was any different than any other programmer? He showed them by offering low-cost classes in custom programming for small businesses. These classes became his marketing platform. Some of his students soon learned how difficult programming customized software could be, and they knew they didn't want to do it themselves. Since they could see that Milburn understood their needs, he got all the business he needed.

Free consultations for corporate employees became the platform for Teri Goehring, an image and color consultant. She offers image seminars for corporations during lunch periods, and sells products to those who attend. The Science of Mind Church became a platform for Jerry Florence. Instead of waiting for a record company to produce his first musical album, he produced it himself and sold copies at church performances. Within two years he'd sold over thirty thousand copies and was booked to sing concerts across the country.

Think of where you could demonstrate what you have to offer on a regular basis to those who need it.

3. Give away samples at first if necessary. Although their marketing became self-liquidating, all the people we've talked about so far began by giving samples of their services. Helen spoke for free at first. David's theater barely broke even in the beginning. James offered his valuable expertise for only a small fee. Jerry's first appearance was free, and often at first he sang for a small fee, but each time he sang the ranks of his loyal fans grew and each time he sold more tapes.

Here's another excellent example of how initially giving away your services or products can help you reach critical mass. When Ted Laux began his book-indexing service with a TRS Model I, he looked through bookstores for books that didn't have adequate indexes. To demonstrate how much more effective these books would be had the publishers used his services, he indexed the books on his own and sent copies to the publishers. Several liked the results, and Ted was in business. His indexing software was his unique advantage, and the postal service became his platform for showing off just what he could do.

4. Showcase what you offer in as many media as possible. The more avenues you can use to demonstrate your unique advantage the better. Although Helen began with trade conferences and a column, she has gone on to produce audiotapes and write many magazine articles. Her next project is a book. Teri has expanded her image demonstrations to trade shows and radio. Jerry has developed a video and holds concert series.

Begin thinking of the many avenues open to show off your work. Where could you speak about your subject? Where could you offer seminars or do demonstrations? What trade shows might you exhibit at? What magazines, newsletters, or newspapers could you write for or arrange a feature story in? How could you use radio or television? After demonstrating her techniques repeatedly on a local television morning show, the bridal-makeup artist Sally Van Swearington has opened two new studios. The Florida financial consultant Brian Sheen has built a thriving practice from his own radio show, as has Dr. Maury Susser with his Los Angeles show, *Questioning Medicine.*

Such results are not unusual. These are examples of what you can accomplish with a concentrated effort sustained over time. If you start now, find your platform, and expand from it into as many arenas as you can, you can develop similar results. It's what happens when you shift your focus from merely surviving project by project to thriving on an abundance of work. You'll be able to generate enough momentum to leap to a new level where everything occurring around you begins working in your favor. Once your efforts reach a critical mass, you'll find yourself accomplishing much more with much less effort.

For more information on how to develop your marketing mindset and tools, we recommend reading our book *Getting Business to Come to You.*

Using Technology to Reduce Administrivia

Technology is the great equalizer. It gives the small the power of the large.

PAUL AND SARAH EDWARDS

Twenty years ago, the information you needed to take advantage of the latest modern technology was expensive, time-consuming, or nonexistent. Just two decades ago, Sarah's father had to travel from Kansas City to New Jersey and spend an entire summer there learning how to computerize the billing for his company. Installing their computer system cost tens of thousands of dollars and took several consultants over six months to accomplish. Today that entire billing system could be run on a personal computer with off-the-shelf software her father could either install himself or hire a consultant to set up within a few days to a week.

Today there's a wealth of relatively inexpensive, increasingly small technology that can free you from the headaches of handling the business side of your work so you can spend your time getting paid for doing what you enjoy.

And this new technology, which can be used at home or in a car or van, is easy to use. Often you can simply turn it on and put it to work doing the things you hate to do or don't like taking your time to do—tasks such as billing, balancing your bank account, invoicing, keeping up your mailing list, taking messages, keeping track of key information, and so forth.

Equipping the Ideal Do-It-Yourself Office

When you're trying to get your work done, having to constantly stop what you're doing to play the role of clerk and gofer can be demoralizing. You can start to feel like a second-class citizen. Having to take out a half hour to drag yourself over to the print shop in the rain to make just one copy that has to go out today, begging friends to print out a proposal for you on their computer so it won't look like schlock, paying $11 every time you have to send something overnight, having a client tell you your answering-machine message sounds like you're drunk, or, worst of all, getting a chance for some really good work only to have the client ask you to fax him or her something, and you don't have a fax—well, it's embarrassing, time-consuming, and demeaning.

You deserve better. You owe it to yourself and to your work to equip your office in a manner that will support you like the professional you are and aspire to become. Fortunately, you can equip your office so that everything around you works just as it would for the CEO of a well-run corporation. Below is our list of the ideal equipment for a single-person office and how each piece of technology we recommend can take the drudgery out of being your own boss. Note, we use the word *ideal*. The things on this list are in no way to be thought of as essential, and not having these items is most certainly never a reason to accept defeat. In other words, you can survive without them, but with them you can thrive.

1. A personal computer that is quick and expandable. A computer is the single most versatile and valuable piece of equipment you can own. It's a staff in a box. It can be a secretary, bookkeeper, receptionist, file clerk, business consultant, financial analyst, tax preparer, graphic designer, and print shop all rolled into one. It can save you hours of time, tons of money, and much misery, yet to date less than half of home-based businesses have one. On the following page are fifty things a computer can do for you, culled from the book *Computer Power for Your Small Business,* by Nick Sullivan.

A personal computer can do all these things for you, and yet by shopping carefully you can buy a fast, powerful, and expandable one for just under $1,000, plus the cost of your printer and software. That means it will pay for itself quickly in reduced costs and increased productivity. Even if you have a high-touch/low-tech business like plumbing, carpentry, psychological counseling, or tutoring, we urge you to invest in a personal computer to help you run your business.

At a bare minimum we recommend using a computer to run the following aspects of your business:

Fifty Jobs a Personal Computer Can Do for You

1. Business planning
2. Market research
3. Market forecasting
4. Cash-flow projections
5. Financial planning
6. Project management
7. Newsletter layout
8. Brochure layout
9. Logo design
10. Graphs and charts
11. Slides and overheads
12. Letters, reports, and other documents
13. Business forms
14. Library searches
15. Find and merge files
16. Place phone calls
17. Answer your phone
18. Record phone messages
19. Set agendas
20. Receive mail instantly
21. Send mail instantly
22. Send faxes
23. Receive faxes
24. Locate resources
25. Track your schedule
26. Store, locate, and search information
27. Record notes
28. Outline projects, articles, and reports
29. Manage telemarketing efforts
30. Build mailing lists
31. Keep mailing lists up-to-date
32. Serve as a tickler system
33. Be an electronic Rolodex
34. Network coast to coast
35. Personalize mass mailings
36. Recordkeeping
37. Record searching
38. Check writing
39. Bookkeeping
40. Accounting
41. Balance your bank account
42. Tax planning
43. Tax preparation
44. File your tax return
45. Budgeting
46. Keep time and expense records
47. Billing
48. Invoicing
49. Inventory Control
50. Print labels

- *Typing.* Do all your word processing on computer, from sales letters to correspondence, flyers, reports, proposals, invoices, statements, and so on.
- *Bookkeeping.* Do your bookkeeping on a program like Quicken, which will balance your bank account, give you instant reports on how you're spending your money, and tally expenses quickly for tax purposes.
- *Mailing list.* Develop a mailing list and keep it up-to-date on computer. This will enable you to announce new products, run specials, send out

newsletters, invitations and news releases, and do other marketing activities quickly and easily.

Of course, you can't begin doing all these tasks on a computer at once, so we recommend starting with the task that is taking up the most time and/or the one that's giving you the most frustration. Once you've computerized that task you can move on to the next most time-consuming or aggravating one.

Other computer-based time-savers you might want to consider include:

- *File-management software.* Studies show we waste more time looking for things we can't find than any other activity. And what's more frustrating than not being able to remember what you named a particular file you created six months ago? File-management software solves this problem. *Gofer, Xtree Gold,* and *Magellan* for IBM computers and *Gofer* and *On Location* for Macintoshes enable you to search through your hard disk and locate files with any key word or phrase you can remember from inside the file you need to find.

- *Phone-dialer software.* This software lets you use a few keystrokes of your computer to dial any phone number that's stored in your computer—all clients and prospects, even thousands of them. Also, if you need to locate an out-of-town address or phone number quickly, software like *Hotline* instantaneously gives you access to the telephone numbers of ten thousand of the nation's largest corporations, government agencies, organizations, associations, colleges and universities, radio and television stations, and newspapers.

- *Time and expenses software.* Packages such as *Timeslips III* and *TimeTracker* can streamline your billing by automatically keeping track of your time and then billing for it without any additional calculations.

We've listed several books at the end of this chapter that spell out in detail how to purchase, set up, and learn to use a computer to carry out the administrative aspects of your business, along with specific software packages that can do these tasks for you. For assistance in shopping for or expanding your computer you can refer to chapter 8 in *Working From Home.*

Finally, once you're using a computer regularly, make it a point to go beyond the bare minimum of what your software can do. Explore and adopt useful new aspects periodically, and be sure to get the newest versions of your software, because each new release is usually updated with new features that can make your work easier in some way.

2. A laser printer. A laser printer is to other printers what a computer is to a typewriter. Laser printers are faster, more versatile, and *QUIET.* They shoot out your documents in seconds in a wide variety of type styles and sizes, and you can be talking in hushed tones nearby and hardly know they're printing.

But best of all, owning a laser printer goes a long way in addressing the number-one concern of self-employed individuals who work from home: the need to project a professional image. If you select a decent laser printer, the documents you produce may be indistinguishable from those coming from a Fortune 500 company.

Although once priced beyond the reach of most self-employed individuals, laser printers are no longer expensive. Every year they come down in price. At the time of this writing you can get an adequate laser printer for under $800. This is another item of equipment that will pay for itself quickly. Bios, handouts, newsletters, flyers, reports, presentations, media materials—virtually anything you want printed—come out camera ready, to use as is or to have professionally printed or copied. For further assistance in selecting your printer, see chapter 8 in *Working from Home.*

3. A copy machine. For as little as three hundred dollars, you can buy a personal copy machine today the size of a briefcase. Not only can these personal copiers produce better-looking copies than you'll get at most copy stores for less money; a copier costing about a thousand dollars can make reductions and enlargements. And think of how quickly your copy machine will pay for itself. How long does it take you to go out to the copy store? How far do you have to drive? How long do you have to wait for your copies? How many phone calls will you miss while you're gone? How quickly will you be able to make needed copies when the machine is on hand? This one purchase will save you innumerable hours and endless frustration. For the features to look for in a copier, see chapter 8 in *Working from Home.*

4. A two-line telephone. A two-line telephone provides you with a wealth of options for simplifying your life. It enables you to have separate lines for incoming and outgoing calls. This means you can place calls and still leave your incoming line open to receive others without the inconvenience of *call waiting,* which is unquestionably disruptive and is highly irritating to some callers. The incoming line can also roll over to an answering machine if you are on the other line.

Alternatively, if you work from home, you can use one line as your personal line and the other for your business calls. Another advantage of a two-line phone is that one of the lines can be used for fax or modem transmission, although if you use these features frequently, you really should have a separate third line dedicated just to fax and modem use. And, of course, a two-line phone saves precious desk space and reduces the cord jungle around your work space.

5. An answering machine or voicemail. A quality answering machine is a must; voicemail is even better. Voicemail turns your telephone into an answering machine, a switchboard, and a phone-mail system like those you encounter when calling many large companies today. In addition to simply recording a caller's message, when you're away, it also records messages while you're talking on another call. Voicemail can also give the caller a number of options. For example, it can relay a specific prerecorded message about your product or service and provide directions or instructions for placing an order. If you are talking on another line, it can tell callers you're busy and take their messages or switch them to another line. So it becomes another alternative to *call waiting.* Voicemail can also be used to take dictation and act as a calendering system as well as a directory that enables you to call in and obtain phone numbers when you're away from the office.

Most local telephone-operating companies are now offering voicemail through their regular phone service for a low monthly charge. You also can set up your own voicemail system with your personal computer and a voicemail card like *Watson* or *Complete PC.* A voicemail board suitable for a small or home-based business runs from $200 up.

6. A fax machine or a fax board. A fax, which is short for *facsimile,* allows you to transmit information over phone lines instantly to another fax machine or computer that's capable of receiving a fax. It takes only twenty seconds to send a page of text by fax. That beats any overnight-delivery service or same-day messenger service for a fraction of the cost. But that's not all. Think of the time a fax can save *you.* You don't have to put your mail in an envelope, address it, stamp it, and get it to a mailbox. You just push a button and it's on its way.

Just think what that means. How much more quickly an invoice can be paid. How many hours—and how much pressure—that saves you when meeting a deadline. How much simpler it becomes to resend something someone claims he or she never received. And you can get a fax machine for as little as $400.

Even faster is a fax board, which turns your computer into a fax machine. With a fax board in your computer, you can send and receive material through the phone line directly. You don't even have to print it out; you can also edit it and send it back without ever printing it out. Another advantage is that you can print out anything you've received through your fax board on your printer and thereby avoid getting copies on the thermal paper used by most moderately priced fax machines.

The only drawback to a fax board is that you can send only materials that you can store in your computer. That rules out sending newspaper clippings, magazine articles, and so on, although you can receive such materials through your fax board. Personally, we now have both a freestanding fax machine and a fax board and find the flexibility of having them both to be worth the investment. A fax board costs from $150 to $400.

For further information about shopping for fax capability, see chapter 8 in *Working from Home.*

7. A high-speed modem. When used with communications software, a modem turns your computer into both a library and a telephone to the world. While it's perhaps less vital than the other things on this list, we've included a modem in the ideal do-it-yourself office because with a modem you can gain access to a significant amount of the information that's been published in the last 15 years and some that's available only on-line. You can do market research, check stock prices, find venture capital, local personnel, investigate companies, and use the processing capabilities of mainframe computers.

By joining an information service like CompuServe, you can also send mail, do banking, shop, pay bills, get airline schedules, and make reservations—all without leaving your desk. By using the Working from Home Forum we operate on CompuServe you can meet and talk with other self-employed people across the country and even in other countries. You can market yourself and get invaluable advice from leading professional experts.

A modem is about the size of book. It plugs directly into the modular jack in your phone; a high-speed 2400 baud modem costs about $150. If desk space is a problem, however, you can have an internal modem mounted on a card inside your computer.

8. An electronic organizer. In chapter 3, we mentioned the value of using an electronic organizer. These tiny vest pocket-sized computers are desiged to be your portable calendar, address book, check register, personal secretary, and planner. The size of a wallet, they replace the multiple items you used to have to carry around in your purse, pockets, or briefcase. But they do the job faster, they don't get dog-eared, and they can be updated easily. The most desirable models can exchange files with your desktop computer and thereby save you the time of entering material twice.

The Sharp *Wizard* and the Casio *Boss* are the most popular models; they cost from $110 to $400. I, Sarah, recently replaced my paper-based personal organizer with the *Wizard,* and I've found that it is easy to use and can do everything my paper system did. It's much smaller and weighs less, so it's much easier to carry in my purse. I also use it as a notepad at meetings and workshops. I can even transfer my notes to my computer using their *PC Link.*

Take a few minutes to identify the tasks that take you the most time and cause you the most frustration. Chances are the equipment we've described or other technology can simplify, streamline, and automate what you need to do.

Breaking Down Myths and Resistances to Technology

While technology can never make up for a poor product or service or for bad business decisions and poor management practices, we can say with certainty that as a general rule those who take advantage of what technology has to offer tend to be more successful on their own than those who try to muddle through by doing everything the old-fashioned way. Technology clearly gives you the power to accomplish much more with less effort.

Yet we do encounter people who for one reason or another resist investing time and energy to bring their office up to the level of sophistication better equipment could help them achieve. Here are several common myths and sources of resistance and how we and others have gotten past them.

I don't need that.   In truth one of us has said this about nearly every piece of equipment we listed above. I (Sarah) was much slower to adopt new technology than Paul. I didn't think we needed a computer at first. We had a Selectric typewriter, and that was enough for me. But within two weeks of Paul talking me into a computer, I found I couldn't live without it. Now I'm as eager as Paul to explore new technology.

If you have an "I don't need that" attitude toward any particular piece of technology, at least allow yourself to take a serious look at how your competition is using it. See if you're missing out and making your life harder than it needs to be.

It's too complicated. I'm not mechanical.   If you're someone who thinks of yourself as low tech, we have good news for you. Much of the equipment we recommend is no longer complex and difficult to use. Using a two-line phone, an answering machine or voicemail from the phone company, a personal copier, or a personal fax is no more difficult than using a toaster. So if technology is intimidating to you, start with these. And if you have any difficulty or need moral support, ask for help from a friend or colleague who's already using one.

IBM, Tandy, and Apple all have computer models available now that are simple to get up and running. Many software packages have a tutorial that walks you through using them. Low-cost seminars are available in most communities to learn major software programs. But if you still have resistance to getting a computer, hire a consultant to walk you through selecting, setting up, and learning to use one. Today using a computer is like driving a car. Just as you don't have to be a mechanic to drive a car, you don't have to be a programmer or techie to master a computer.

One area where you may want help if you're at all squeamish around technology is in configuring your laser printer to work with your computer, your software, and the needed type fonts. If you buy your printer from a full-service computer store, you may be able to arrange for their personnel to set it up for you. If not, hire a consultant. Newer items like voice-mail boards and modems can wait until you're comfortable with easier-to-use technology.

I can't afford that.   In regard to technology, it's particularly easy to think that the price tag will be too high. Many people are not aware of how dramatically the prices for the items we've described have dropped and continue to drop. Since they first came onto the market their prices have been dropping at the rate of about 20 percent a year.

In fact, by shopping right you can get a computer, a laser printer, a copy machine, a fax, an answering machine, and a two-line phone for under

$2,500. If your money is tight, however, or nonexistent, consider using a separate credit card for financing equipment purchases. Purchase one item at a time on that card, beginning with the one that will pay for itself most quickly. For example, if you can charge more or land a bigger contract with a laser printer, your new printer will pay for itself with your first sale. And since interest on business debt is tax deductible, Uncle Sam can even pick up part of the tab.

One woman found that once she purchased a laser printer, she was able to get a book contract—with an advance—that had been eluding her for years. A carpenter was able to take on two extra clients a month in the time he previously spent doing his accounts by hand, and thus was able to pay for his computer and software within six months.

To get her business under way, the typesetter Tina Linert leased her specialized equipment, as did Dorothy Baranski when she opened DorBar Executive Services. Others have had customers purchase the equipment they needed and then leased it back from the customers. One woman brought in a partner who financed the equipment so she could expand her video-production business.

Gloria Parks was especially eager to start a desktop publishing business, which, of course, depends entirely upon having a top-of-the-line computer system. She had just lost her job unexpectedly, however, and had neither the credit nor the cash to purchase the system she needed. At first the situation looked hopeless. But then she had an idea. She approached several print shops that were not yet providing desktop publishing and told them that if they would purchase the equipment, she would handle all their desktop-publishing needs and make payments on the equipment from the revenue. It worked. One shop had been wanting to add desktop publishing for months, and this idea saved them the expense of hiring additional staff.

You may be thinking that hiring a consultant to help you computerize will also be expensive, and it can be. But it doesn't need to be. Get a referral from the store where you bought your equipment, from local college or university computer instructors or from your peers. We've found excellent, very reasonably priced assistance in these ways.

Cutting Down on Cleaning Up

Technology can also help you cut down on the time involved in cleaning up. You can free your time and energy for more important tasks and still keep your home/office professionally neat and clean by using labor-saving appliances. We've actually found, however, that many time-consuming cleaning tasks are unnecessary if you don't make the mess in the first place. Here are several ways you can keep your home office clean without taking up your time.

60-Second Cleaning Secret

Premoistened towels. Virtually every surface in your home and office, from countertops to monitor screens, telephones to disk holders, gets dusty and dirty, smudged and smeared. An easy way to avoid lugging around spray bottles, paper towels, and dust rags is to use pretreated or premoistened towels. These towels have the cleaning product already applied. All you have to do is pull one out like a tissue, use it, and toss it.

We keep an entire set of these towels in each area of our home and office, and they are a godsend. Scott has a line called *Viva Plus,* which comes in three varieties: one for dusting, one for the kitchen, and one for the bath. Dow makes a line called *Spiffits* which includes an all-purpose cleaner, a glass cleaner, a wood polish, and a scouring towel. Fantastik *(S'Wipe's),* Lysol, and Pine-Sol also offer premoistened towels for surface cleaning. Fuji Film makes a premoistened towel for cleaning computer and other electronic components.

1. Dirt that doesn't get through the door doesn't need to be cleaned up. Good-quality mats at the door and covered or elevated entryways keep dirt, mud, and water out.
2. Well-insulated doors and weatherproofed windows let in less dust.
3. Using liquid-soap dispensers instead of bars of soap prevents soap-scum buildup on sinks.
4. Deep sinks prevent splattering.
5. Brushed brass plating on faucets doesn't show spots that must be polished.
6. A shower stall or tub wiped down immediately stays clean.
7. Mildew doesn't grow as much in well-lighted bathrooms with plenty of circulation.
8. Food doesn't get caked on dishes that are cleaned off at the moment they're used.
9. Laundry folded when it comes out of the dryer usually doesn't need ironing.
10. Clothes hung up at the moment you take them off don't get piled up to be put away.
11. Magazines and papers read or skimmed, clipped, and filed when they arrive don't accumulate into a major catch-up project.
12. Receipts filed when you return from the store don't pile up for sorting.
13. Semigloss latex enamel paint and vinyl wallpaper don't spot, and they clean easily.
14. Fabrics treated to resist stains are easier to clean and need cleaning less often.

15. Neutral colors for all surfaces are easier to clean than dark or white ones.
16. Tile with dark grout saves hours of bleaching and scrubbing.
17. Streamlined furniture and fixtures don't collect dust and dirt like ornate ones, and they can be cleaned more quickly.
18. Plenty of storage units, drawers, racks, cabinets, and closets prevent messes by providing a place to put everything away in, on, or under.

For more tips on messes that don't need to happen see *Make Your House Do the Housework* by Don Aslett and Laura Aslett Simons (Writers Digest Books, 1986).

You're the Boss

The next time you start to feel like your business is running you instead of the other way around, *stop*, take a break, and ask yourself what you need to do to turn the tables. You're the boss. By applying the basic principles we've outlined in this chapter you should be able to decrease the time you have to spend running your business. Once you get the most time-consuming aspects of marketing and administration operating automatically in the easiest, most efficient ways, you'll find that you can concentrate your energy on your work, your health, and your quality of life.

Resources

CompuServe Information Service. The largest of the on-line computer networks. A membership package is available at computer stores across the country. To access the Working from Home Forum, enter GO WORK when you log on.

The Complete Guide to CompuServe. Brad Schepp and Debra Schepp. New York: Osborne McGraw Hill, 1990. Introduces many resources on CompuServe Information Service.

Complete Handbook of Personal Computer Communications. Alfred Glossbrenner. New York: St. Martin's Press, 1984. The in's and out's of getting on-line with your computer—from what equipment you need to the many information services that are available via computer.

Computer Power for Your Small Business. Nick Sullivan. New York: Amacom, 1990. Outlines how to use a personal computer for running virtually every aspect of your business—from planning and financial management to making presentations and doing your mailing list.

Getting Business to Come to You: Everything You Need to Know About Public Relations, Advertising, and Sales Promotion for the Small and Home-Based Business. Paul and Sarah Edwards and Laura Douglas. Los Angeles: Jeremy P. Tarcher, 1991. Introduces key marketing strategies used by over one-hundred successful *propreneurs* and provides practical information for getting more business without having to spend your time selling.

Home Office Computing Magazine. Scholastic Inc., 730 Broadway, New York, NY 10003. A gold mine of information about how to succeed on your own including reviews of the latest software and equipment as well as articles on marketing and other business-management skills.

How to Get Free Software. Alfred Glossbrenner. New York: St. Martin's Press, 1989. How you can get good software free for virtually any task you want to use your computer for.

How to Look It Up Online. Alfred Glossbrenner. New York: St. Martin's Press, 1987. How to use your personal computer to search for virtually any information you might need.

How to Use a Computer in Your Home Office. Hal Schuster with Paul and Sarah Edwards. Las Vegas, NV: Electronic Cottage Press, 1990. A guidebook for starting and operating a business with a personal computer.

Make Your House Do the Housework. Don Aslett and Laura Aslett Simons. Cincinnati: Writer's Digest Books, 1986. A must for anyone who wants to do less housework. It is filled with practical suggestions for preventing your home from getting dirty.

The Personal Computer Book. Peter McWilliams. Los Angeles: Prelude Press, 1990. Is an update of the famous first edition that came out in the early 1980s and which became the bible for getting acquainted with the world of personal computers. It can be understood by the computer novice yet it thoroughly presents the in's and out's of becoming computer literate.

Working from Home. Paul and Sarah Edwards. Los Angeles: Jeremy P. Tarcher, 1990. See especially chapters 7 and 8.

PART 3
∎∎∎∎∎∎∎∎∎∎∎∎∎∎∎∎∎∎∎∎∎∎∎∎

Becoming the Boss
You've Always Wanted to Have

*Happiness . . . has a direct relationship to
the freedom in life to make choices to do the
things I want to do.*

KEN KRAGEN

If you've been blessed with having had
outstanding coaches, parents, teachers, managers, or mentors, you are indeed
lucky. Your job of managing yourself now that you're on your own will be
easier. You've undoubtedly incorporated a great deal from them about how to
get yourself to do what you need to do. You probably have a sense of what
you can put up with from yourself, what you can let yourself get away with,
when you need to draw the line, and how you can get yourself to go the extra
mile. Whenever you're at a loss as to how to motivate yourself, you can go
inward and ask yourself what these people would advise you to do.

If you're like many of us, however, you haven't had the benefit of such
expert coaching and direction. Many of our authority figures demanded too
much and expected too little. Not knowing what to do, they threatened,
ignored, tolerated, abused, belittled, denigrated, and otherwise manipulated
us into performances that fell far short of what even we know we're capable
of. If that was your experience, when you look inward for assistance in
getting yourself to do what you need to do, you risk becoming as ineffectual as
your previous role models. You may rebel, and sabotage or otherwise defeat
your own efforts.

In this case, what are you to do? How can you find the means by which to consistently draw out the best in yourself? What can you do to inspire performances that will surprise and delight you? To find the answer, we began studying highly effective coaches, teachers, managers, and directors. And we noticed something very important: the best ones don't treat every player or performer they work with in the same way. In fact, the same person can be a screaming terror with one person and a gentle, tender, supportive parent figure with another. Sometimes they show this range of behavior even with the same person, offering a loving hug at one moment and raving angrily at another.

Why such erratic behavior? And is it really erratic? In watching the most effective coaches, teachers, and managers, we've observed that they approach their protégés much like an expert jockey approaches a prized racehorse. The best jockeys learn to ride each horse as if they were playing a fine instrument. They learn to respond to every nuance, every trait, every characteristic of the horse. Sometimes they apply the whip. Sometimes they nudge and talk softly to the horse. Sometimes they dig their heels into the horse's side. Sometimes they shout angrily. Sometimes they almost sing to the horse. And sometimes they do all of the above, but only at the precise moment that it will catapult the horse to the front of the field.

That's how we must learn to manage ourselves. We must become so familiar with ourselves—our whims, our needs, our emotions, our patterns, our preferences, our strengths and weaknesses—that we can literally feed ourselves the exact words, schedule, food, routines, and resources we need to nourish our competence and enable us to operate consistently at our best.

Isn't that what the top sports coaches are able to do for their athletes? Don't they literally prescribe a tailor-made training schedule? Don't they provide a tailor-made diet? Don't they lay out a tailor-made practice routine or workout? Don't they whisper just the right words at just the right moments? Isn't that what the top directors do in their own way for their actors? Isn't that what excellent teachers do for their pupils? Isn't that what top managers do for their staff? And isn't there a direct relationship between what they put into their protégés and what they are able to get from them?

Like these professionals, you will get out of yourself exactly what you put in. To keep yourself on track, you must be there for yourself. You must be the one who knows how to respond when situations get you down. You must be the one who offers the consolation, guidance, respect, and recognition you need to believe in yourself. You must be the one you can turn to when you are at a loss. You need to have effective solutions and answers for yourself.

That's what this section is about—learning to motivate yourself effectively, helping yourself through the emotional roller coaster being your own boss can be, and being there with the answers to keep yourself going when problems arise.

CHAPTER
FIVE

■■■■■■■■■■■■■■■■■■■■■■■

Motivating Yourself to Do What Needs to Be Done

*Once you get to the pros, coaching is not
about telling people what to do; it's about
managing personalities.*

NORMAN VAN LIER,
*former player for
the Chicago Bulls*

There's probably no greater power than
the power to follow through on what you say you want to do. Whether it's
being able to hit a tennis ball just where you want it to go, deliver a project on
time within budget, or get yourself to stop smoking, being able to count on
yourself to deliver what you want to accomplish is truly a gift. But once you're
on your own, it's also an essential skill.

Yet how often we make promises to ourselves, set goals, make New Year's
resolutions, or swear we'll do something—or never do something again—only
to let ourselves down. According to a 1989 report in *USA Today*, for example,
90 percent of Americans make New Year's resolutions, but studies by Alan
Marlatt from the University of Washington in Seattle show that almost four
out of five people fail to follow through on their resolutions.

When you like what you're doing and you're committed to a clear purpose,
of course, following through on what you set out to do is less of a problem.
But aren't we quite sincere in making New Year's resolutions? So how do we
know we'll be able to do better on our own? What about the days when you
just don't want to do what you know needs to be done? What about the

things you don't like doing . . . the things you want to put off . . . the things you will get to later? All the best-made goals, schedules, routines, plans, and to-do lists are useless if you can't get yourself to turn them into action.

This is the same issue every professional athlete or performer must face in any important competition or performance. In every game, in every match, in every contest, in every show, they each have to ask, "Will I be able to perform at my best upon demand?" To make sure they can, they have to mobilize themselves every day to train. They have to go through endless repetitions of moves or lines until they can do what it takes under the pressure of competition or production. And that's essentially what we have to do to make it on our own. But, of course, athletes and performers have coaches, directors, and managers to help them.

Coaches need to understand those they coach so well that they can inspire, motivate, energize, catalyze, outfox, outmaneuver, outwait, outpsych, or one way or another get their charges to call forth the best within them precisely when they need it. And now that you're on your own, that is your job, too. By becoming your own boss, you now must step into that role and serve as your own coach, mentor, and manager.

Becoming Your Own Coach, Mentor, and Adviser

In other words, you have to get to know yourself very well, so well that you know exactly what will get you going, what will calm you down, and what will help you focus; how to make sure you follow through on what needs to be done when you'd rather not, how to keep yourself going when things take longer than you expected, and how to keep yourself going when you feel like quitting or become impatient.

If you begin to think of yourself as your own protégé—and your most important project—you'll be able to notice what you respond to and what you don't. You'll begin to respect your preferences and needs. You'll learn to take them into account rather than to fight yourself or try to bury the aspects of yourself you don't like.

Three Steps to Becoming an Effective Self-Manager

To become a reliable mentor/coach for yourself you must take three steps: (1) you must identify the peculiarities of what motivates you; (2) you must discover what you need to hear and learn how to say it in such a way that you'll listen; and (3) you have to determine what you can do to assist yourself to function at your best consistently. In this chapter, we'll discuss each of these steps in detail and provide practical guidelines for managing yourself. But first, review the tips on the next page for how to make sure you can count on yourself to follow through on what you actually want and need to do.

Making Sure You Can Count on Yourself to Do What You Say You'll Do

- **Distinguish between goals and commitments.** A goal, the dictionary tells us, is "the object of some effort." To get more clients is a goal. To have a current up-to-date filing system is a goal. A commitment, however, is "the act of resolving to put forth an effort toward some object." In other words, goals are what you want to accomplish; commitments are what you promise to do to make sure you achieve your goals.

- **To assure that you reach your goals, commit to take only those steps you know you can count on yourself to carry out.** Be sure that whatever you commit to doing is something you actually want to do and that you will do. In other words, don't make commitments to yourself or others that you doubt you will follow through on.

  If you're a person who has a difficult time saying no, ask yourself, "Is this something I want or am clearly willing to do?" If not, don't commit to doing it. You can do that, after all. What's the worst thing that can happen if you say no? Even if you can imagine something awful, how likely is that to happen? Obviously if something negative is likely to happen, then saying yes is justified and you'll be motivated to find a way to do it, even if it involves getting help from others.

  Here's an example of what we mean. If your goal is to double the number of clients you serve but you *hate* making cold calls and have never been able to get yourself to make them, don't resolve to make ten calls a week. Resolve instead to find some other way to get clients. You might commit to joining a networking group, attending a seminar on selling through seminars, or advertising by direct mail.

- **Make bite-sized, realistic goals and commitments.** Dream big, but take one small step at a time. If you dream of becoming a best-selling novelist, for example, you might set a goal of writing and publishing a short story and commit to enrolling in a class on short-story technique.

- **Set completion dates for your commitments and track your progress.** Also, flag a date sometime before the date you've set so as it approaches you'll be able to revise your commitments accordingly. For example, if you agreed to complete three interviews by the end of the month, cue yourself midmonth. If they're not scheduled yet, take appropriate action.

- **Give yourself slack, but don't let yourself slack off.** Making a commitment doesn't mean you must be imprisoned by it. You can always decide en route to go somewhere else, and you can always choose an alternative route for getting there. The only things that really matter are that you do get where you want to go, and that you enjoy the trip along the way.

Identifying What Motivates You

Know thy self.

THE ORACLE AT DELPHI

There are actually a wide variety of ways people motivate themselves. For example, the event planner Marsha Hanscom learned quickly that the best way to motivate herself was to set up incentives or prizes for herself. "If I have something special I can work toward, I get a lot more done," she says. She entices herself with promises of rewards for reaching her goals. For instance, she once told herself that if she had a particular exhibit all filled by a certain date, she would send herself to an upcoming national conference. She hit the goal and took the trip!

Diane Vaughn, who has a thriving counseling service, is motivated by the satisfaction she gets from the work she does. All she needs to do is think about how much joy her work brings her and she finds it easy to do whatever is required to make sure she succeeds. Jeffrey Kline, a sales trainer, knows that money is what motivates him. "The more money I can make, the better I produce," he told us. Photographer Ron Allenberg, however, finds that showing everyone what he can do is what keeps him going: "So many people told me that I shouldn't do this—that I'd never make it. Now all I have to do is think about how much I want to prove they're wrong, and I'll do whatever it takes." Here are some other insights self-employed individuals have had about how to motivate themselves:

When things look bad, I get discouraged and don't want to do anything much. So I've learned to tell myself the good side of whatever's happening. I point out why it's not as bad as it looks and how it could even be better than I thought. Then I feel like working all the harder.

When I'm under the pressure of a deadline, I get so much done; but without a deadline, I don't think I'd get anything done. It's got to be a real deadline, though. I can't just make something up. So what I do is get myself into situations that involve firm deadlines.

I ask myself what will happen if I don't do this, and if it doesn't look good, then I want to do it.

I think about the kind of person I want to be, and if I'm not living up to who I aspire to be, that's a real motivator. When I am living up to my image of myself I feel great and I gladly do more of what it takes to do even better.

Facts and figures are what motivate me. I track my progress like I'm keeping a scorecard. And I watch what my competition is doing. I like to make sure I stay out in front.

Knowing what de-motivates you is equally important. Gil Petersen, a soft-ware engineer, discovered for example, "If I tell myself I *have to* do something, it's like the kiss of death. I'll do just about anything else. And boy, has that gotten me in trouble. Now if I don't want to do something, I just tell myself I don't have to do it. And usually, once I know I have the choice, I'll go ahead and do it if it really does need to be done."

Kim Freilich dislikes doing billing for her publicity business. "It's so time-consuming," she moans. "But I think of it as dumping the money out of my pockets and counting what will be coming back to me. That gets me through it."

To begin identifying what motivates and de-motivates you, pay attention to what you complain about, what you get excited about, what gets you down, and what picks you up. Then cater to yourself as you would to a prized client. Don't sell yourself short and let yourself get away with less than you know you can do, but make it as easy as possible for yourself to excel. Ask yourself the following questions. Then listen to your responses and observe your be-havior to see if it confirms your answers.

There are no wrong answers to these questions. The idea is to learn what you respond to. The two of us work best, for example, when we believe we're

---

What Motivates You?

1. What is most important to you about what you're doing? What makes it worthwhile? What makes it a drag?
2. How could you make doing something you need to do worth the effort? What would make you eager to get it done?
3. Which spurs you to do better: compliments and positive feedback about what you've done well, or criticism of your performance and feedback on what you need to improve?
4. Are you more likely to strive to prevent negative things you fear might happen or to work toward attaining a positive outcome?
5. Do you thrive on competition? Does the opportunity to do better than someone else spur you on or intimidate you?
6. Are you more interested in improving your own performance or achieving more than someone else?
7. Do you work better with the pressure of a deadline, or do deadlines get you clutched?
8. Do you work more efficiently when you wait until the last minute to meet your deadlines, or do you like to start early and finish ahead of time?
9. Do you like to begin with the most pleasant tasks, or do you prefer to get the worst over first and save the best for last?

---

doing well. Comparing ourselves negatively with others leads us to start doubting ourselves. We've spoken with people, however, who start sloughing off when they think they're doing well. Comparing themselves negatively with others keeps them on their toes. Of course, with some effort you can change such motivation patterns, but when possible, it's easier to simply use the patterns you have to your own advantage.

Knowing What You Need to Hear and Saying It in Such a Way That You'll Listen

Once we are destined to live out our lives in the prison of our mind, our duty is to furnish it well.

PETER USTINOV

We all have a constant stream of conversation running in our heads. At any given moment this conversation either helps us carry out our intentions or works against us. If you begin to listen to this conversation and observe its effects on you, you will be amazed at how you can not only improve your performance, but greatly increase your enjoyment of whatever you're doing, by simply changing what you're saying to yourself.

Think, for example, of the following alternative sets of inner chatter that might take place if you wake up late one morning.

Scenario 1: "Boy, are you a sleaze. You'll never amount to anything. Didn't I tell you you'd be goofing off the minute no boss was looking over your shoulder? How could you have overslept again? You'll never make it on your own. If the few clients you have ever found out how lazy you are, they'd take their business elsewhere. You might as well forget today anyway. You've already blown it again."

Scenario 2: "Oh, it's late. Did I have anything I had to do this morning? Let's look at the calendar. Oh great! I'm free. Well, I guess I can oversleep once in a while. But it doesn't really matter because, if I need to, I can work some this evening. I'm feeling so rested, though, I'll probably get more work done now anyway. Let's see, what did I want to get done today? I think I'll go on up and start making a few calls."

Inner dialogue or self-talk like this is actually one of the major ways we coach ourselves. Which one do you think will get the best results? You can begin listening to your current chatter to see how well you're coaching yourself. Do you think a good coach would be saying the things you're saying? Even more important, however, notice how you respond to what you're saying. Does it make you feel more confident, more effective, and more eager to do what you need to do? Or does it work against you? Do you actually perform better based on what you say? Or does it erode your performance?

In addition to such ongoing inner chatter, begin to notice what you say to yourself in response to specific problems or difficulties you encounter. If, for example, your work is harder than you thought it might be, what do you say to yourself about that? If you don't want to do what needs doing, what do you tell yourself? If you make a mistake of some kind, how do you respond?

The conversation you have with yourself at times like these is the equivalent of the pep talk a coach gives his or her team at halftime. How well do your pep talks work for you? Do they send you back to the game more committed and determined to succeed? Or do they cause you to fall into an emotional sinkhole? Do you go back in with an angry attitude and a chip on your shoulder, or with a greater desire to excel? Do you hit the court running, or do you drop out temporarily?

Being able to be give great pep talks to yourself is a valuable skill when you're on your own. In fact, a study of top executives showed that the most effective ones all have aphorisms or favorite sayings that they repeat to themselves now and then—mini–pep talks like "When the going gets tough the tough get going," "Hang in their baby; you can make it," and "Where there's a will, there's a way." Although these examples aren't particularly original, they work well for the people who use them.

We suggest that you, too, take a moment when needed to talk with yourself and pretend that you're the coach of your own team—because you are. Think of what you need to hear and tell it to yourself. Find stories that will inspire and encourage you. Look for incidents, quotes, lyrics, or ideas that will help you proceed with confidence and resolve.

What to Do When You Don't Feel Like Doing What Needs to Be Done

What do you do with yourself when you know what you need to do, but you don't want to do it? At one time or another, we've all faced a rapidly approaching deadline only to find ourselves doing everything under the sun but what we need to do. And as you've probably already discovered at times like this, begging, pleading, blaming, and shaming do not work, at least not for long. Trying to force yourself to do it doesn't work either. Now that you're on your own, you *know* you can do whatever you want, even if it doesn't seem like you can. So when you don't feel like doing what needs to be done, you've got to find a way to get yourself to do it willingly.

In other words, you need to find out what would make doing the task at hand sufficiently desirable that you become actively involved and get it done. That means you have to believe that it's worthwhile, possible, and intriguing enough to activate your participation. Here are several avenues to consider:

1. Ask yourself what you want to do now. Sometimes you're perfectly willing to do something at a later time; you just don't want to do it now.
2. Ask yourself when you would be willing to do it.

3. Ask yourself if you still want it to be done. If not, why not? Does it really need to be done?

4. Ask yourself if you're willing to live with the consequences of not doing it.

5. Ask yourself what you would be willing to do. Sometimes there is part of it you're willing to do, and once you get started you may find that's all it takes to get you going.

6. Ask yourself how else it could get done. You may find yourself having plenty of energy and interest, for example, in arranging for someone else to do it.

7. Ask yourself how you will feel once you have done it. Sometimes the prospect of having done it will activate you.

8. Ask yourself why you don't want to do it. Sometimes you can alter aspects of what needs to be done to make it more appealing.

9. Ask yourself what would make you want to do it.

10. Ask yourself how long you would be willing to do it. Sometimes you may be willing to do a little at a time.

11. Get up and do it. That's how the accountant Michael Russo says he handles difficult things he doesn't want to do: "Just do it. Set it up, and put it in motion."

Getting in Peak Condition and Keeping Yourself There

> *Achieving peak performance begins with the discovery,*
> *complete acceptance, and development of skills to ex-*
> *ercise consciously the power of volition. Volition is a*
> *potential until it is harnessed . . . a potential that you*
> *activate . . . through discipline and dedication.*
>
> CHARLES GARFIELD

We once saw a bumper sticker that read, "The more prepared I am, the luckier I get." It reminds us of our favorite definition of *luck:* what you get when preparation meets opportunity.

When you watch the winning horse at the Kentucky Derby or the winning car in the Indianapolis 500, it's easy to overlook the preparation that's gone into those instant victories. Like all success, the moment of victory arrives in the twinkling of an eye, and we are thereby tempted to chalk it up to luck. Actually, all such victories begin with thousands of hours of preparation over weeks, months, and even years before the glorious day—hours devoted to laboriously grooming and training the horse, meticulously building and testing the car.

In studying successful performers from all fields, you'll notice that they, too, have groomed and prepared themselves mentally and physically for opportunity. When that magic moment arrives in which they can have it all, they're ready. They're able to remain calm and and cool under pressure. They're able to summon the energy they need exactly when they need it and to maintain it for as long as it takes. They can concentrate fully on the moment at hand and not be distracted from what they know must be done. And at the same time, nothing of importance gets past them. Their senses are alert and finely tuned to respond quickly and precisely to the demands of the moment. Operating from this finely tuned state, they appear to be very lucky—just like the highly successful entrepreneurs and propreneurs we've met.

In fact, in reading about highly successful entrepreneurs, professionals, and craftspersons, it's easy to think of them as leading charmed lives. When hearing about how Debbie Fields launched Mrs. Fields' Cookies, or how Famous Amos rode the chocolate-chip-cookie wave to fame and fortune, or how the businessman Harvey MacKay and the psychologist Wayne Dyer became household names, it's easy to think, "Boy, did they have all the luck!" But we've met and personally interviewed each of these people, and many others as well. And guess what? They weren't any luckier than average. They are ordinary people, doing extraordinary things.

Yes, they each began with their particular advantages. But so do all of us. They also each had their own handicaps and their ups and downs. They faced the same things we all face and they were up for it. They were ready to capitalize on the opportunity when luck struck.

What Makes the Magic?

So what is it that enables peak performers to function optimally under such pressure, to know what to do and when to do it, to come from behind, to make the difficult look so easy? We wanted to know. We wanted to be able to produce such extraordinary results ourselves. So over the past ten years we talked to nearly 400 highly successful individuals—from athletes to entertainers, from artists and entrepreneurs to propreneurs—and we've observed two things.

First, of course, they're all competent. A strong degree of competence seems to be a given. But, as the peak-performance researcher Charles Garfield found in his studies of the world's greatest athletes, competence, although essential, accounts for only 10 to 40 percent of any performance. What separates the peak performers in all the fields we've investigated from others who were equally competent is that they had conditioned themselves to be able to do the following five things—all at the same time.

1. They are *relaxed* under pressure.
2. They operate from a *high state of energy.*
3. They remain *focused* intently on their desired outcome.
4. They anticipate a *positive* outcome.
5. They are fully *present* in the moment.

If you watch peak performers, you'll see these traits in action. And while they are characteristic of the most successful among us, they can be developed by anyone over time through consistent conditioning, repeated experience, and a commitment to attain them. All of us can train ourselves to function from this peak-performance state on a regular basis.

As your own coach, mentor, and manager, you're now in a position to condition yourself to perform optimally by cultivating these five traits. When the client calls, when it's time to negotiate the deal you've been waiting for, when you get the big contract—when an opportunity strikes—you can be ready to make the most of the moment. Like the athlete, you can be at your peak, energized, focused, calm, cool, and relaxed. Your files and records can be sufficiently in order that you have all the facts, figures, and materials you need at your fingertips when you need them. And when all those things come together just right, it will look easy.

So how's your luck these days? Are you prepared for success? Are you ready to seize whatever opportunities come your way? This mini-quiz can provide a snapshot of where you stand. Take a moment to see how you score. Then we'll discuss what you can do to enable yourself to work even more consistently at your peak.

You can think of the various statements on the quiz as indicators of the

---

Are You Ready for Success?

Give yourself 2 points for every statement you strongly agree with, 1 point if you agree somewhat, and no points if you disagree.

1. I get out of bed eager and raring to start the day.
2. I know exactly what I intend to accomplish by being my own boss.
3. I am good at the work I do and confident that I can do it well.
4. I spend my day concentrating on the important tasks that will assure that I'll reach my goals.
5. I am relaxed and inwardly calm throughout the day.
6. I have plenty of energy to do what needs to be done.
7. I am not easily distracted. I can concentrate on the tasks at hand.
8. I quickly grasp the situations I encounter and can make decisions quickly and decisively.
9. I can count on myself to do what needs to be done to achieve my goals.
10. At the end of the day, I still have energy to enjoy my favorite activities.

If you scored 18 or over, you are fit for success. If you scored 10 to 17, you're on the right track but need to step up your training to attain your personal best. If you scored under 10, you're out of shape and need to put yourself on a success regimen at once.

---

extent to which you're in condition, so to speak, to work optimally and thrive on your own. We find the quiz helpful in identifying the areas in which we need further conditioning, much like a coach is continually assessing the extent to which his protégé is ready for competition and pointing out which areas need work.

Today, peak-performance training is virtually a science. Top athletic and artistic coaches across the country have a wealth of techniques to draw from to help condition their protégés to perform again and again at their peak. It's not surprising that many of the most successful self-employed professionals and propreneurs are using some of these same techniques in their work. Here's a five-step program we've developed for conditioning yourself to work at your peak.

A Five-Step Regimen for Peak Performance

> *Each time you exercise, you come back stronger. Before long, you flat out get tough, both mentally and physically.*
>
> RAFER JOHNSON
> OLYMPIC DECATHLON CHAMPION

Preparing yourself to work at your peak is much easier when you're on your own, particularly if you're working from home. On your own at home, you have more flexibility in scheduling your work and greater control over the course of your day, making this basic five-step program much easier to follow.

Step One: Remain Relaxed under Pressure

> *If you are relaxing and subconsciously thinking about your coming race, you are going to perform with just about 100 percent efficiency.*
>
> MARK SPITZ
> OLYMPIC SWIMMING CHAMPION

Do you find that sometimes you're hot and sometimes you're not? We all have times when we drag through the day, times when nothing seems to go right. We can't be hot all the time. The trick is to be hot when you need to be.

When you need to be at your best, when you need to perform at your peak, you want to feel relaxed and confident. You want to be calm, alert, and in charge. Unfortunately, it's too often true that the more important the moment, the higher the pressure and the less relaxed and composed we feel. At key moments, instead of enjoying a state of relaxed confidence, you may feel your heart racing and your palms sweating. Your brain may feel like it's either stuck in slow motion or on fast forward.

We know about this experience firsthand. It's happened to us all too often. Actually, it's a common experience for most people who are on their own. After all, we are usually doing things that are new to us. You may not even know any other people who have done what you're doing. In Chapter 6, we'll go into detail about how to turn this fear and anxiety into confidence. But here are a few quick and easy techniques we and others find useful to get and stay relaxed at any time throughout the day.

Learn to notice quickly when your body is beginning to feel tense. Notice where in your body you feel tense, tight, hyper, creepy, queasy, shaky. Then take action to return to a relaxed state immediately, *before* the tension builds up.

Take several long, deep breaths. Slow, deep breathing sends a signal to the brain that all is well; your brain then floods your body with the chemical signals that accompany a relaxed state. So anytime your day gets harried and you start to feel uptight, take a few slow, deep breaths. Count from 1 to 10 as you inhale and from 10 to 1 as you exhale. Do five to ten of these relaxing breaths until your breathing becomes calm and rhythmic.

Shake out the tension. Take a moment to shake out the areas of your body that begin to feel tense and tight. Shake out your hands, arms, head, feet, legs, and finally your whole body. Do this until you feel some relief.

Take a break in a relaxing locale. Research shows that being in a natural setting can reduce stress. The geologist Dr. Roger Ulrich has found, for example, that even viewing scenes of nature reduced muscle tension, blood pressure, and heart rate in stressed individuals and helped them recover from stressful events, including surgery, more quickly.

The environmental psychologist Stephen Kaplan found that you can get the stress-reducing advantages of nature simply by spending a few moments looking out the window or walking through a garden. Watching sunrises and sunsets is particularly relaxing. And if you don't mind getting wet, standing in the rain is an unusually renewing experience. So when you feel uptight, go outside. Lie under a tree on the grass. Sit in the breeze on the porch. Walk in the park, or if you have water nearby, stroll by the river, lake, or ocean.

Take a mental mini-vacation. If you cannot get away even for a few minutes, close your eyes and imagine that you are in one of your favorite natural environments or some other relaxing place. Perhaps imagine yourself watching the sun set over the ocean, sitting by a bubbling brook in the mountains, or curled up in your favorite nook.

Play relaxing background music. Recent research shows that the human brain and body are highly sensitive to sound and especially to music. Certain types of music have a particular rhythm and cadence that has been found to induce a calm, relaxed state of mind even when played softly in the background. In fact, the musicologist Dr. Stephen Halpern claims that listening to the right music can take you from a highly tense state to one that is relaxed yet alert, in as little as thirty seconds. Robert Ornstein, author of the book *Healthy Pleasures,* calls this phenomenon *musical valium.*

Eat right.   Good nutrition can help you stay relaxed, too. Judith Wurtman, a researcher at the Massachusetts Institute of Technology, has found that certain foods pick you up or relax you. In her book *Managing Your Mind and Mood through Food,* she recommends that to feel more relaxed, you should eat complex carbohydrates like breads, muffins, pasta, cereals, potatoes, and grains. And Dr. Charles Tkacz of New York's Nassau Mental Health Center stresses the importance of the B vitamins in managing stress, while Dr. Robert Haskell of San Francisco recommends vitamin C as a stress reducer. Whole grains and leafy green vegetables are high in B vitamins. Foods rich in vitamin C include sweet red and green peppers, brussels sprouts, strawberries, cauliflower, and salmon.

Use your natural alarm clock.   According to Rob Krakovitz, the author of *High Energy,* the sound of an alarm clock starts your day in distress. It blares you awake and puts your system into panic. He maintains that when you go to bed early enough, you can program your internal alarm to wake you up without a commotion. Using this natural alarm clock to awaken you works wonders. It helps you ease your way gently but quickly, into the day.

Musical Valium

Classical
- Bach's Air on G String, Aria from *The Goldberg Variations,* and *Largo* from Harpsichord Concerto in F Minor
- Pachelbel's Canon in D
- Hayden's Cello Concerto in C
- Debussey's *Claire de Lune*
- Vivaldi's Largo from "Winter" from *The Four Seasons*

New Age
- Stephen Halpern, *Spectrum Suite*
- Ron Dexter, *The Golden Voyage*
- Richard Del Maestro, *Relax*
- Soundings of the Planet, *Music Makes the Snow Melt Down*
- Alliance, *Music of the Heart* (instrumental version)

Enjoy a pet break.   Stroking and playing with a pet can help reduce stress and even extend life. Petting an animal actually reduces blood pressure, as does watching fish swim around in an aquarium.

Take a short nap.   Researchers at a large Athens hospital found that people who took at least a 30-minute nap daily were less likely to suffer from heart disease. This correlates with evidence that countries where the afternoon siesta is commonplace have a lower incidence of heart disease. The entertainer George Burns told the *Los Angeles Times* that a daily nap is one of the secrets to his longevity.

Meditate daily.   If there were one thing you could do that was proven to reduce stress, improve your ability to learn, prevent insomnia, enhance your relationships and job performance, improve your memory, normalize your blood pressure, leave you feeling happier throughout the course of the day, and slow down the aging process, wouldn't you spend twenty minutes a day doing it? It sounds like a prescription for health, wealth, and happiness, doesn't it? And maybe it is.

A large body of scientific research now shows that daily meditation is one of the best, most reliable ways to condition your mind to function in a perpetually calm and relaxed state. Actually, the research is startling. It shows that meditating regularly lowers levels of stress hormones and plasma cortisol and reduces cardiovascular risk. As a result, it can improve your mood, reduce stress, lower your blood pressure and cholesterol level, improve your sleep, slow the aging process, increase your productivity, and speed up the rate at which you learn. And all in only twenty minutes a day! To find out more about meditation, refer to the resource list at the end of this chapter.

Step Two: Get Energized! Stay Energized!

> *Create in you an irresistible energy, putting wings on your heart that will allow you to fly beyond all self-imposed limitations.*
>
> GERALD JAMPOLSKY, M.D

Fatigue is the number-one symptom people complain about to their doctors. Yet the most successful people seem to have boundless energy. They always seem ready to take on any challenge. They jump out of bed ready and raring to go, and they're still going full steam ahead come evening. How do they do it? Here are several ways to get charged up and stay that way.

Get plenty of R & R.   Sometimes people question why we put so much emphasis on making sure you don't overwork. Perhaps it's because we both tend to be overworkers. But more than that, it's because we know that you can't be at your best when you're tired, worn out, and dragging. It's like overtraining. If you overtrain before a competition or performance, you're burned out when the actual event arrives.

It's an illusion to think you'll get further by overworking. When you're overworked, you don't think at your best, or make the best decisions. Research shows that overworkers actually produce less in more time.

A management consultant we'll call Rita is a good example of what happens when you ignore your need for R & R. She had been out on her own for only a couple of years, and was doing quite well. Her strategy had been to assume a leadership role in her professional association and thereby build her reputation as a leader in her field. It was working. She had served as the local chapter president and gone on to a leadership role at the national level. Through the contacts she was making in the organization she had been able to get several key clients.

When she was offered the chance to head up the association's annual national conference, she jumped at the opportunity, even though she had a major contract under way with pressing deadlines. She believed that doing a good job of producing this conference would be an ideal way to showcase herself and her skills. To meet the schedules for both her contract and the conference, however, she really had to burn the midnight oil.

On the day of the conference, she had done it all. She had completed her project, and the conference was clearly going to be a success. The speakers were excellent. The registration was strong. Now was her time to shine. And, of course, she was introducing the keynote speaker and giving a speech herself on the future of the field. But that morning when she took the podium, she hadn't slept for three days straight. She hadn't had a day off in three months, and the entire week before she'd slept only four to five hours a night.

The strain of such a schedule came crashing in on her at that moment. She stumbled through the introduction of the keynoter. She lost her place repeatedly during her own presentation, and under the pressure of it all her voice cracked nervously throughout. Fortunately, she was able to save face because people respected the fine job she had done. But what should have been a glorious victory for her was instead tinged with embarrassment.

And that was not the end of it. She became ill immediately after the conference and lost a month of work while sick in bed. She also had to go back and tie up loose ends on her project, handling details that hadn't been given sufficient attention. By the end of the year, Rita was burned out on her business. She was wondering if she wanted to continue operating at the level of success she had created for herself.

This may sound like an extreme case, but as your own boss it's your job to make sure that something similar doesn't happen to you, even on a smaller, less visible scale. You are the one who must make sure you pace yourself so you can be at your best when you need to be.

Keep the pressure in bounds. According to research by Joseph Procaccini of Loyola College in Baltimore, unrealistic expectations are the real culprit in burnout. Burnout occurs when the demands we put on ourselves outweigh our energy supply. On the job, we might blame overly demanding bosses for the burnout we experience. But on your own, it's your own unrealistic demands that slow you down and sabotage your performance.

High expectations are a good way to motivate ourselves to go beyond unnecessary limits. But success requires a delicate balance between the energy we have available and the demands we place on ourselves. When energy and demand are equal, we perform at our peak. If we don't believe fully in our ultimate success, however, we tend to make unreasonable demands on ourselves in order to compensate, and ultimately our performance suffers. On the other hand, when we believe fully in our ultimate success, we instill in ourselves the confidence to work at a sensible pace, and our performance improves.

The poet and publisher Rusty Berkus of Red Rose Press is an excellent example of this point. Rusty's staff members were pushing her to take on major speaking engagements to help sell her books of poetry. She refused to bend to the pressure, however, because she had never spoken before large audiences and public speaking made her anxious. But she did believe in her ability to learn and knew that in order to become an accomplished speaker, she needed to begin with smaller, more informal audiences with whom she could make mistakes and learn without risking her reputation. That is what she did, and now she speaks successfully to increasingly large audiences.

Know how much sleep you need and make sure you get enough. Don't shortchange yourself for more than one or two nights in a row. For some people, eight hours of sleep is a must; for others slightly less or slightly more is required. The goal is to get enough sleep each night that you arise feeling refreshed, but not so much that you feel sluggish. You can find your peak level by noticing how you feel each morning. Schedule your most demanding work for those times of day when you are at your peak. Leave less arduous tasks like sorting mail and filing for low-energy periods.

Insist that you take at least one day off a week. You need this break to relax and recharge. Taking off two days a week is even better. If for certain *short* periods you can't squeeze out a day off every week, insist on at least a day a month.

Make sure you are enjoying what you do. There's nothing like loving what you do to boost your energy. Usually when you first go out on your own you're excited and turned on by what you're doing, but sometimes after doing it day after day, you don't like it as much as you thought you would. Or after a while, you may feel the need to go on to other things. When this happens, if you force yourself to continue doing what you've been doing, you'll start dreading Mondays again. You'll begin dragging through the day, going through the motions, and sloughing off. So watch for signs that your creative

---

How to Have a Good Night's Sleep
with Everything Hanging over Your Head

- **Hang your work problems on the coat rack when you leave work.** At the end of the day, as you close the door on work, imagine putting your concerns in a special box or basket where you can pick them up in the morning. Write out a to-do list or an issues-to-address list for yourself so you'll feel confident you won't forget about something important overnight.
- **Chase yourself out of the office at a reasonable hour.** Good bosses make sure their employees go home. Insist that you leave ample time between work and sleep. Allow at least an hour or two to unwind from the workday before trying to sleep. Do relaxing, pleasurable activities before retiring.
- **Don't work in bed.** Reserve your bed for sleeping and other pleasurable, relaxing activities.
- **Avoid stimulating food and beverages later in the day.** Caffeine, sweets, and salty and fatty foods keep you wired.
- **Keep your bedroom restful.** Philip Goldberg and Daniel Kaufman, the authors of *Everybody's Guide to Natural Sleep*, recommend keeping the bedroom quiet, dark, and comfortably cool (between sixty-four and sixty-six degrees Fahrenheit).

---

energies are waning, and allow yourself to find ways for your business to evolve with you.

Eat high-energy foods. In her book *Managing Your Mind and Mood through Food*, Judith Wurtman identifies foods her research shows will boost your energy and make you more productive. For high energy, increased mental alertness, and greater motivation, she recommends a diet of protein-rich foods like fish, chicken, and lean beef, low-fat dairy products, dried peas and beans, grains, seeds, and nuts. Also, she suggests that you leave out or minimize energy drainers like alcohol, sugar, salt, coffee, and junk food, which seem to charge you up but actually stress you out. Keep healthy, high-energy snacks on hand like pumpkin seeds, almonds, carrots, hard-boiled eggs, grapes, and whole-grain bread.

Get plenty of exercise. Do an aerobic exercise (swimming, running, cycling, dancing) at least twenty to thirty minutes every other day. Choose an activity you enjoy. Being on your own, especially if you work at home, allows you more options for fitting exercise into a busy day. Choose whatever times work best for you. You can use your exercise time as a work break or as a way to start or end your day.

Instant Energy Builders

When you start to feel tired and burned out, bring yourself back to life in a few seconds with one of these high-energy tips.

- Put on some lively, exhilarating music. Sing along. You can't feel sluggish while singing "Zippity Do Dah," especially if you get up and dance or move around to the music.
- Give yourself a 60-second round of vigorous applause. Stand up. Take a bow. Whistle and stomp your feet.
- Count from one to ten as loud as you can.
- Try this high-energy drink from Dr. Rob Krakovitz's book *High Energy*. Mix a half teaspoon of vitamin-C crystals with diluted fruit juice (half juice, half water).

Step Three: Build Your Concentration

> *I always felt that my greatest asset was not my physical ability, it was my mental ability.*
>
> BRUCE JENNER,
> OLYMPIC DECATHLON CHAMPION

Watch the faces of the players during the world basketball championships. Notice the expressions of the Wimbledon finalists. Observe the pitcher who's about to pitch a no-hitter. Take note of the Olympic gold medalist as he or she prepares to dive. What do you see on all these faces? The same thing: concentration—the ability to focus all of your energy on accomplishing the task at hand. How do these peak performers develop the ability to focus, to concentrate on their goals no matter what's going on around them? How do they respond readily to any event that's pertinent to the task at hand and ignore all else? Here's what we've observed.

- They know exactly what they want to do and what it takes to do it. They aren't asking themselves, "Do I really want to get that shot in now or should I wait until later?" They aren't wondering, "Should I put the ball in this hoop or some other one?" They know what they need to do.
- Their goal—be it getting the ball over the net or making a shot—is the sole focus of their efforts. Have you ever noticed that when being interviewed after a stunning victory, performers often appear to be in a trance of some kind? Their eyes are glazed. Sometimes they don't remember all of the events of the game and talk somewhat randomly.

member all of the events of the game and talk somewhat randomly. They seem disoriented because they are returning from a state of total concentration in which *all* their attention was on their goal.

■ They turn the performance over to the moment. The preparation, practice, study, strategy, and so on are behind them, and they give 100 percent of their energy and attention to what is going on second by second, shot by shot, stroke by stroke. They aren't looking back at what they did the last time. Nor are they looking ahead at what might happen the next time. They're doing what needs to be done right *now* to achieve their goal.

We can each develop this ability to concentrate totally, but it requires a commitment and a willingness to set up our lives so that we can devote our full attention to the tasks at hand. For example, you can do any or all of the following.

Make adequate child care arrangements so you aren't distracted by family and other parental responsibilities. Some people mistakenly think they can work with children underfoot. Occasionally the nature of your work is such that you can, but often there are aspects of your work that require 100 percent of your attention.

Set up time signals so you aren't having to continually watch the clock. You can use a digital watch to alert you when it's time to do other activities. You can set a clock radio, program your TV, or use a wake-up service to signal you. Sarah used a cuckoo clock in her therapy office to signal when to begin closing her sessions. This freed her to concentrate totally on her clients without constantly glancing at her watch. The piano instructor Margy Balter sets a timer to let her know when sessions must end.

Use an answering machine or answering service so you can be free to work without interruption from constant phone calls. When you need to focus on key tasks, set aside a time of day to return phone calls instead of taking or making them at random.

Take definite action. Don't vacillate. Once you set on a course of action, act. Then evaluate. If you're always doubting and questioning yourself each step along the way, you'll never learn what actually works and what doesn't. Commit to a course of action and observe the results. Research shows that people who overanalyze miss the boat.

Get the cooperation of family and friends so they will not be making demands on you during times when you need to be focused on your work.

Locate your office or work space away from disruptions and distractions. Attics, garages, back rooms, and rooms off the garage make ideal home offices. Offices at the end of corridors or set off from customer areas can help you concentrate more effectively.

Step Four: Become an Optimist

Nothing splendid has ever been achieved except by those who dared believe that something inside them was superior to circumstance.

BRUCE BARTON

Worry is one of the biggest drains on our energy. It saps enthusiasm and confidence faster than any other activity. Mark Twain once claimed he had many problems, most of which never happened. And isn't that the truth? Most of the things we worry about never happen, but a nationwide survey found that 42 percent of those interviewed report worrying a lot and spend at least 25 percent of their day worrying.

Alan Loy McGinnis, the author of the book *The Power of Optimism,* defines worry as the misuse of our imagination. Instead of using the imagination to project positive outcomes, the worrier imagines dreaded disasters and defeats. Optimists, on the other hand, use their imagination to rehearse success. And indeed we find that the most successful individuals from all walks of life do this routinely. According to Robert Ornstein and David Sobel, the authors of the book *Healthy Pleasures,* not only do optimists imagine a rosy future, they remember their successes much better than they recall their failures. They also dwell on the pleasant. They skip over, although they don't ignore, their shortcomings.

In the emerging new sciences of psychoneuroimmunology and psychobiology, this phenomenon is called *positive illusion.* And you see it in world-class competition of all kinds. The world champion goes into competition thinking he or she will succeed. Top ice skaters, skiers, gymnasts, divers, and other performers imagine themselves completing their programs flawlessly. They are all optimists. They *anticipate* success. They don't hope for it; they *expect* it.

The power of positive illusion occurs in the worlds of commerce, politics, and art as well. Warren Bennis, a professor of business administration at the University of Southern California, has spent a lifetime conducting pioneering research into the nature of leadership: what it is, who has it, and how we can foster it. For his best-selling book *Leaders: The Strategies for Taking Charge*—a study of the barriers to successful leadership—he interviewed hundreds of leaders from all walks of life such as John Sculley, Norman Lear, Gloria Steinem, and Sydney Pollack. In his subsequent book, *On Becoming a Leader,* he pulled together all his research on the process by which people become effective and inspiring leaders. One trait he found all the great leaders to possess is what he calls *unwarranted optimism*—the ability to see a positive future even in the face of contradictory evidence.

Research is now confirming that optimists are more successful in all areas of life. Recent studies show that optimists excel in school, have a better love life, make more money, have better health, and may even live longer! Dr.

Michael Scheier of Carnegie-Mellon University in Pittsburgh has found that optimists also do better in the face of stress. They take action sooner; break big problems into smaller, more manageable ones; stick to their goals longer;

Creating a Supportive Work Environment

A supportive work environment can help you concentrate and work at your peak. Design and furnish your work space so that it is a place you like to be. Make sure it nourishes rather than fatigues or distracts you. Now that you're the boss, give yourself the equivalent of the corner office. Make sure it has a window, plants, artwork, music, and other things that sustain you. Consider the following.

- **Lighting.** According to a Harris Poll, lighting is the number-one contributor to productivity. For best results, use natural light when possible, or full-spectrum bulbs. Avoid glare, and light various work tasks appropriately. For specific lighting information see *Working from Home*, pages 132 to 136.

- **Soundproofing.** Columbia University found that, of all environmental factors, unwanted noise has the strongest correlation to job stress. Other studies suggest that people who work in noisy settings are more likely to become discouraged than those working in more quiet environments. So find a sound level at which you can remain alert but still are able to concentrate. Mask street and other unpleasant noise with background music or a white-noise generator. Soundproof windows, doors, and noisy equipment. For more information about soundproofing see *Working from Home*, pages 131 and 132.

- **Office furniture.** Poorly designed furniture can cause irritating aches and pains and eat away subtly at your concentration. Furniture should be comfortable and ergonomically designed to avoid muscle strain and fatigue. For more information on selecting the right office furniture see *Working from Home*, pages 128 to 131.

- **Aromatherapy.** Psychologists at City University of New York have found that odors affect how we feel and how well we think. Peppermint, for example, stimulates productivity. Orange is relaxing; lavender is energizing; spiced apple helps reduce stress. So treat your office to your favorite fresh flowers, potpourris, incense, and oils to help you work more productively.

- **Color.** Dr. Alexander G. Schauss, a clinical psychologist and the director of the American Institute for Biosocial Research, has found that the colors in our environment produce strong psychological and physiological effects. For example, red is energizing; blue is relaxing; yellow stimulates thinking and creativity. When researchers painted classroom walls yellow on three sides and blue in the back, student IQ scores rose an average of 12 points, and teachers felt more relaxed.

and believe others can help. Optimists also report less fatigue, depression, dizziness, muscle soreness, and coughs than pessimists when facing the same stressful events.

So perhaps it's time to put aside our expectations that we be totally realistic. Having an unrealistically positive view of ourselves seems to be a correlate of greater success. Fortunately, having such a positive outlook can be cultivated and learned. Although the latest research suggests that Pollyanna may have been onto something and rose-colored glasses may not be so bad, it doesn't mean we should look at life through rose-colored blinders. So just what does having a positive outlook mean? Below is a list of traits that Alan Loy McGinnis finds healthy optimists possess. Which ones describe you?

If you tend to be pessimistic by nature, here are a few things you can do to make optimism a regular habit.

Stop hoping and start anticipating. Think for a moment of something that you want very much to come true. Now close your eyes and *hope* for it. Take time to notice what you think about as you experience this feeling of hope. How do you feel? Now open your eyes. Clear your mind. Then close them again. This time *anticipate* what you want to happen. Again take time to notice what you think about and how you feel as you experience anticipation. Then open your eyes and compare the two experiences.

Most people feel much better *anticipating* the results they want. *Hoping* usually involves imagining two outcomes: the one you want and the one you don't. It's usually accompanied by an uneasy sense of yearning. *Anticipation,* on the other hand, usually involves thinking of only one result: the one you want. It's usually accompanied by a sense of excited expectation.

Twelve Characteristics of Tough-Minded Optimists

1. Optimists are seldom surprised by trouble.
2. Optimists look for partial solutions.
3. Optimists believe they have control over their future.
4. Optimists allow for regular renewal.
5. Optimists interrupt their negative trains of thought.
6. Optimists heighten their powers of appreciation.
7. Optimists use their imagination to rehearse success.
8. Optimists are cheerful even when they can't be happy.
9. Optimists believe they have an almost unlimited capacity for stretching.
10. Optimists build lots of love into their lives.
11. Optimists like to swap good news.
12. Optimists accept what cannot be changed.

Reprinted with permission from *The Power of Optimism,* by Dean Loy McGinnis, Harper and Row, 1990.

If you must worry, do it on schedule. The Pennsylvania State University psychologists Thomas Borkovec and Elwood Robinson suggest that chronic worrywarts contain their worry by setting aside thirty minutes a day in which they can worry. All worry is to be saved for this one period, during which they can worry as much as they please.

Associate with optimists. Optimism is contagious, so cultivate positive, upbeat friends and acquaintances. Avoid spending time with naysayers, complainers, and doomsdayers. Join upbeat organizations and groups; avoid downbeat ones.

Listen to upbeat songs. Have you ever noticed that popular vocal music generates intense feelings—usually sad, wistful, lustful, or romantic ones? What if you were to put this same emotive power of music to work to generate joyful, optimistic, empowering, stimulating, and exciting feelings? Some songs on the popular market do have this effect. Whitney Houston's "One Moment in Time," Bette Midler's "Wind beneath my Wings," "Love Lift Us Up Where We Belong" from the soundtrack of *An Officer and a Gentlemen,* and "The Rose" by Amanda McBroom are a few examples. In addition, today there are growing numbers of New Thought vocalists whose albums are devoted to inspiring and empowering their listeners.

Step Five: Be There Now

> *When completely focused on the present, logical and*
> *analytical processes are suspended, and as this occurs,*
> *the peak performer has the sense that all actions are*
> *occurring automatically and effortlessly.*
>
> CHARLES GARFIELD

Do you ever feel out of it? Have you ever missed an opportunity because you didn't see it coming? If so, chances are you were distracted, lost in thought, living in your own world, listening to yourself talk, planning ahead, reminiscing, or daydreaming when the vital clues of great things passed you by. Doing such things, even frequently, is okay, of course. In fact, daydreams are a great way to relax and get away from it all. But when the situation calls for you to be on your toes, you need to be fully present—in touch with what's going on around you—and able to respond quickly and appropriately.

Have you noticed how the most successful individuals are able to react quickly to the events around them? Nothing seems to get by them. They can respond to any challenge at a moment's notice. They have all their antennae up. Their senses are tuned to hear, see, and sense everything around them. In the field of neurolinguistic programming this state of awareness is referred to as *being in up-time.*

According to the peak-performance researcher Charles Garfield, the key to

A Stay-Up Music Guide

These artists create music to motivate and inspire. The names of our favorite albums appear in boldface. Our favorite selections from each album follow in quotation marks. Write to the addresses listed for a catalogue and information on ordering these albums.

Songs of the Heart, Vol. 1 and 2 (Alliance, Box 3021, Beverly Hills, CA 91212; (818) 988-2684): "I Wanna Fly," "I Love Myself," "Life Begins Again"

Live and Well (Alliance): "Stand Up for Truth," "Brand-New Day," "Love Sets Us Free"

That Kid Can Fly (Michael Byers, Insight Productions, Box 4459, Glendale, CA 91222; (818) 241-0522): "I Set Myself Free," "Someone Must Be Grinning Down on Me," "Someone Was There"

The Universe Is Saying Yes/A Beautiful Song (The Coopers, Universal Songs Unlimited, 13334 Bessemer Street, Van Nuys, CA 91401; (818) 780-6536): "I'm Gonna Wake Up," "Nothing's Gonna Take This Dream Away," "A Brand-New Song," "I'm Ready to Fly"

I Believe in You (Stephen Longfellow Fiske, 635 California Avenue, Venice, CA 90291; (213) 396-8205): "You Are a Star," "I Believe in You," "I Remember Who I Am"

Funny Tunes (Stephen Longfellow Fiske): "Bumper Sticker," "New Age Man" (humorous)

Songs My Neighbor Knows by Heart (Dale Gonyea, Gonyea with the Wind, Box 27143, Los Angeles, CA 90027; (213) 661-3210): "I'd Like to Play Carnegie Hall," "Frazzled," "Help I'm Turning into my Parents" (humorous)

Loving Yourself (with Louise Hay; Jai Josefs, 2210 Wilshire Boulevard, Suite 659, Santa Monica, CA 90403; (213) 451-3734): "I Love Myself," "Road to Prosperity," "Remembering and Forgetting"

Warriors of the Heart (Jai Josefs): "I Release the Past," "You Can Go On"

Pepper Street (Pepper Street, 3435 W. Magnolia Boulevard, Burbank, CA 91505; (213) 842-8384): "Guardian Angel," "Here's to Life," "Turning Point," "Where Does the Time Go?"

One Dream (David Pomeranz, Upward Spiral, Box 93907, Los Angeles, CA 90093; (213) 650-7822): "One Dream," "Come Home," "Hit That Target," "It's in Every One of Us"

White Light (Gail and Ed Tossing, HeartSong, Box 2455, Glenview, IL 60025): "Wake Up and Dream," "Let Your Music Soar"

successfully focusing on the present is learning to be attentive to your senses, and to the quality of what you are sensing rather than to your interpretation of the meaning. So the first way to begin honing your skills of awareness so you can operate more often in up-time is to become more aware of what you are and are not aware of. Here are a few simple exercises from John Stevens's book *Awareness* that you can use to heighten your sensory awareness.

Become an observer of your awareness. Take a moment to observe where you have your attention. Say to yourself, "I am aware of . . ." and finish the sentence with whatever you become aware of at the moment. Do this for a few minutes. You'll notice how quickly your attention moves. As it does, identify whether what you are aware of is:

■ An inner sensation: a pain, an itch, a feeling, an emotion, a tightness, a fullness, a hunger, a thirst. Peak performers are quickly calibrating feedback from inner sensations.

■ An outside stimulus: an object or event you see, touch, taste, smell, or hear. Peak performers block out superfluous stimuli and are hyperalert to relevant ones.

■ Mental activity: thoughts, explanations, interpretations, guesses, comparisons, plans, remembered events or activities, anticipation of future activities, daydreams. Mental activity is down time. It takes you into your head and away from your present experience. Thought stops performance.

Focus on each area of awareness. Begin by noticing your inner sensations. Notice how your body feels. Are you relaxed? Where does your body feel tight? How do you feel right now? Mad? Sad? Glad? Scared? Excited? Bored? Agitated? Peaceful? How do your toes feel? Your stomach, shoulders, fingers, elbows, earlobes?

Now shift your attention to your thoughts. What are you thinking about? What do you think of this activity? What do you think about what you're thinking? Maybe you're thinking about what you will have for dinner. Or something you forgot to do today.

Now shift your attention to outside sensations. Look around the room. What do you notice? What do you hear? Do you suddenly become aware of sounds you didn't hear before? A clock ticking? The heat or air conditioning running? Is there talking in the background? Can you smell anything? Now move around and touch things around you. Notice the sensations—soft, smooth, hard, sharp, rough, cold, hot. As you do this, notice if you begin evaluating or thinking about these things or if you just let yourself experience them.

Finally, shift your awareness back and forth between inside and outside. Between sensations and thoughts. From one sense to another. Which ones do you notice most easily? Focus on those that you are less sensitive to.

Exercises like these and the "Five-Minute Warm-up" on the next page can help you get out of your mind and into the moment, where you can perform at your best. If you feel self-conscious about doing such exercises, go to a track

A Five-Minute Warm-Up for Peak Performance

Haven't you noticed that professional artists and athletes warm up before they perform? Obviously it helps them perform better. So why don't we warm up to function more effectively? Why do we just assume that somehow we'll automatically be in peak condition to work? Why not spend a few minutes warming up our mind and body, especially at times when we want to be at our best? Here's a five-minute routine we created for getting relaxed, energized, focused, positive, and present.

Minute 1: Relax. Stand up. Shake out your entire body, from head to toe. Close your eyes. Take a deep, relaxing breath. Breathe in slowly to the count of ten and then out to the count of ten. Complete ten such breaths. Ride the wave of your breath for one minute.

Minute 2: Energize. To get your energy moving, start clapping. Keep clapping louder and faster. Then begin stomping while you clap. Stomp and clap faster and faster, louder and louder. If you need to warm up somewhere silently, try the quiet version of this exercise—finger snapping. Snap you fingers quickly with both hands for one minute.

Minute 3: Focus. Now you're relaxed and energized. But you don't want to be a loaded loose cannon. You want to focus your energy toward accomplishing your goals. With your eyes closed take a minute to visualize your goals and dreams as if they were already happening. Imagine you're living your dream. Go into every detail. Savor the full experience of it for close to a minute. Then focus on what steps you will take today to make those dreams a reality.

Minute 4: Anticipate success. With your eyes still closed, prepare for a successful day by taking another minute to review your past successes and the things in your present life that give you great pleasure. Cultivate an attitude of gratitude toward the many things for which you are grateful. Imagine once again the future you anticipate enjoying. Imagine yourself managing whatever problems you encounter. See yourself responding skillfully to any unexpected developments. Feel the excitement as you anticipate achieving your goals.

Minute 5: Get in touch. Before opening your eyes, begin to connect with your environment. Hear and sense what's going on around you. Slowly savor the sounds and sensations. Now open your eyes and take full notice of your environment. Allow your attention to linger over the objects, sights, and sounds about you. See colors. Notice textures. Let the day spring to life. Think of the people you will be contacting. Connect with your memory of them. Imagine yourself making contact with everyone you meet or talk with. Resolve to take the time to look them in the eyes, to reach out a hand to them, to tell them something about yourself and find out about them.

Now feel a wave of calm and boundless energy charging through your body. Acknowledge that you are alive, and relish the moment. Imagine that energy carrying you like a river effortlessly through the day.

meet and watch the performers warming up. You'll notice them doing similar types of activities. Or visit a theater or dance company and watch how the performers prepare for the curtain to go up. They, too, will be doing exercises like these.

Making Success Automatic

You'll find as you begin conditioning yourself using the above suggestions that you'll be able to access a peak-performance state whenever you need to. When you need to perform optimally you'll be able to move into the highly productive state. Over time, when the pressure is on, when the stakes are high, you'll automatically relax, feel energized, focus, anticipate the best, and remain in the moment. If your heart starts racing or your energy starts lagging, you will automatically say and do the right thing to slow yourself down or charge yourself up.

Conditioning yourself for peak performance is like setting the automatic thermostat on your heating and air-conditioning system, or like setting your car's automatic speed control. When more heat, cool air, or gasoline is needed, the system notifies itself to kick in. Once the optimal level is reached, however, it cuts back. And so it is with learning how to keep yourself in a state at which you can perform optimally.

When we've asked top athletes and entertainers like the Olympic gold-medal-winning ice dancers Jayne Torvile and Christopher Dean how they were able to excel under such intense competition, they have frequently told us that the discipline of having performed the same moves, or the same routines, over and over in practice and competition enables them to do it almost automatically. In this same vein, the basketball star Isaiah Thomas told Arsenio Hall that when he's at this best, it's like he isn't even there. He's so in tune with the goal and the present moment that the ball is going into the hoop even before it leaves his hands.

As your own coach and manager, you can train yourself to achieve these superior results as well. It's a matter of making sure you can count on yourself to do what you want to do and what you tell yourself and others that you will do. It's a matter of knowing what motivates you and how to tap that motivation when you need it, and then being in peak mental, physical, and emotional condition.

Taking Care of the Coach

Since as your own coach and mentor you need to be there for yourself with the answers, the direction, the support, the guidance, the reassurance, the appreciation, the expectations, the demands, and the resources, what do you do when you—the coach—become discouraged, baffled, or at a loss? What if you don't have the answers? What if you don't know what to tell yourself?

What if you find situations in which you can't manage yourself? What if you fly off the handle? Give bad directions? Make mistakes?

Unlike professional coaches, you can't decide to drop yourself as a client. Although you might like to, you can't take another job with some more talented, compliant, or cooperative protégé. You can't even fire yourself. This job is yours for life—unless, of course, you want to take another salaried position and turn yourself back over to someone else.

So if you get fed up with yourself on occasion, just keep in mind that you're the best you've got. And remember, some people are much harder to supervise and motivate than others. The moment you get out on your own, any authority issues you have are now with yourself. If you tend to rebel or act out when things don't go the way you want, you'll be rebelling and acting out against yourself. If you tend to be recalcitrant, lazy, or stubborn, guess who will have to handle it? You, of course.

Obviously, you can't be perfect either as an employee or as a coach, boss, and mentor. Making it on your own is a learning process. Learning to be your own boss is like learning anything else. You have to get the hang of it. There are many professional organizations and groups you can join that are filled with others who are meeting similar challenges. In fact, when Sarah and several other psychotherapists founded a mental-health institute in Kansas City, they created a group that met every Monday afternoon; its sole purpose was for care givers to support, nurture, encourage, and sympathize with each other so they would be able to begin the week with renewed confidence and commitment.

Forming such a support group for yourself can be a godsend and is not difficult, because many people who are on their own share this need for a sense of mutual team support. Look for noncompetitive individuals who share your level of commitment and who are excited about other people's success. Join with them and you will all benefit.

If you discover that you're really giving yourself a hard time—messing up deals, losing business by abusing drugs, alcohol, money, or sex, or just doing a bad job, get some professional help. You may have observed, as we have, that many of the most successful performers in all fields are in therapy. Sports teams now even hire team shrinks. This isn't because successful people are sick or have more things wrong with them than anyone else. It's because success demands more of people than mediocrity, and the most successful people and the most successful coaches don't want to see talent and potential bound up in unnecessary limitations. They want to do whatever they can to free themselves of such limitations. They know what miraculous things are possible when ability soars untethered.

Resources

Awareness. John Stevens. Lafayette, CA: Real People Press, 1971. A classic book of exercises designed to increase your awareness of internal and external reality.

Everybody's Guide to Natural Sleep. Philip Goldberg and Daniel Kaufman. Los Angeles: Jeremy P. Tarcher, 1990. A comprehensive guide to how to overcome sleep problems using natural methods.

Healthy Pleasures. Robert Ornstein and David Sobel. New York: Addison-Wesley, 1989. A fascinating book about how the simple pleasures of life are actually good for your health. It documents the latest laboratory research with practical suggestions about how to live a life you enjoy.

High Energy. Rob Krakovitz, M.D. Los Angeles: Jeremy P. Tarcher, 1986. How to overcome fatigue and maintain peak vitality.

How to Stay Up No Matter What Goes Down. Sarah Edwards. Here's How (Box 5172, Santa Monica, CA 90409). Thirty three-minute motivational pep rallies for renewing your resolve, determination, enthusiasm, and confidence.

The Inner Winner. Dennis Waitly, Ph.D. Nightingale Conant. This audiotape album consists of affirmative messages accompanied by musical segments.

Managing Your Mind and Mood through Food. Judith Wurtman. New York: Harper & Row, 1986. This book outlines how what you eat affects your mood and identifies foods that can help you be more focused and alert.

Mastering the Information Age. Michael McCarthy. Los Angeles: Jeremy P. Tarcher, 1990. A course in working smarter, thinking better, and learning faster, this book outlines many steps you can take to perform at your peak in an age when information can be either overwhelming or empowering.

Never Be Tired Again. David C. Gardner and Grace Joely Beatty. New York: Harper & Row, 1988. A nutrition, fitness, and lifestyle program that can triple your energy level in seven days.

On Becoming a Leader. Warren Bennis. New York: Addison-Wesley, 1989. Using interviews with leaders from all walks of life—from Norman Lear to Gloria Steinem—Bennis identifies the basic ingredients of leadership.

The One-Minute Manager. Kenneth Blanchard and Spencer Johnson. New York: Berkley Books, 1986. The most basic of guides for how to be an effective boss. If you apply its simple principles to managing yourself, you'll love your new boss.

Peak Performance. Charles Garfield. Los Angeles: Jeremy P. Tarcher, 1984. This book lays out the basic findings of Garfield's research into the mental training techniques of the world's greatest athletes. It includes how they relax, use mental rehearsal, and build concentration.

Positive Illusions. Shelley E. Taylor. New York: Basic Books, 1989. This book presents the latest scientific research documenting how mental and physical well-being is actually enhanced by unrealistic optimism about oneself, the world, and the future.

The Power of Optimism. Alan Loy McGinnis. New York: Harper & Row, 1990. McGinnis has created an action plan to bring out the best in yourself, take charge of your life, and keep your enthusiasm high—based on what he has found to be the characteristics of tough-minded optimists.

The Relaxation Response. Dr. Herbert Benson. New York: Avon Books, 1975. Sets forth a simple meditative technique for handling stress, anxiety, and fatigue and explains physiologically why relaxation affects us so positively.

The Silent Pulse. George Leonard. New York: Dutton, 1978. Sets forth the fascinating thesis that each of us has at the heart of our existence a silent pulse that can literally be in synchronization with the universe around us. It's beautifully written, and puts a new perspective on how we relate to ourselves and the world.

TM: Transcendental Mediation. Robert Roth. New York: Donald I. Fine, 1987. Comprehensive summaries of many research studies on the effects of meditation on performance, health, self-esteem, learning ability, and productivity.

What to Say When You Talk to Yourself and **The Self-Talk Solution.** Shad Helmstetter. New York: Pocket Books, 1987. A comprehensive program for replacing this negative chatter with positive self-talk. (Many tape albums on the same subject.)

Working from Home. Paul and Sarah Edwards. Los Angeles: Jeremy P. Tarcher, 1990. See especially chapters 6, 7, 12, and 13.

CHAPTER
SIX
■■■■■■■■■■■■■■■■■■■■■■■

Riding the Emotional Roller Coaster

*I learned to master the trembling of my
limbs, to control my heartbeat and my
breathing, to wipe away the sweat that
burned my eyes. . . . I was intoxicated by
the satisfaction of having overcome my fear
of the unknown.*

DOUCHAN GERSI

Being on your own is an emotional ex-
perience. Usually it's quite literally an emotional roller coaster, with moments
of soaring exhilaration, intense apprehension, overwhelming opportunities,
paralyzing fear and doubt, gut-wrenching disappointments, and unbelievable
elation—punctuated with periodic moments of deep satisfaction, unbearable
impatience, momentary rejection, alternately devastating and delightful surprises, fleeting frustrations, intriguing curiosity, and a growing sense of confidence and self-assurance. In other words, on your own you know you're
alive!

Being on you own is such an emotional experience because you're usually
living every day on the edge of your greatest fears and joys. Much more is at
stake. Your ego, your self-confidence, even your very survival may seem to
hang in the balance from day to day, at least at first. Any day can bring a big
break. One phone call can make your week, your month, or even your year.
Or the same call can be a cancellation, a rejection, or a bad turn of luck that
crushes budding hopes.

And there's so much more to prove. There are the people who believe in you, the people you don't want to let down, the people who said you couldn't do it, the people who discouraged you from trying. And then, of course, there's yourself, the part of you that believes you can do great things and the part of you that doubts; the part that's confident and the part that's concerned.

There's also usually no one around to constrain your emotional reactions. There's no one to put on a show for. In a salaried position, the boss, co-workers, and subordinates are around for you to impress and keep up a stiff upper lip for. On you own, your true feelings are free to come out, and they often do, sometimes to your surprise.

But, of course, business books don't talk about the emotional aspects of being your own boss. Somehow being emotional—especially *overreacting* or feeling *out of control* of your emotions—is an embarrassing, almost taboo, subject. To reveal that you're having unfamiliar and unexpected emotions is like admitting to some flaw in your personality. Certainly the experiences of politicians like U.S. Representative Pat Schroeder and the former U.S. senator Edwin Muskie demonstrate that in this country we construe emotional expression as a sign of weakness. Both were confronted with highly negative public reactions to a tearful speech.

Actually, having strong emotional reactions is a natural and normal aspect of being human, especially at times when you move out of what the motivational speaker and author Jim Newman refers to as your *comfort zone*—the range of experiences, events, and environments with which you are familiar and at ease. So is it any wonder we have strong emotional reactions to becoming our own boss? Being on our own takes almost all of us right out of our comfort zone and into highly unfamiliar, unpredictable, and capricious circumstances.

Having strong emotional reactions, however, is not the problem. In fact, it can be an asset. Recent psychological studies show that organizations that employ personnel with narrow, limited emotional responses are devoid of creativity and therefore stagnate. The problem is that we get very little preparation for dealing effectively with our emotions. The most common approach we learn for dealing with emotions is to avoid having them.

With a few exceptions, like rooting for our favorite sports team or cutting up on New Year's Eve, we learn to keep our emotional experiences within a narrow range that is considered acceptable and manageable. We are encouraged to limit our experience of intense emotions to feeling them vicariously through television, books, and film. People who express their emotions outside these acceptable bounds are often referred to as hysterical. As a result we have virtually no experience in handling unfamiliar and unpredictable levels of intense emotions in a work context.

So what are you to do when suddenly you feel panic about pressing deadlines and having more work than you think you can handle? How should you react to feeling hopeless after being turned away repeatedly by prospective clients? What can you do when you're furious about an unexpected and seemingly unfair cancellation? How do you deal with the hostility you feel about having to ask again and again for a client to send you a check? The assumption is that somehow we're supposed to handle all these things in a cool, calm, and collected manner.

But being on one's own has upped the ante, raised the stakes, and demands that we access a wider variety of emotional responses than we're used to. Now as the boss you've got to know what to do with the wide range of your moods, reactions, overreactions, escalations, dispositions, and morale. And that's what this chapter is about—handling the rich array of emotional reactions you experience. In this chapter you'll gain a new perspective on your emotions, from which you can view them as powerful assets that can guide you to precisely that right response to any emotionally charged situation.

A New Perspective on What to Do with Your Feelings

> *At the very instant that you think, "I'm happy," a chemical messenger translates your emotions, which have no solid existence whatever in the material world, into a bit of matter so perfectly attuned to your desire that literally every cell in your body learns of your happiness and joins in.*
>
> DR. DEEPAK CHOPRA

It was with a great sense of relief that we first learned about the unique perspective toward emotions we're about to describe. We did so from reading Leslie Cameron-Bandler and Michael Lebeau's book *The Emotional Hostage.* We recommend it to anyone who wants to become the master of his or her fate. Leslie is one of the pioneers of neurolinguistic programming—the study of internal reality. In applying her discoveries, along with findings from the new field of psychoneuroimmunology and the work of acting coach Gene Bua, we've discovered a way you can greet your emotions as trusted friends and valued resources. Using the concepts we describe here, you need never again feel at the mercy of your emotions. Instead you can call upon them to enrich and enhance the quality of your life.

Emotions as Valued Messengers

We now believe that all emotions, those that have been thought of as negative as well as those considered to be positive, are designed to serve as physiological road signs that point us toward appropriate action. Once we can learn to read their language, we no longer need to get waylaid in negative emotional pit stops for hours, days, or even a lifetime. Instead, we can use emotions as way stations where we can stop to ask directions and get fueled up for the journey ahead.

Instead of thinking of negative feeling as impediments to getting where you want to go and therefore as something to be avoided at all costs, you can view them as biochemical messengers bearing supplies and valuable directions that tell you what you need to do next to get to where you want to go. Understanding the role of emotions in this new way is enormously helpful to those who are self-employed and routinely find themselves outside their comfort zone, faced with a broader, richer, more intense range of emotions that are hard to hide, avoid, bury, or ignore.

Physiologists now recognize that our emotions flow naturally and powerfully from our perceptions, traveling through our nervous system and our bloodstream, simultaneously flooding every cell of our bodies with their vital messages. You've probably heard of the classic *fight/flight reaction*. It provided the first indication of how our emotions function to prepare the body for action, and was identified near the turn of the century by Dr. Walter Cannon of the Harvard Medical School. Cannon described how the brain, when it registers a threat of some kind, floods the body with chemicals that prepare us to stand and fight or turn and run: blood pressure increases, heart rate increases, rate of breathing increases, and more blood flows to our arms and legs. Every cell becomes charged with energy and prepares for action.

Over the years, scientists have suggested that the fight/flight mechanism is actually an anachronism, a vestige of an era long past when humans lived in the wilds and needed to flee from or fight off the dangers they encountered. The interpretation has been that this mechanism is no longer suitable to our modern world, when fighting and running are rarely appropriate responses to the daily threats we encounter. Therefore, the theory goes, we try to avoid or repress this fight/flight reaction, and that takes a heavy toll on our bodies. As we try to stop or repress this reaction, we interrupt the flow of energy the body has generated for us to use. Holding back and storing up this energy takes a lot of effort, and over time we end up fatigued and worn out. Now research shows that ultimately such stored-up emotional energy can even lead to chronic stress, high blood pressure, hypertension, and disease.

But what then are we to do with all the emotional energy our bodies keep manufacturing? If we can't run or fight, if we can't repress or avoid, is our only hope, as some might suggest, to evolve toward a more functional human being who, like Spock on the popular television series *Star Trek*, doesn't have these bothersome responses? We believe that would be a grave loss and that, in fact, it's not our human physiology that's outdated; it's our understanding and use of it that need updating.

Instead of calling this innate human physiological reaction the fight/flight response, for example, we should think of it as a *ready state*. In this ready state, empowering energy surges through our bodies. But we need not limit the use of this energy to running away or clubbing someone just because these would be our most primitive prewired responses. We can use the same energy to think on our feet, take immediate action, and carry out any number of other productive responses.

As twentieth-century human beings, we have access to a wide variety of emotional and behavioral reactions. Centuries of social and psychological evolution have provided us with a greatly expanded repertoire of responses that go far beyond simply fighting or fleeing. If you think back to the last time you experienced a fight/flight response, do you remember how energized, alert, and excited you felt? It's almost like an electrical charge. Can there be any more empowering state of being? In some ways, doesn't it resemble the peak-performance state we discussed in Chapter 5? It's like Luke Skywalker's light sword—a force so powerful we have to learn how to wield it. And that is, in fact, exactly what today's top performers in all fields are learning to do. They are learning to direct and command that energy, speeding it up or slowing it down according to their needs.

To take this interpretation a step farther, what if this ready state is not just the way our body responds to fear or threat? What if every emotion we experience produces its own unique and equally precise ready state, which brings us an ample source of the exact type of energy we need to respond appropriately? The latest research in psychoneuroimmunology indicates that this is in fact the case. Research now shows that, whatever emotions we experience, our entire body prepares us appropriately for the circumstances at hand.

When you feel angry or sad or happy or scared, your entire physiology reflects these emotions. All the cells in your body are angry, sad, happy, or scared. How could a mechanism as sophisticated and efficient as this have become outdated? Certainly the human body would not be prewired so exquisitely to carry out such an intricate and precise process if this process were not designed to serve us.

From psychoneuroimmunology we learn that there's nothing inherently harmful in our emotions themselves. Any harm comes about because instead of making productive use of our feelings, we allow them to rage through us like a forest fire or repress them until they burn us out. In reality, our emotions are as natural—and as vital—as breathing, digesting, eating, or sleeping. Instead of trying to hide them, deny them, ignore them, and avoid them, we can learn to consciously utilize them just as man learned to use fire to light the darkness and to fuel the engines of industry.

Each emotion is like a biochemical gift that comes with instructions and a full set of batteries. In other words, there are two components—one mental and one physical—to each emotion. The mental component is the message or signal that tells you what you need to do, and the physical component is the energy or fuel that activates whatever behavior is called for. If we ignore the message, we simply flail about in the energy—ranting and raving or wallowing and sinking—until it passes through us. On the other hand, if we try to stop the physical energy from surging through and carrying us into action, we become immobilized. Our task is to listen to the messages our emotions bring us and to use the energy they generate within us to initiate the behaviors that will produce desirable results for us.

Let's use the feeling of *disappointment* as an example. Disappointment flows from the sweet memory of a desired experience that is now lost. Think about a time when you were disappointed. What had you lost? And what feeling came over you when you realized it was gone? Usually disappointment engenders a sinking, empty feeling that, if we allow ourselves to experience it fully, eventually carries us to an *acceptance* of that which can never be. Disappointment puts us in the ready state for letting go, so we can move on and fill ourselves again with what can be.

In fact, the word *emotion* derives its meaning from the Old French word *esmovoir*, meaning "to set in motion," "to move the feelings." Emotions are feeling in motion. And they do move. Once you experience them, they flow on. Their energy carries you somewhere else, and you can participate in that journey. Disappointment moves to *acceptance.* Acceptance opens you to new desires. In fact, the quickest way to stop feeling some way you'd rather not feel is to go *through* the emotion. If you allow yourself to experience the feeling, it will take you somewhere else. The way we get stuck in our feelings is by trying to stop them and not experience the accompanying emotion.

Checking the message. But remember, our emotions arise from our perceptions. If we falsely perceive something, we will experience the feeling and put ourselves into a ready state for a situation that doesn't exist. For example, if we falsely perceive that something is lost to us forever when in fact it is not, we end up accepting the loss of something that is actually still possible and available to us. We give up on what we could still achieve.

Here's a great example from our own lives. We had an opportunity for our local radio show to be picked up on a national network. We were excited. That excitement generated plenty of energy to make all the necessary arrangements to get the first show on the air with just a few days' notice. We'd aired two successful shows when we were notified that our appearing on another show prevented us from continuing on the station. Our hearts sunk. We were disappointed.

But if disappointment serves to prepare us for loss, what had we lost? Only that one opportunity. We did have to accept that. But we didn't need to accept defeat in placing our show. There were still many other opportunities, and once we realized that, our disappointment shifted quickly to *hope* and then to *frustration.* And that was great!

Surprisingly, frustration is a very functional emotion. It makes you feel uncomfortable, like you just sat down on a hotplate or like something sat down on you, trapping and constraining you. It brings up a rush of energy for breaking through whatever roadblocks you've encountered. Frustration says,

"Something is in the way of what you want. Here's the energy you need to do something about it!"

It took a full year before we found the right station. But over that year, our quest was fueled by the energy engendered by an intense desire kept alive by hope and an ongoing feeling of frustration. All that emotion was useful. Thank heavens for our frustration and impatience. Where would we be today without them?

We probably wouldn't have found another radio station had we allowed ourselves to mistakenly accept defeat, because *acceptance* is like a low-power vacuum that sucks aways your energy. It prepares you to withdraw your energy, to let go, to give up. Had we accepted defeat we wouldn't have had the necessary energy to keep sending out proposals and relentlessly talking up what we wanted.

As you can see, recognizing the message each emotion brings can guide you to take the appropriate action and assist you in using the energy it brings appropriately. Knowing, for example, that disappointment is designed to help you let go means that whenever you begin to feel disappointed, you can check out the message to be sure that in reality what you desire is lost. If it is, you can use that sinking feeling to let go of what cannot be.

But if what you seek is only delayed until some unspecified time in the future, you need not give it up (although you certainly can if you choose). Instead, you can move on to other emotions, like *frustration* and *determination,* associated with not yet having what you know is possible. And you can use the energy from those emotions to help you get there.

Using the energy. The energy each emotion brings has its own unique qualities—a rhythm, tempo, intensity, and scope of its own. Some emotions slow you down; others charge you up. Some take you into the future; others propel you into the past. Some engage you; others detach you. And you can use whatever energy an emotion brings to move yourself to virtually any other state you wish. But particular types of emotional energy move more easily along certain paths.

Think, for example, of how easily you can move from feeling happy to feeling hopeful, and from feeling hopeful to feeling enthusiastic. Or how easily you can move from feeling disappointed to feeling hopeless. Undoubtedly you've moved through these emotional chains yourself at times. Then think of how difficult it is to move from feeling disappointed to feeling happy. How many times have you told yourself or others to cheer up when you or they were feeling too disappointed to do that. Or how often have you wanted to feel confident but instead, despite your best efforts, you felt anxious?

Fortunately, even in cases like these you don't need to wait for outside circumstances to move you from one mood to another. Remember, emotion is about movement, the movement of feeling. A feeling will carry you along on its appropriate course. You don't need to fight it, nor do you need to simply go passively along for the ride. If you know the route, you can use the energy of that emotion to propel yourself to wherever it is you want to go.

Actually, there are many routes you can take to get from one emotion to another. You have undoubtedly already learned ways to move in and out of certain emotional states. But there may be some emotional states you tend to get stuck in and have a hard time moving on from. We all do at times. For such times we've developed the Emotional Road Map that follows. Using concepts from Cameron-Bandler and Lebeau's *The Emotional Hostage,* we've developed a road map for dealing with the most common feelings self-employed individuals tell us they have a hard time handling. The Emotional Road Map points out the valuable signals each of these emotions brings and suggests ways to allow the energy of each emotion to take you to the appropriate action it's suggesting.

The Emotional Road Map

Most people don't know it's possible to enjoy . . . all their emotions. The key lies . . . in the emotions themselves. Each emotion is a slightly different riddle that has embedded within it the clues you need to benefit from it.

LESLIE CAMERON-BANDLER AND MICHAEL LEBEAU

The road map that follows provides a step-by-step guide for identifying the useful messages and valuable energy each of the so-called negative emotions brings. The guide suggests how you can use that energy to respond productively and move on. While these are certainly not the only productive ways to respond to these emotions, we have found the road map to be useful for ourselves and others we've shared it with.

At no point are we trying to say that you should or shouldn't feel any particular way. There is no particular way you *should* or *shouldn't* feel, but denying your feelings can be very costly when you're in business for yourself. In reality, you can feel however you wish for as long as you wish. But you don't need to be enslaved by your feelings or trapped by them until your external circumstances change. Our goal is simply to assist you in understanding what you are feeling and in getting the energy of that emotion moving in a direction you desire.

Like any road map, this one can be dull reading unless you've got somewhere you want to go, so we suggest that in using this map you turn directly to the emotions you're personally grappling with.

================== **From Angry to Satisfied** ==================

Anger is a signal that you perceive some harm or threat to your well-being. It signals that you need to take action to stop or prevent what's happening. If damage has already been done, it says that you need to take action to right the damage or prevent it from occurring again. Anger can also be a signal that you think some important standard or value has been violated.

Anger is an intense, fast-moving emotion. What a rush of energy it brings you! Plenty to make sure you safeguard yourself from any further insult. The value of all this energy is lost, however, if you just flail around in it, yelling and carrying on ineffectively. Haven't you seen people yelling pointlessly at store clerks? Perhaps you've done it yourself. Most of us have at one time or another. Whether you feel like yelling at yourself or someone else, the message of the anger is "Back off! Shape up! See to it you don't do that again!"—in a way that produces results.

Anger is never a comfortable energy to receive from someone. It's not supposed to be. Making someone feel sorry or making that person miserable is rarely sufficient, however, especially in a business situation, where you may need to do business with the individual again or where your reputation is affected. To be effective you need to use your anger in a way that assures you that people know what you expect of them and that they can't cross the limits you've set to protect your well-being and values. Here's one road map for getting results when you feel angry.

**Anger → Gratitude → Outcome → Curiosity →
Reassurance → Satisfaction**

1. Direct the energy you're feeling into verifying for yourself that indeed there is some actual or potential harm to your well-being. Just getting angry because life isn't going the way you want it to is a real waste of time and energy. If there's no harm done, ask yourself if you would rather be right or get on with your life. This one question will save you a lot of unnecessary trouble.

2. If there is actual harm or potential harm to you, be grateful that you've seen this danger signal so you can act now to protect yourself.

3. Shift your energy to what you want to accomplish with your anger. Define the outcome you desire from your anger. Do you want people to stop doing something? Do you want them to rectify something? What action do you want them to take? Generally having them admit that they're wrong or getting an apology will not accomplish what you need. You need a commitment from them to stop or not to repeat the action, to cover your costs, make corrections or repair damage, and so forth.

4. Then begin to become curious about what you can do to elicit that action in order to stop, prevent, or rectify any harm to you. Generate possible actions you can take and select the one you believe will be most effective.

5. Prepare yourself to take action with confidence. This is an important step because often there is a sense of helplessness involved in anger. If you have difficulty dealing with anger, recall times in the past when you have stopped or prevented harm to yourself, and feel reassured that you can do that again. Acknowledge that it's okay to express your anger and that you can effectively protect yourself with it. Now imagine yourself taking the action you've identified until you feel satisfied that you've found a solution to the situation and are confident you can carry it out.

6. Find effective anger role models. If you grew up in a dysfunctional family where expressing anger was dangerous or where you never saw anyone express anger productively, you need to find some anger role models. That is, you need to see someone safely and effectively expressing anger. Look for such people among highly successful individuals who are well respected and admired by people who work with them repeatedly, by choice. We also recommend observing highly effective animal trainers. You will see how such trainers command respect and get results from their animals with appropriate anger and how they also convey their affection and respect for the animals even while they're angry at them.

The acting coach and director Gene Bua is one of the most effective people we've met at expressing his anger. When Gene's angry about something, you know it. And it's unpleasant. It's always caused by your failure to do something you're fully aware he expects of you and that you have agreed to do. But once he's expressed his anger, it's gone. It's been effective and it's over. There's not a trace left. His energy flows right on to the next issues at hand.

For example, all his students sign a contract before their first class spelling out the payment policy. And when people don't pay their tuition on time, Gene gets angry. He says something like this in a loud, angry voice: "I expect you to give me your checks at the beginning of the first class of the month! I do my part in this agreement. I'm here every week. I teach the class. And I should not have to chase you down to get paid!" And then that's that. But his message is delivered so powerfully that any late checks are on his chair within minutes.

Breaking an Anger Habit

As the Greek Stoic philosopher Epictetus said, "If you do not wish to be prone to anger, do not feed the habit." Often people with high standards and high expectations spend a lot of time being angry that life is not as it should be. They are constantly comparing the way things are with the way they think they ought to be and then feeling angry about the disparity. This, of course, is their right, but often such anger habits greatly diminish the quality of their lives and the lives of those around them.

To break this anger habit, you can shift your attention from making negative comparisons to finding similarities between how things should be and how they actually are and feeling grateful about these. You can ask yourself what difference it really makes that something isn't just as you think it should be. Often we think that things have to go a certain way if we are to obtain our goals. Actually there are many routes to the same goal, and amazingly, there is no necessity that they go any one particular way.

Sometimes highly perfectionistic people are afraid they can't handle things unless everything goes according to their plans. In such cases, building self-confidence by remembering times when you handled emergencies and unexpected events well can assist you in developing tolerance for the unexpected and enable you to respond more easily to whatever happens.

As the noted family therapist Virginia Satir reminds us, "Life is not the way it's supposed to be. It's the way it is. The way you cope with it is what makes the difference."

■━━━━━━━ From Depressed to Encouraged ━━━━━━━■

Depression literally slows you down and is the most draining of emotions. When you feel depressed, the past, present, and future all look bad. Your entire body goes into a withdrawal ready state. Temporary depression is an appropriate part of the grieving process and can be expected at time of major loss. It helps you to retreat so you can heal from your loss. Under such circumstances, it's important to allow yourself to retreat and not try to force yourself into feeling good.

Depression at times other than a loss, however, is a strong signal that you need to change your life in some significant way. It means your life is not providing you with sufficient gratification for you to want to continue it as it is. It tells you that you are pulling away, and the sooner you take action to create better circumstances for yourself, the easier it will be for your depression to move on. (*Note:* We are not speaking here of clinical depression, which requires medical and/or psychotherapeutic treatment. If depression continues uninterrupted over several weeks, you should seek professional help.)

Because depression is such a low-energy emotion, the first step in pulling yourself out of it is to generate enough energy to begin taking some action. Here's what we recommend.

Depression → Encouragement

1. Begin by identifying something that is better now than it once was. It can be anything, even a very small thing, like how now you don't have to take your children to day care, or how you can sleep as late as you want. No matter how bad things look, Sarah always reminds herself of the stomachaches she used to have every day from the stress of her salaried job. Now she hasn't had a stomachache in years. Paul always remembers how much he used to dislike practicing law; now he enjoys what he does.

2. Project what is better now into the future. Imagine a future that continues to reflect the improvement you've noticed—a future, for example, of spending time with your children at home, of mornings getting up feeling rested because you can sleep as late as you want, of no more stomachaches, and of work you enjoy.

3. Identify something else that is better now and then repeat the above process. Do this over and over until you have built a future that dispels the depression and creates a growing sense of encouragement. This shift will probably not be immediate. But keep using this process. Cameron-Bandler describes it as being like lifting a heavy object from the ocean floor; you have to keep pumping more and more bubbles of air into it to get it to rise.

▬▬▬▬ From Disappointment to Hopeful ▬▬▬▬

Being on your own is filled with *disappointments,* small and large. Knowing how to manage feelings of disappointment is virtually a self-employment survival skill. And actually, as we mentioned previously, it can be a valuable sign that can help direct you toward getting more of what you want.

Disappointment is a signal that you need to decide whether to carry on striving toward something or let it go. It's how you feel when you're expecting something you want and don't get it. It helps you recognize when something is over or isn't going to happen and signals that you need to reevaluate and renew your resolve to take action toward what else you want. It's a passive, low-energy emotion that's an ideal ready state for helping you let go of something that is not possible. Here's what you can do when disappointment strikes.

Disappointment → Possibility Test → (Letting Go) → Acceptance → Hope → Frustration → Patience → Determination → Anticipation

1. Ask yourself if having what you want is still possible through your own efforts. Give your desire Cameron-Bandler's and Lebeau's possibility test on the following page.

2. Accept what cannot be. If what you want is no longer a possibility, it's time to let go and accept that the situation is out of your hands.

How to Know What's Possible

Before giving up hope, before succumbing to disappointment, ask yourself the following questions.

- Is there still something you can do to make this happen?
- Can you think of a time you or anyone else has ever done this?
- Can you imagine circumstances under which you could do it?

If the answer to any of these questions is yes, your dream is still possible. Now you must decide if you still want to pursue it. If you do, go for it. If not, let it go and move on.

---

3. Allow your energy to move on.   Once you let go and accept the impossibility of what you wanted, you'll find that your energy will start to shift as you begin moving toward feeling *hopeful* that the situation will change at some time in the future. You'll begin feeling a desire to pursue other, more feasible goals.

On the other hand, if the possibility test indicates that what you want is still possible, disappointment is not the most productive feeling, because it prepares you for giving up. However, once you recognize that what you want is still possible, your emotions will begin to shift. You may begin to feel *hopeful* and *desirous*. And you may start to feel *frustrated* that you haven't yet attained your goal. Frustration will provide you with the energy to continue striving toward the outcome you desire. When you feel frustrated:

1. Remind yourself what a useful and energizing, albeit uncomfortable, emotion frustration is.

2. Take a deep breath, and focus on the fact that what you want is still possible.

3. Recall times in the past when it didn't look like you could do, be, or have what you wanted, but through your continued efforts you ultimately did get what you wanted. This will help you move into an I-can mindset.

4. Resolve to be patient while renewing your determination to achieve your goal.

If you continue imagining the desired outcome you are now determined to attain, you may begin to feel a renewed sense of enthusiasm and excitement and begin anticipating the outcome you're striving for, and begin looking forward to enjoying it.

■■■■■ From Discouraged to Feeling Encouraged ■■■■■

Discouragement is a feeling that arises when you take on what for you is a highly challenging goal and your progress is slow or nonexistent. Some fields, such as many of the arts (acting, dance, comedy, creative writing, screenwriting, and so on), are by nature discouraging because the odds of success are so low. Unless you are unusually well prepared and well connected, only the most determined and persistent will succeed. Those who get easily discouraged may give up before they get the chance to make it.

To feel *encouraged* we need to perceive increments of progress toward our goals. If, we shoot so high or undertake something so difficult that we repeatedly fall short of our goal and can sense no progress toward it, we begin feeling discouraged. It's a sign that we need to aim at a target that we can actually hit and feel like we're making some headway toward our eventual goal. As your own boss it's your job provide yourself with this sense of progress. The best coaches and teachers don't make demands beyond the reach of their protégés; they help them keep stretching by setting attainable goals and then continually extending them.

In other words, if you're getting nowhere in obtaining a place on the podium at your national convention or are falling far short of your goal to earn $10,000 a month, focus instead on something you can reasonably expect to accomplish. You might aim to speak to a number of regional programs this year or to do $5,000 of business a month. As you attain these goals, you will feel increasingly encouraged and can then set your goals higher and higher as you progress.

Here's one roadmap for shifting from feeling discouraged to encouraged.

Discouraged → Pride → Curiosity → Anticipation → Encouraged

1. Compare where you are now with where you were some time in the past and note the progress you've made. When the road to success becomes long and weary, it's easy to miss the progress you *are* making. Focus on this progress until you get some sense of accomplishment.

2. Compliment yourself on your accomplishments, and allow yourself to feel proud of the movement you've made.

3. Become curious about what you know you can do next that will take you one step further.

4. Imagine other times in your life when you ultimately achieved your goals by taking one step at a time.

5. Imagine yourself carrying out the next step successfully until you begin anticipating further progress and feel encouraged about reaching your ultimate goals.

From Feeling Like a Failure
to Feeling Like a Success

Feeling like a failure often follows having made a mistake or not having accomplished a goal. It is not a signal to quit or give up, although this is a common misconception about this emotion. Rather, it's a signal that you need to do things differently in the future.

The feeling of failure is actually one of the most basic of human survival tools. Without it, we could not master anything. No one ever learns to do something perfectly on the first try. As the writer James Joyce observed, "Mistakes are the portals of discovery."

Does the baby who falls give up trying to walk? Does the child who fails to tie his shoe give up forever on tying shoes? No. In fact, think of how quickly and eagerly the young child pushes you aside to try again. On its own, the feeling of failure tends to flow naturally into wanting to try again. The desired outcome fuels this drive to do it until you succeed. The brain is busily calibrating, assimilating, and making thousands of necessary adjustments so you can do it better the next time. So what happens as we grow up? Somehow the natural urge to go forward toward completion that comes from the feeling of failure gets sidetracked.

At some point in our lives or in a particular area of our lives, we decide that we are no longer learners, that we ought to have mastered certain things and should have nothing else to learn. And we decide that if we don't do these things correctly we have *failed*. Failure becomes a finality instead of being an intermediary step to success. Or after having experienced multiple failures, we come to equate failure with ruin and feel hopeless and defeated, giving up instead of feeling eager and determined to continue on.

Therefore, building a history of success for yourself is very helpful in being able to remain resilient in the face of failure. The parent who takes a child to the swimming pool, for example, and throws him or her in the water before teaching the child to swim is creating a dramatic and memorable failure for the child. But don't we do that to ourselves sometimes? Don't we throw ourselves into situations without the experience or preparation we need to assure our success? We can create ample opportunities for success by making sure we are prepared and by agreeing to do things we now we can accomplish. Then occasional failures are just a misstep from which we can quickly recover and carry on.

Whenever you feel like a failure you want to recapture the natural feeling of forward movement that failure can bring with it instead of spiraling downward into defeat and despair. To do this we suggest taking the following steps when you've made a mistake or failed to accomplish a goal.

Failure→ Pride→ Satisfaction→ Reassurance→ Successful

1. Feel pleased with yourself for having had the courage, fortitude, and confidence to have taken action in the first place. People who wait until they're perfect before they act wait forever. Only those who try will ever succeed.

2. Forgive yourself for having caused any negative consequences from your mistake (to yourself or others). Correct any problems or damage as best you can.

3. Remind yourself that mistakes and failures are a learning opportunity, and take pride in learning from your experience.

4. Feel the satisfaction of having acquired new insights and abilities from your experience, and feel reassured that with them you will perform more successfully in the future. Imagine yourself doing so, and instill yourself with a feeling of *success.*

■■■■ From Fear or Anxiety to Anticipation ■■■■

Confidence is the antidote to fear.

ALEXANDER ROMAN
SPORTS PSYCHOLOGIST

All the people we've met experience some fear and anxiety when they move out of their comfort zone into the unknown, especially when, as is the case in being on your own, the stakes are high. You can bet that all your heroes have been fearful and anxious at one time or another. Reportedly Johnny Carson is still nervous every night before his performance on *The Tonight Show*! If he can still be nervous after all these years, surely you can understand your feeling nervous about your major undertakings. So give yourself a break: don't panic or get down on yourself if you are feeling anxious or fearful as you leave behind the once-presumed security of the paycheck.

Fear and anxiety are normal reactions to a totally unfamiliar future. They are a signal that you can foresee a future that might hold a danger for which you are not prepared. They signal that you need to begin preparing to cope with or avoid possible upcoming negative consequences. So trying to ignore them is foolhardy. Thank goodness they're there to alert you now so you can take needed action to make sure things go well in the future.

As is true of all emotions, fear and anxiety have several characteristics that can help you work with them. Fear is an intense, active, fast-paced emotion that arises from thinking about the future. Actually, it provides you with an incredible amount of highly-charged energy, although you may feel the impulse to use it to either freeze or run.

But you can calm your fears by shifting your attention from the uncertainty of your future to the reality of your present. You can also reduce your fear to a more manageable level by simultaneously taking several deep, relaxing breaths while you concentrate on your present situation. Here's a step-by-step process you can use to walk yourself through a fear attack.

Fear or Anxiety → Safety → Curiosity → Feeling Capable → Self-Confidence → Anticipation

1. *Bring your attention into the present.* Since fear signals a possible future danger, when you start to feel anxious, immediately shift your attention away from the dreaded future to the present and concentrate on the here and now. You can take action only in the here and now anyway, so it's a good place to be when you feel apprehensive.

2. *Notice that you are safe for the moment.* For example, if you are feeling anxious about an upcoming speech, stop thinking for the time being about your future moments at the podium and recognize where you are right now and that you are just fine.

3. *Focus on what you can do now* to protect yourself from negative future possibilities. Once you begin feeling safe in the moment, click into your curiosity and ask yourself what you can do now to safeguard yourself against the future you fear. What could you do to prepare for the imagined future situation? What are you afraid will happen? How could you prevent that? Become intrigued and fascinated with answering these questions. Begin breaking down what you can do into small, specific, steps. For example, if you're going to be speaking before a group of potential clients, how can you make sure you are sufficiently well prepared that you will succeed? If you're anxious about having enough business next month, what steps can you take now to bring in business? If you are afraid you won't meet an important deadline, what steps can you take now to avoid the problem?

4. *Recall times in the past when you have taken the needed steps* to meet a future challenge until you begin to feel capable. Other than for the purpose of identifying what you can do to prepare now, avoid repeatedly recalling times when you were not prepared.

5. *Then imagine yourself preparing to meet this challenge or threat,* mentally rehearsing until you feel confident in your ability to do so.

6. *Begin anticipating the experience of success* you've been rehearsing. As you anticipate meeting the challenge, you may well begin to look forward to doing it.

Now let's take a few minutes to talk about using this process to respond to a few of the most common fears and anxieties we face on our own.

Performing under Pressure:
Mastering Performance Anxiety

George finally had the opportunity to give his first sales presentation to a Fortune 500 company. He was a manufacturer's rep, and he'd been working for months to get this appointment. Now he had it! But the minute he put it on the calendar, he was gripped by paralyzing anxiety. He kept imagining that all the figures would get turned around in his head. He saw himself standing before these important people and losing his place, not being able to find the papers he needed, and so on. He became so anxious that he had to lie down on the floor and try to recover his balance.

He called us for advice. "I'm immobilized," he reported. "What should I do?" "Look around the room," we suggested. "Is there anything frightening there?" Of course there wasn't, and soon he was feeling much better. He was perfectly safe at the moment. From the safety of his office, we suggested that he ask himself what the worst thing that could happen at the upcoming meeting would be. The worst thing he could imagine was that he'd make a fool of himself and wouldn't get the account. "So," we asked, "could you live through that?" And of course he could. "But" we asked him, "how likely is that to actually happen?" It wasn't very likely. Although he had missed sales, he'd never actually made a fool of himself in a sales presentation.

By now he was actually laughing, and we asked him to begin thinking of ways he could prepare himself for success. Mastery is a cure for performance anxiety. Once you know that you can handle anything that might come along, the anxiety of doing it will go away. There's nothing like experience to take off the pressure.

Begin with identifying what you know you *can* do. Then challenge yourself to go one step beyond that. In George's case, he was taking a bigger step than he was actually prepared for. He was going from working with small accounts to a Fortune 500 account all in one leap. So before he showed up we suggested he begin extending his track record as follows.

1. Build a history of success. Do what you do until you know you can do it well consistently. Begin with volunteer or small projects until you have a string of positive memories of successfully doing whatever is involved. If you can't actually do multiple performances, mentally rehearse your performance repeatedly. Charles Garfield found that mental rehearsal is one of the key strategies world-class athletes use to achieve peak performances. George actually had a number of successful sales presentations from the past that he could mentally review.

2. Get the bugs out of whatever you need to do well in a series of dry runs where mistakes don't matter. Would an Olympic athlete go into competition with a new routine he or she had never done well in practice? Would a concert pianist go on stage to play a piece he'd never rehearsed? Confidence goes up and nervousness comes down with each successful experience you have. George, for example, arranged to do a dry run of his presentation before several colleagues from a field similar to that of his prospective client. This rehearsal uncovered several areas where he wanted to gather more information.

3. Mentally replay the string of positive memories you have built before and during times when you need to perform at your best. When doubts creep in, remember that you have done what you will be doing before and therefore you can do it again. Give yourself the evidence of this by mentally reviewing your past successes.

4. Convince yourself you'll do a good job. If you're convinced you'll do a good job, you'll feel confident and your anxiety will disappear. Think of several things you know you can do well. Perhaps you're a good driver or a good tennis player. Now ask yourself how you know that you'll do a good job with these tasks and how many times it took you to demonstrate this to yourself before you were convinced. What can you do now to convince yourself that you'll do a good job at this task? Take the necessary steps to convince yourself, because once *you* are convinced, everyone else is more likely to be, too. If you believe, so will others.

5. Fear, anxiety, and excitement feel very similar. All three of these emotions put you into a high state of energy. But remember, a high state of energy is one of the cornerstones of a peak performance. So turn your anxiety into *excitement.* Instead of using the impulse you feel to run away, use it to run headlong toward what you want. Let the energy you feel flow through you into your performance. It's okay to feel so much energy. Don't sit on it or try to contain it. Use it and it will empower you.

Overcoming the Fear of Failure

No one wants to fail. But fear of failure is never an excuse not to proceed. No one succeeds without the risk of failure. So don't let yourself off the hook just because you fear failure. Use your fear instead to help insure your success by alerting you to possible pitfalls and directing you to take whatever steps you can take to avoid them.

When Lionel left his job in mortgage banking to do investment counseling, he had a wife and two children to support. The children were still so young that neither he nor his wife wanted her to take a job. So he very much wanted his new business to work.

The truth of the matter was that Lionel had been asked to leave his job, and he was fully aware that he had engineered his dismissal. He just didn't feel he was cut out to work for someone else. This was his big chance. But he was terrified of failing. He just didn't know it. He was so afraid to look at the possibility of failure that he almost defeated himself: "I was so afraid of failing that I didn't want to see even the most obvious potential problems. I couldn't face them. I took any work that came along, even if I didn't like it and had to charge much less than I knew I was worth. I pretended that everything was fine. But it wasn't. My wife saw problems coming, but when she would point them out I thought she wasn't being supportive of my business. I was angry and resentful, and most of all, I was envious of people I knew who were doing better than me."

Fortunately, Lionel wanted to succeed so much that he was finally willing to admit his fear of failure. Admitting his fear was the turning point. Then he could begin to look at what he feared and take steps to make sure he could handle those situations effectively. He sought the advice of colleagues and attended several marketing seminars. In the process, he realized that he had to take a stand on the type of work he was willing to do and the fees he needed to charge. He also got a lot of encouragement. "If I had just paid attention to the way I was feeling in the beginning, it would have saved me and my family alot of agony. But the important thing is that I did it. I am my own boss and I have been for five years!"

Russell Seeley served as CEO for a major corporation before leaving to form his own consulting firm, which works with other manufacturing companies. Seeley attributes his success to the fact that he never ignores possible problems. "You've got to be willing to look the problems square in the face," he told us. And, as with Lionel, that's what a fear of failing can help you do. It can get you to look at the problems, and once you've taken steps to prevent them as best you can, you're chances of success will go up.

Also, keep in mind that people are often more interested in what you do when things don't go well than in how you respond when everything is going smoothly. So handling a particular failure or problem well, should one occur—rebounding and going on—can be very impressive. It can actually strengthen your reputation and improve your skill and knowledge.

Conquering the Fear of Success

Fear is a signal that you perceive danger ahead. While there's no inherent danger in success, if you are fearful of it, that's a sign you are perceiving it to hold some danger for you. So let your fear lead you to the thought or stimulus that's convinced you success is dangerous in some way. This thought will most likely be linked to some early experience or decision in your life, and therefore if you have difficulty identifying what you fear about success, psychotherapy can often be quite useful in helping you identify the source of your fear.

Once you know what you fear, either you will recognize it as harmless and your fear will diminish, or you can use your creativity to protect yourself from whatever potential harm there may be. For example, when a women we'll call Meredith went out on her own to publish a magazine, she was gripped with fear every time things started going too well. As Sarah talked with her, Meredith remembered that when she was growing up, her father died of a sudden heart attack the night he received an award for his many business and civic contributions. In her young mind, she had linked his death with success. In fact, she remembered some relative shaking her and saying, "He worked himself into the grave."

As she recalled these events, the line "I don't want to be successful like Daddy" ran through Meredith's head. Once she realized this, she could reassure herself with plenty of external evidence that many successful people live long lives. And she could, of course, see to it that she did not work herself into ill health.

Mike's situation was different. He was living near poverty when he came to talk with Sarah. He restored antique automobiles, but he had set up his business so he couldn't possibly succeed. When Sarah suggested changes that could make the business profitable, Mike became very apprehensive. As they talked, he remembered how his father had failed at his one attempt to start a business. After that time his father had never been quite the same. "The light had gone out in his eyes," Mike recalled. Suddenly Mike realized he feared that his own success would be a painful ongoing reminder to his father of that past failure. "It would be like opening an old wound, and just seeing me would be like rubbing salt in the wound," Mike said.

How clever Mike had been to set his business up so he could do it without really succeeding at it! By doing it that way, in Mike's mind, his father could feel sorry for him instead of threatened by him. Of course, before Mike talked this out, he had no idea he was sabotaging his success. He decided to speak with his father and discovered that the man wanted Mike to succeed, so much so that he volunteered to help him out in the shop.

Getting Past the Fear of Rejection

Whether it's being turned down for a loan by one bank after another, losing out on one proposal after another, being passed over for a much desired contract, or having another manuscript returned, making it on your own usually means coming face to face with *rejection*. No one likes it, but everyone has to deal with it. And it's rarely easy at first. Rejection is an evil-eyed dragon that stalks us all until we cool its flaming tongue and remove its razor-sharp fangs. Here's our list of potions for taming this demon. Each is a question you can ask yourself when the pain of rejection begins nipping at your heels. They've become standard tools of our trade, as valuable to us as our personal computer.

1. Do you still want to do the work you're doing? When faced with repeated rejection, you're often tempted to say something like "Hey, I don't need this!" or "Who needs to put up with this?" And of course you're absolutely right. As your own boss you don't have to put up with anything, unless you want to. You have choices. You didn't have to start this business. You don't have to keep it going. You're free to quit anytime you want.

2. How much do you want this? Okay, so you still want to do it. But how much do you want to do it? Do you want it enough to put up with whatever it takes for as long as it takes? We've found that the more rejection a particular venture involves, the more you need to want to do it. So to test your resolve, use a scale from one to ten, with one meaning you don't want it at all and ten meaning you want it more than anything in the world.

We've found that if you don't score at least an eight or above, chances are you don't want it enough to stick with it through the long-term rejection many solo ventures require, and you owe it to yourself to do something that means more to you.

3. Are you taking this too personally? Like artists, it's easy for propreneurs to overidentify with their work. This is particularly true in a service business like consulting or in creative fields like writing. There's a tendency to think that the bank or the customer is rejecting you and judging you personally as inadequate. In actuality, most business rejections have less to do with you than with the circumstances. Or, as Laura Huxley put it so nicely in the title of her book, "you are not the target." If you can remain sufficiently detached and realize you are not the target—that this isn't even about you—you're more likely to ascertain what the actual circumstances are and know what steps to take next.

Banks, for example, have different guidelines. Contractors have different selection criteria. If you find out which of their needs your proposal didn't meet, you can make the necessary modifications or approach other sources whose criteria you could meet.

4. Are you being realistic? Selling yourself, your product, or your service is often a numbers game. What looks like rejection may simply be a matter of statistics. For example, novices at selling are often surprised to learn that there is a sales/rejection ratio for most businesses. For example, it will take a certain number of calls to get an appointment and a certain number of appointments to get a sale. Only experience will determine what your ratio is. So if you need to make twenty calls to get one appointment and five appointments to get a sale, you need not consider the first 19 calls to be rejections. They're simply par for the course, and each one takes you closer to your goal.

5. Is that "no" really a "no"? Before letting the claws of rejection impale you, always consider that a no is not necessarily a no. While we were growing up, most of our parents told us, "When I say *no* I mean no. And I don't want to hear another word out of you." So most of us learn to take *no* seriously. But in a grown-up world, no isn't necessarily so.

Do you know that some businesspeople routinely say no at first simply to determine if the person is serious enough to pursue the issue? And you would be amazed at how many people change their mind after talking with you for a while. Times change. Circumstances change. We've come to hear *no* as meaning *not now.*

We learned this lesson the hard way. When first beginning to sell radio advertising for our Los Angeles show, we were taking no to mean no, only to discover that companies that said no to us were advertising on other shows shortly thereafter. We were actually making sales for representatives of the other shows, who walked through the open door we'd left behind by not coming right back again. Since that time we've made many sales that begin as one or even several no's.

6. *Who's the best judge?* Is your product a good one? Is your service valuable? You know the answer to those questions if you stop to think about it. To feel rejected is to let someone else provide those answers. When based on reactions from your market you can see room for improvement, welcome the feedback and make the needed changes to make your product as good as you know it truly is meant to be. Then go back. If possible, thank those who made the suggestions and show them what you've got.

7. *What can you celebrate right now?* It can be hard to keep moving ahead when you encounter one rejection after another. There's no reward for your efforts. So we've learned to celebrate every milestone along the way to our goals. Success is a process. If you wait to celebrate until the end, there'll be nothing left to celebrate.

8. *Who thinks you're great?* One of the antidotes for the fear of rejection is a little support from your friends. When you're feeling your worst, ask yourself, "Who thinks I'm great? Who always believes in me?" And get together with them fast. We have a support system of people now who believe in us and our work. When setbacks or rejections occur, we get together with the folks who think we can't possibly lose. This loose-knit group of friends acts as an informal mutual admiration society; we get each other through the tough times.

When you get thank-you letters or notes of appreciation from friends or customers, save them. Put them in a "stroke file." At times when you're getting a lot of no's, get out those notes and remind yourself there are people who value and appreciate your work so much they were moved to be sure you knew about it.

9. Can you take matters into your own hands? Nothing can finish off a venture more effectively than having to wait endlessly for someone else's okay to get underway. Entertainers and writers usually face this type of chronic rejection. They can't get a part until they're in the union and they can't get in the union until they get a part. The successful ones don't wait for someone to discover them. They find some way to perform. They may, for instance, volunteer to appear in trade films or organize their own theatre group.

Remember, success is always attracted to a moving target. So if you're not getting the break you want, rather than feeling rejected, take charge. Don't let your success rest in the hands of someone else. Don't wait for another no. If the bank won't give you the loan you need to expand, raise your own funds. That's what the singer and songwriter Amanda McBroom, who wrote the popular theme song for the movie *The Rose,* did in order to cut her first album. If you can't seem to get a bid, volunteer to do a project for someone who could influence your future customers.

A researcher with a new computerized scanning system for the health field found that prospective clients remained skeptical despite his best efforts to sell his service. Rather than feeling rejected, he started demonstrating the system free of charge to key professionals. Within six months his practice was thriving.

■■■■■■■ From Guilt to Self-Confidence ■■■■■■■

Guilt is a much maligned emotion because it can spiral downward to feelings of *worthlessness, hopelessness*, and *despair.* Actually, however, guilt can be a very valuable emotion. It is a signal that you have violated one of your own personal standards. It informs you that you have let yourself down, that you have not lived up to what you expect of yourself, and it provides you with the opportunity to take steps to insure that you won't violate that standard again.

If you are sufficiently tolerant of imperfection, as any good boss would be, you need not feel worthless when you admit to not having lived up to something you expect of yourself. You can break the downward spiral and look forward instead of doing better in the future.

Guilt is also complicated by the fact that sometimes it arises when we're trying to live up to someone else's standards or expectations instead of our own. For example, a woman might feel guilty about working late because her parents told her family should always come first. Here's one road map for dealing with guilt.

Guilt → Curiosity → Reassurance → Self-Confidence

1. Ask yourself if you have, in fact, violated your own standards or whether you are feeling guilty because you haven't done what someone else thought you should do.

2. If you are feeling guilty because you are trying to meet someone else's expectations and have failed, identify what your own standards are in this situation and act accordingly. If you haven't actually broken your own standards, you will probably no longer feel guilty and, if necessary, can clarify with others what they can and cannot expect from you.

3. If you have violated your own standards and expectations, begin, with a sense of **curiosity,** *to evaluate whether this is a standard that you still want to maintain.* If it is, with *respect* and *appreciation* acknowledge that you want to make sure you will not violate this standard again.

4. Recall times in the past when you successfully lived up to your standards even though it was difficult, and feel reassured about your ability to live up to your personal standards now.

5. Then imagine yourself taking the necessary steps in the future to live up to these standards in the most difficult situations, and feel pleased and confident about your ability to do so.

Confidence Builders

Here are a few things to do when you need to boost your self-confidence.

- Adjust your posture to one that is confident.
- Remember a time when you felt and acted confident.
- Talk to yourself, telling yourself that you're great, reminding yourself of things that you appreciate about yourself.
- See yourself doing something amazing, such as climbing a mountain or flying a plane.
- Identify something within the situation that you are already confident about.
- Feel your own backbone, and imagine it to be a steel rod.
- Identify a clear outcome for yourself in the situation.
- Play a particularly affecting piece of music in your head, one that makes you feel confident.
- Think of people who make you feel confident and imagine them small and sitting on your shoulder, talking into your ear.

Reprinted from *The Emotional Hostage* by Leslie Cameron-Bandler and Michael Lebeau. Future-Pace, 1986.

From Hopeless to Determination or Acceptance

Hope springs eternal in the human breast.

ALEXANDER POPE

Emotions often occur on a continuum from small to large, from weak and mild to strong and intense. Disappointment, for example, is mild in comparison to hopelessness. Yet hopelessness is milder than depression. These three emotions are similar in that they all involve proceeding into a future without something you desire. They are all low-energy emotions that prepare you for letting go.

Hopelessness is more final than disappointment, however, and not as bleak as depression. It's the appropriate emotion to feel when you've done *everything* you can do and it isn't enough. It occurs when you cannot envision a future that includes something you've wanted and prepares you for giving up any expectation of attaining it in the future.

Therefore, the first thing you need to do when you feel hopeless is to ask yourself if, in fact, there is nothing else you can do. Is there any possibility that you can still do something? If there is, imagine the future you want and allow yourself to feel the frustration of not yet having accomplished it yet. Feel challenged and determined to discover what remains to be done and to do it.

Hopelessness → Frustration → Feeling challenged → Determination

If you have done all there is to do, however, it's time to heed your feeling of hopelessness and let go. You can help yourself let go of something that has been important to you by doing the following.

1. Recall times in your life when you have let go of desired outcomes and were freed to go on to other things that were satisfying.

2. Feel reassured by these memories and accept what cannot be attained.

3. Now imagine yourself in the future walking away from this goal and moving on with confidence toward other things that you *can* accomplish. In this case your road map will look like this:

Hopelessness → Reassurance → Acceptance → Confidence

When Susan and Peter left the public-relations firm they were working at when they met and married, they were excited about their plans for launching a nationwide seminar program that would help couples rebuild shaky relationships. They prepared brochures, took out ads in the paper, created lots of media exposure for their inaugural seminar, and held a small but successful first seminar.

Unfortunately, the expenses of holding the seminar exceeded the money they brought in. There was no money left for promoting a second one. Still hopeful, however, they used telemarketing—working the phones themselves until they finally filled another seminar. It, too, was a success for those who attended, but again expenses still exceeded income.

After several months, Susan and Peter were exhausted and on the point of bankruptcy. As weeks passed, their dream of a national seminar looked increasingly hopeless. They had done everything they could think of. And although it was painful, they decided to let go of that dream before it did them in. Once they accepted that their future would not include national couples' seminars, they were free to begin thinking of what else they could do. Since they were both highly skilled public-relations specialists, they decided they would open their own PR firm, doing publicity for seminar leaders.

By shifting their focus to the history of success they'd had in PR, they began envisioning a new future, one in which they were running a successful firm and were able to proceed toward that goal with confidence. Their subsequent success in PR provided them with the funds to conduct, through their church, free seminars for dysfunctional families. Susan now says, "This work is actually much more gratifying than the original seminars we'd planned. When everything seemed so hopeless, it was actually just a sign that we needed to proceed in a different direction."

■━━━━━□ **From Inadequacy to Self-Confidence** □━━━━━■

Many high achievers make a habit of comparing themselves with very successful people because they aspire to such levels of achievement. Too often, however, in making these comparisons they focus on the ways in which they fall short. As a result they end up with a chronic feeling of *inadequacy,* and of course, people don't perform at their best when they're feeling inadequate.

Feeling inadequate is usually the result of comparing what you can do or have done with what someone else can do, has done, or thinks you should do. It's a passive emotion that tends to stop you in your tracks. It prepares you to withdraw from the action before you get in over your head and allows you time to regroup and get better prepared.

This ready state can be valuable if you are truly not prepared to accomplish something you're about to undertake. We know of several cases where it has alerted people to turn down a contract or project they were truly not equipped to take on. A computer consultant we'll call Phil is a good example of someone who did not heed such a warning signal. Phil came to us after a disastrous failure. He had been approached to lead a large nationwide training program that would introduce a complicated software package to several thousand employees. He did not know much about the package, and he didn't like what he did know. But he really liked the prospect of six months of steady work at a good fee. The fee was so good, in fact, that he could live off the income from it for an entire year. He couldn't resist taking the project.

As soon as he signed the contract, however, what had begun as a vague feeling of apprehension swelled, and he began feeling very inadequate. He felt he would need weeks to learn the program adequately, and he had only days. He should have heeded the signal there and then and done what he could to salvage what was looking like an impossible situation. Unfortunately, he didn't. The first session went so poorly that he was fired immediately.

In any situation where you begin to feel inadequate, the first thing you need to do is to restore your sense of adequacy so that you can make the necessary decisions to proceed successfully.

Inadequacy → Feeling Capable → Self-Confidence

1. Remind yourself of your own capabilities, accomplishments, and past demonstrations of competence. Focus your attention on what you know you can do and have done well. Review your strengths in detail.

2. Continue reviewing your strengths and assets until you begin to feel adequate to the current situation.

3. Act from your own sense of competency.   Once you are feeling adequate again, you will have access to what you can contribute to the situation and proceed with confidence.

In Phil's situation, there were many alternatives. He could have asked for additional time. He could have offered to do portions of the training and provided someone else to handle other aspects of it. Or he could have told the company honestly that this program was not his strength and referred them to someone else. In the process he could have highlighted his own unique areas of expertise so the company could call upon him in the future should it need assistance with other programs. Experience shows that turning away work you cannot do adequately commands respect and builds your reputation as someone who can be trusted.

Breaking an Inadequacy Habit

Of course, turning down work that you can actually do because you suffer from a chronic sense of inadequacy is another matter. For example, we once worked with a nutritionist who had a modest private practice. Joanna was frustrated with her income, but was convinced that she couldn't raise her fees. Also, she felt that many of the patients who came to her needed to be referred to a well-known nutritionist with whom she had studied.

When we asked her why she couldn't raise her fees and why so many patients needed to be referred out, her reasons were as follows: she didn't have a doctorate; she had never written a book; she had never done a research study; she didn't have an ongoing research study to put her clients in. She planned to do all these things eventually, but felt she had to build up her income first. Clearly she didn't feel *adequate* at this point.

In reality, Joanna was perfectly capable of handling 98 percent of the people who came to her and could command more than double her current fee. But she was living in the shadow of her mentor, to whom she was constantly comparing herself. This mentor was thirty-five years her senior and had an outstanding international reputation. He had written many books, lectured at many schools, and even received professional awards for his pioneering work. Obviously Joanna, only five years out of graduate school, didn't stack up well in her comparisons.

In this case, instead of serving as a valuable signal, her feelings of inadequacy had become needless and habitual and were diverting Joanna from moving ahead with her success. This is one reason swimmers and runners are often trained not to look backward or sideways to see how they're doing. They are taught to put all their attention and energy into getting across the finish line as quickly as they possibly can.

If, like Joanna, you have a habit of comparing yourself negatively to people whose success or skills you admire, here's what we suggest.

1. Make sure those you use as role models are people you want to be like. If you tend to aspire to be like someone other people think you should be like, you are doomed to feel inadequate. An intellectual sister who is always comparing her success to that of her athletic brother, for example, is setting herself up to feel inadequate. The brother has a completely different set of skills and abilities than hers and she has no desire to acquire them. You'll never feel adequate if you're comparing yourself to someone whom you don't want to be like. Look around for people to admire who are sufficiently like you that you would want to be like them.

2. Compare yourself positively. Instead of noticing the ways you don't measure up to those you admire, notice the ways in which you are similar. Even if you find this hard to do at first, search until you find the similarities. You will. We truly admire only people who reflect an image of what we already know is the best in ourselves. So we have to train our eyes to see what's similar.

3. Use their achievements to set goals for yourself. If you would like to do what those you admire are doing and have done, whenever you see or hear them doing those things say to yourself, "That's for me!" "That's what I'm going to do!" "That's how I'm going to be!"

4. Imagine yourself doing those things that you admire. Using Joanna's situation, for example, she would imagine herself working successfully with new, challenging clients, raising her fee and having people gladly pay it, writing a book, speaking internationally, or doing her own research project.

5. Resolve to learn how to do the things you aspire to do. Take action to master skills and carry out those tasks.

6. Try on your role models for size. As you watch them at work, imagine yourself inside their skin, doing what they're doing. How does it feel to be them? Then imagine how *you* would do it. How would you integrate your own skills, values, and personality? In your mind, experience yourself on that podium or behind that desk or receiving that award.

7. Act as if. In the course of your day, act as if you had already achieved the stature of your role models. Notice how this colors the way you walk, talk, and perform.

From Feeling Irresponsible to Assuming Responsibility

Irresponsibility is one of those feelings that our society holds in contempt. Sometimes if we don't live up to our own demands, we begin accusing ourselves of being irresponsible, which leads to our feeling guilt, shame, or anger, and resentment. Actually, feeling irresponsible is a signal that one of the following is true.

- You don't believe anything needs to be done.
- You don't think it's yours to do.
- You don't believe you are capable of doing it.

Once you determine that something needs doing and that there's no one better qualified to do it than you, the feeling that you can't do it will usually shift and you will probably begin feeling responsible and start considering how to go about it. So when you start feeling irresponsible, give the situation Cameron-Bandler's and Lebeau's responsibility test that follows on the next page.

If you agree that something does need to be done and you are the person to do it, but you feel you can't do what needs to be done, you'll probably start feeling inadequate. In that case you will want to develop the confidence you need to proceed. Refer to the road map for *inadequacy.*

"I kept feeling like I should do my own taxes," Maxine, who works as a paralegal, complained. After all, she knew tax law, and her taxes did need to be done. She'd already asked for one extension. Why wasn't she doing them? She felt irresponsible and guilty. It wasn't until her boyfriend pointed out to her that she was actually one of the most responsible people in the world that

Knowing What You're Responsible For

- Does anything actually need to be done?
- Are you the most qualified person to do it?
- Are you able to do it?

she realized that she needed an expert to handle the tax aspects of several investments she'd made. She truly wasn't the best qualified person to complete her taxes that year. Had she given herself the responsibility test as soon as she began feeling irresponsible, she would have saved herself a lot of time and discomfort.

From Lethargic to Motivated

Lethargy is an emotion you may feel when faced with tasks you know should be done but don't want to do and therefore you lack the necessary will or motivation to carry them out. It's a passive, slow, low-energy feeling that signals disinterest or lack of involvement in what you feel needs to be done. It's a signal that you don't find the tasks at hand desirable and want to withdraw from them.

Instead of passively hoping that your mood will change or resentfully doing what you don't want to do, you can heed the signal your lethargy is sending and begin asking yourself some questions designed to make the tasks at hand more desirable so you'll want to become actively involved. Here's a way to use that energy to get going again.

Lethargy → Curiosity → Motivation → Determination → Ambition

1. Ask yourself if this work is worth doing. Is the outcome worth the effort? If the tasks at hand aren't worthwhile, why are you expecting yourself to do them? Why not let yourself off the hook? You'll be amazed at how quickly your energy and your emotions will shift.

2. If the tasks are worthwhile, ask what aspects of them you have at least some mild interest in. Begin asking yourself questions about what's involved, questions that have some importance to you.

3. As you are asking these questions, pick up your tempo somewhat. (Playing some moderately paced music in the background while you work may help.)

4. You'll probably begin to feel curious about your answers.

5. Shift the feeling of wanting to know the answers to feeling that you must know the answers and you will begin to feel motivated and determined to find them.

6. Finally, think about how finding what interests you about these tasks will help you achieve your goals and you will undoubtedly begin feeling ambitious.

From Feeling Overwhelmed to Feeling Capable

Feeling overwhelmed is a signal that you are trying to take care of too many tasks all at once without setting priorities. When you are feeling over-whelmed you are probably aware of *many* tasks you *must* do *immediately.* Doing many things simultaneously is, of course, impossible, but your mind and body are probably racing from one thing to another, trying to do them all, like a whirl of energy not knowing where to land.

As time passes and the pressure builds, feeling overwhelmed can spiral downward into feeling immobilized and hopeless. But to focus and utilize this maelstrom of energy before it spirals downward you can do the following when you first begin to feel overwhelmed.

Feeling Overwhelmed → Focused → Motivated → Capable

1. Slow your tempo at once by taking a deep breath.

2. Remind yourself you have all the time in the world.

3. Begin breaking the overwhelming situation down into the various tasks and start setting priorities—what needs doing first, second, and so on.

4. Then **focus** *on only the one task that must be done first.*

5. Switch your thinking from **I must do this** *to* **I can do this.**

By this time you'll probably feel motivated to begin the first task and capable of moving on to the next one once that's completed.

From Feeling Stuck to Making Progress

Feeling stuck is a signal that you need to step away from whatever approach you're using and find another option. Feeling stuck is a way of telling yourself that you've got to do something differently. It's a passive but high-energy emotion. Therefore, taking *any* action will usually help get you moving again. Here's what you can do when you feel stuck.

Feeling Stuck→ Appreciative→ Curious
Reassured→ Confident

1. **Appreciate** *all the bound-up energy you're feeling,* and begin using some of it to feel curious about various alternative actions you could take.

2. **Recall times in your life** when you were able to come up with new options that worked out well for you. Do this until you feel reassured about coming up with options for this situation.

3. **Then imagine yourself** generating new options for this situation until you feel confident about finding a new direction.

4. **Generate at least ten options,** no matter how outrageous they might seem, that would represent progress toward your goal.

5. **Select and take some action now** on the one you like most.

Diane had been trying to get a computer for over six months. First a friend was going to get one for her through his job. But after several months of delay, he told her the discount policy his office had offered was no longer in effect and he couldn't get it after all. Then her boyfriend told her he knew someone who thought he could pick up a surplus computer for her. Several months later, still no computer.

"I feel stuck," she told a friend. "I just don't seem to be able to get a computer even though I know it would really help my business. I just don't have the money to pay full price for one." Her friend's response was enlightening. She said, "Thank goodness you're getting fed up with your situation, Diane. You've got to try some other approach. What if you were going to be shot at dusk unless you had a computer? What would you do?" Immediately Diane knew what she'd needed to do. She sold her camera and her exercise bike, realizing she never used them. And while she didn't get it all done before dusk, within the month she did have her computer!

Handy Guide to the Emotional Road Map

All emotions, no matter how unpleasant, are valuable signals designed to point you in the direction you need to go and supply you with the precise energy best suited to responding appropriately. Use this summary as a reference for how to put unpleasant emotions to work in your best interest.

Feeling	Message	Direction
Anger (page 159)	You face some harm or threat; take action to stop or prevent it.	Gratitude Curiosity Reassurance Satisfaction
Depression (page 161)	Focus on improvements.	Encouragement
Disappointment (page 162)	Carry on or let go.	Possibility Check Hopefulness
Discouragement (page 164)	Set shorter-range goals.	Pride Curiosity Anticipation Encouraged
Failure (page 165)	Learn, go on.	Test Pride Satisfaction Reassurance Successful
Fear Anxiety (page 166)	You face a future that holds danger you are not prepared for; prepare to cope or avoid negative consequences.	Safety Curiosity Feeling capable Self-Confidence Anticipation

Feeling	Message	Direction
Guilt (page 174)	You have violated a personal standard; take steps to assure you won't do so again.	Curiosity Reassurance Self-Confidence
Hopelessness (page 176)	It's time to let go.	Possibility Check Determination Acceptance
Inadequacy (page 177)	You're comparing yourself in an unfavorable way; consider your assets.	Feeling capable Self-Confidence
Irresponsibility (Page 180)	You aren't convinced; evaluate the situation	Assuming responsibility
Lethargy (page 181)	You're faced with tasks you know you should do, but don't want to; get involved.	Curiosity Motivation Determination Ambition
Feeling Overwhelmed (page 182)	Too many large tasks at once; break the situation into smaller tasks and prioritize.	Focused Motivated Capable
Feeling Stuck (page 182)	You're out of options; step away and find new ones.	Appreciation Curiosity Reassurance Self-Confidence Progress

When You Don't Like the Way You Feel

As you can see from the Emotional Road Map, each emotion brings us a particular energy with its own unique qualities. Like with other forms of energy we can harness the various energies our emotions bring us and use them to carry us from one place to another. As we come to understand the qualities unique to each emotion, we can use them like a throttle to help us shift from one feeling to another along the Emotional Road Map. Following are some of the qualities emotions have that we've found to be particularly helpful in learning to ride the emotional roller coaster.

Working Your Emotional Throttle

1. Tempo. Each emotion has a characteristic speed associated with the energy it brings us. Some speed up our psychological and physical systems. Others slow us down.

Slow-paced emotions

lethargy, boredom, apathy, discouragement, patience, calm, acceptance, satisfaction, dread, caution, and contentment

Fast-paced emotions

anxiety, excitement, impatience, enthusiasm, frustration, panic, restlessness, exhilaration, and anger

To feel more energized, you might arouse your enthusiasm by thinking about the many wonderful and exciting possibilities that could await you. Once you literally speed up your movements and thoughts, your emotions will shift as well. Playing background music with a quick tempo, or calling up a high-energy, enthusiastic, fast-talking friend can also pick up your mood.

If you wish to calm yourself down, you can slow your emotional pace by thinking about areas of your life with which you are content. Or you can think of and allow yourself to experience things in your life that you find satisfying. You can also breathe more slowly and deeply, play background music with a gentle slow tempo, or call up a friend who is usually calm and relaxed.

2. Involvement. Emotions also require varying degrees of engagement. Some are passive: they have no forward movement; they pull your energy down. Others are active: they have direction; they move you forward and carry your energy toward an outcome.

Passive emotions

hopelessness, apathy, satisfaction, calm, boredom, depression, resignation, and self-pity

Active emotions

friendliness, ambition, determination, frustration, curiosity, fear, disgust, and agitation

If you wish to become more involved in something, cultivate active emotions. Activate your curiosity or interest, for example. If you're feeling bored, become involved with what pleases you. If you're feeling apathetic, become dissatisfied or agitated about the absence of something engaging. On the other hand, if you need a break and could use some perspective and distance from your circumstances, move toward less involving, passive emotions. You might focus on what you find satisfying, for example, or what you feel grateful about.

3. Intensity.   Some emotions are more intense than others. For example, the following emotions lie on a continuum from less intense to more intense:

disappointment → sadness → grief
satisfaction → happiness → joy
concern → upset → anxiety
curiosity → interest → arousal

If you want to move into a particular feeling state you will probably be able to do so more easily by beginning at the less intense end of the continuum. If, for example, you want to become more interested in something, you might begin by exploring your curiosity about it. If you want to feel happy you might begin by attending to what you find satisfying.

4. Time.   Some emotions are associated with a particular time span. Some are rooted in recalling the past. Others relate to the here and now. Still others relate to imagining or projecting into possible futures. Some arise from comparing various aspects of the past, present, or future. For example:

Past-oriented	Present-oriented	Future-oriented
regret	curiosity	anxiety
nostalgia	boredom	ambition
disappointment	lethargy	concern

One easy way to shift from one emotion to another is to shift your attention to a different time span. If you are feeling anxious, you can shift your attention to the here and now. If you are disappointed, you can shift from thinking about what has been to what could be. If you are feeling bored or lethargic, you can imagine what you would be doing in a more exciting future, which may give you the energy to start doing some of those things in the present.

5. Comparison.   Many emotions arise from various mental comparisons you are making of how well what you have or want matches, or doesn't match, your ideal. For example:

Reality match	Reality mismatch
agreeable	frustrated
fulfilled	disappointed
satisfied	guilty
content	humorous
grateful	envious
pleased	inadequate

One of the most common ways we make ourselves feel miserable is by comparing the way things are with the way we think they should be. Such comparisons produce *dissatisfaction, frustration, disappointment, inadequacy, discouragement,* and *impatience.* In fact, some of the most miserable people we know are people who have very high standards and expectations that both they and life continually fail to live up to.

Of course, all these emotions can also motivate us to work harder in order to match our desires with reality. In fact, that's why and how people who have high standards and expectations become driven to achieve them. Fortunately, however, you can have high standards and expectations and still enjoy the present if you combine your efforts to achieve them with *tolerance, gratitude, anticipation,* and *patience* and focus on the progress you're making toward your goals to give yourself feelings of *achievement, appreciation, satisfaction,* and *accomplishment* as you go along.

In fact, you can feel more successful anytime you want without abandoning your ultimate goal by simply switching your attention to what you're doing that is working and what is happening that does match the way you think things should be. This will lead to feelings of *satisfaction, accomplishment, pride, gratitude,* and *fulfillment.* At any moment, of course, there are things that match and things that don't. So you always have a choice of which to focus on.

Success seems to be a matter of striking a balance between desire and contentment. The accountant Michael Russo has found this balance. He told us, "You are always breaking through your comfort zone. There's a piece of you that wants to stop and just digest what you've accomplished, which is fine. But you can't stay there too long. You have to keep jumping and taking those risks. But the more you jump the easier it gets, and you realize you can handle anything that occurs."

6. Possibility, Necessity, and Desirability. Varing emotions arise depending on how we view something —whether we see it as possible, necessary, or desirable. For example, when we believe we *have* to do something, *need* to do something, or *should* do something, we feel emotions like *resistance, determination, guilt, tenacity, desperation, drive, pressure, challenge, a sense of being overwhelmed, regret, obligation,* and *motivation.*

Therefore, turning a task into a *necessity* by setting a deadline, or making it *unnecessary* by allowing it to be optional, can dramatically alter the way you feel about it. Notice, for example, how differently you feel when you are told you *must* do something as opposed to being told that you *can* do something. What happens when it becomes a choice instead of a requirement? How do you respond to possibilities versus necessities? Are you more inclined to do something if you *can, should,* or *might* do it? Feelings often associated with possibility thinking include *optimism, caution, curiosity, disappointment, confidence,* and *hope.*

Now notice how much different you feel when you think of something as impossible as opposed to possible. What happens when your focus shifts from what you can or could do to what you can't do. Although some people are challenged by doing the impossible, the feelings most often associated with impossibility thinking are *helplessness, despair, discouragement,* and *inadequacy.*

Most of us can produce a dramatic shift in the way we feel by simply shifting from thinking, "I can't do that" to thinking, "How could I do that?" This one simple shift can be a quick way to move from feeling disappointed to feeling curious, for example.

Desirability or willingness also affects how we feel. When you want something, for example, you might tend to feel *motivated, patient* or *impatient, ambitious* or *determined.* If you don't want to do something, you might feel *resistant, lethargic,* or *stubborn.* So giving yourself a choice, or making things more desirable, interesting, and intriguing, can help you shift the way you feel about what you're doing.

7. *Extensiveness.* Our emotions are also affected by how much of the situation around us we are paying attention to. For example, feeling *overwhelmed, inadequate, discouraged,* or *in awe* are usually a result of attending to extensive amounts of available experience. On the other hand, feeling *fascinated, irritated, grumpy,* or *disagreeable* usually arise from attending to small details.

So if you feel *overwhelmed* or *discouraged,* one way to shift your feelings is to break a big project down to small tasks. And if you're feeling *irritated* and *disagreeable,* you can shift your focus to the bigger picture. How significant are the little things that are bothering you, for example, in the overall scheme of life? The more you know about your own preferences, the easier it is to focus on experience around you in a way that will be manageable and productive for you.

Designer Emotions: Preselecting Your Feelings

We said earlier that emotions flow from perceptions and that if you have perceived a situation inaccurately, you will be emotionally charged and ready to respond to a situation other than the one at hand—somewhat like showing up to a party in the wrong suit of clothes. Actually, it's easy to misperceive a situation because our perceptions are colored by the *premise* from which we approach a situation. All the assumptions, expectations, and definitions we're operating from affect the way we experience whatever we encounter. In fact, the premise from which we approach a situation can even shape the experience into exactly what we expect it to be.

For example, let's imagine that you are calling a client to collect an overdue bill. Here are three possible premises you could be holding in your mind as you place the call.

Premise 1: "No one ever pays me on time. This guy is just trying to bilk me out of my money. I'll probably never get this check, unless I take him to court. People want to get away with as much as they can."

Premise 2: I bet Harold is having a hard time with his business right now because of the recession. I'm sure he's feeling bad about being so behind on his account. I wonder what kind of arrangements we could make to help him out."

Premise 3: I wonder why I haven't gotten this check. I think I'll call and find out. There are so many possibilities."

How would you be feeling when Harold answered the phone if you were operating from each of those premises? From premise 1, you might be feeling *angry.* From premise 2, you might be feeling *compassionate.* From premise 3, you'd probably be feeling *curious.* What do you imagine you would say during your converstion with Harold if you were operating from these different premises? How do you think Harold would respond? Do you think the outcome of the conversations would be different? Chances are they would.

By paying attention to and even predetermining your premise at any given moment, you can totally alter your emotional reality, your behavior, and your results. In other words, we can create our own emotions. This does not mean we're suggesting that you be dishonest or deny your real feelings. We have just said that all feelings bring a valuable message and are worth attending to and utilizing. What we are saying is that you will experience different emotions depending on how you are perceiving your circumstances at any moment, and that the emotions that flow from those perceptions will cause you to act differently and therefore produce different results for you.

So if you are going into an important meeting or placing an important phone call, why not check your premise first? Exactly what is the situation? How do you want to approach it? What aspects of reality will assist you in approaching it in the way you desire? For example, here are two very different scenarios from actual situations.

Terry and Carolyn are both accountants. Both have been on their own for less than six months. They belong to the same professional association. In fact, they've met each other. Sarah talked with them separately on the same day.

Later in the week Terry was meeting with the chief financial officer of a moderate-sized company. If she could get their business, it would be her largest account to date and it would cover her operating expenses for the first year. As she was driving to the meeting, these thoughts were racing through her mind: "These big firms are a man's world. It's so hard for a woman to be taken seriously in this field. They always treat me like I'm a little crumb on their table. They're locked into using a large firm. I sure hope I can crack through their armor." By the time she got to the meeting she was filled with anxiety and an underlying hostility.

Carolyn also had an important meeting that week with a prestigious potential client. On the way there, her mind was racing with excitement: "This is the chance I've been waiting for. Everything I've done in the past five years has prepared me for this meeting. I know the industry figures. I know their position in the marketplace. There is so much I can do for them!" Carolyn almost danced her way into the lobby.

You can probably imagine the conversation these two women had later that month when they ran into each other at the association's dinner meeting. Do they live on the same planet? How could a nearly identical situation be such a struggle for one person and such an opportunity for another? Obviously, their premises are showing.

Of course, it's much easier to see someone else's premise at work than to recognize your own. We're grateful each time we hear disparate stories like these, because it reminds us again and again to check out where we're coming from.

Checking Your Premise

If you are repeatedly getting results you don't want, or if you frequently feel emotions you'd rather not be feeling, check your premise. If you usually feel scared or apprehensive when you make a sales call, check your premise. What are you saying to yourself about sales calls? If you routinely get angry when bills arrive, check your premise. What are you saying or thinking to yourself about bills? If you feel tired every time you look at the piles that need filing, check your premise. What are you saying about filing? Here are several possible premises and the feelings they're likely to elicit.

Alternative premises for sales calls

	Possible emotions
I've never been able to sell.	inadequacy
I love showing my portfolio to people.	excitement
I know I can help these people.	confidence
People hate to part with their money.	anger

Alternative premises for bills

	Possible emotions
These bills will put me in my grave.	fear
Boy, have I invested a lot this month!	pride
Everyone always wants theirs.	anger
Let's get these paid.	determination

Alternative premises for filing	**Possible emotions**
I shouldn't have to do this grunt work!	resentment
I can't wait to get this put away.	motivation
I'm so tired. I can't look at this mess.	overwhelmed
I wonder how I should organize all this stuff.	curiosity

Listen carefully to what you say about yourself, your customers, the economy, your field. And recognize that the premise you take into everything you do will determine the way you feel about it, how you approach it, and, to a large extent, the results you will get.

Adjusting Your Premise

When you hear a negative, self-defeating premise running around in your head, consider whether you can find any evidence that would support your adjusting your premise to a more positive, self-affirming one. For example, if you hear yourself saying, "No one can make money in this economy!" ask yourself if that's actually true. Aren't some people making money? Who is making money? Is anyone in your field making money in this economy? If some people are, perhaps you could, too. What can you do so that you, too, can make money? After finding the needed evidence, you might adjust your premise regarding the economy to "Some people are making money. Why not me?"

If you're a woman and you hear yourself saying, as Terry was, "This is a man's world," you might ask yourself if there aren't some women who have done well in the world. Do you know of any successfully self-employed females in your field? If they are doing well, perhaps you can, too. If there aren't any people like yourself who are doing well, then ask yourself if you know of other people who have done things that had never been done before. If they could do what they did, couldn't you do this? And you might adjust your premise to "The world is opening to me, too."

A Premise for All Occasions

1. Remind yourself of who you are. "I am a woman/man."
2. Remind yourself of what you do. "I am a _____."
3. Remind yourself of who it is you're meeting with—"a man or woman who does what?"
4. Remind yourself of the situation. "Our reason for being here is to _____."
5. Remind yourself of life's infinite possibility. "And anything can happen."

At the very least, you can always adjust your premise to a neutral position in which anything is possible. Sarah created one of her favorite premises based on one she learned from the acting coach Gene Bua. When she is about to go into an important situation she runs through this routine: "First I remind myself of who I am and what I do. I say to myself: 'I am a woman. I'm a writer, speaker, and radio personality.' Then I remind myself of who I'm meeting with, saying, 'He is a man. He has his own business. He needs to let others know about his business.' Then I remind myself of our situation: 'We are meeting to discuss how I can help him promote his business.' Then I close the premise by reminding myself, 'And anything can happen!' "

As you come to appreciate and consciously use your emotions to help accomplish your goals, you'll find that the roller coaster of events even the most difficult day brings can be stimulating and challenging instead of debilitating and stressful. You'll also be better prepared to figure out what you need to do about whatever comes your way.

Resources

The Emotional Hostage: Reclaiming Your Emotional Life. Leslie Cameron-Bandler and Michael Lebeau. Moab, UT: Real People Press, 1986. In our view one of the most important books ever written because it gives you the tools and understanding to create a world of full emotional choice.

Human Possibilities. Stanley Krippner. New York: Anchor, 1980. Shows how athletes use relaxation and mental imagery to build confidence, prevent prestart fever and nervousness, rest fully, accelerate reaction time, and relieve fatigue.

Love Is Letting Go of Fear. Gerald Jampolsky, M.D. New York: Bantam Books, 1979. A book about choosing peace of mind every day and every minute. It's a classic.

Release Your Brakes. Jim Newman. PACE Organization (Box 1378, Studio City, CA 91614), 1988. Newman, who originated the concept of the comfort zone, sets forth how we use our emotions to put on the brakes and prevent ourselves from achieving our fullest potential. He then introduces his method for taking off the brakes and testing our limits.

Don't Tell Me It's Impossible Until After I've Already Done It. Pam Lontos. New York: William Morrow & Co., Inc., 1986. An inspiring and motivational story of how changing your outlook can dramatically change your results and other techniques for doing the seemingly impossible.

CHAPTER
SEVEN

■■■■■■■■■■■■■■■■■■■■■■

Staying Up No Matter What Goes Down

*If you continue toward your goal, it will
happen but not necessarily on your time
schedule.*

KEN BLANCHARD

Now that you're the boss, not only do
you have to keep yourself motivated and on track; you've also got to be the
one with the answers and the solutions. There's no one to refer things up to
or delegate down to. You're the one who must evaluate your progress and
assess your performance. You have to help yourself understand and respond
to your circumstances no matter what they may be, on a day-by-day, minute-
by-minute basis. In other words, you have to be the *supervisor*—the one who
oversees and directs, the one with *super-vision.* You have to be what we call a
contextual coach; in fact, it's now one of your most important roles.

Here's an example of the vital role contextual coaching can play. In 1984
the Olympic-gold-medal–winning gymnast Tim Dagget broke his leg, less
than a year before the qualifying tournament for the 1988 Olympics in Seoul.
Tim's coach helped him put this major setback into perspective so that he
could decide whether or not to try to compete.

With guidance from his coach, family, and doctors, Tim decided he would
try to prepare for the competition. Here's how Tim says he was able to frame
the task ahead of him at the time: "There are a multitude of things I can do to
qualify for the Olympic Games while I'm recovering. There are also things I
have no control over at all . . . and if I dwell on those points or worry about
them then I'm taking away from the time I could be spending on the things

that can get me to Seoul. Everybody in the world isn't going to be an Olympic champion. Maybe my leg won't recover in time for Seoul, but the feelings and memories I'll have from just trying will be good enough for me."

As you can imagine, this premise enabled him to work effectively toward his goal and to come out a winner whether he ultimately qualified or not. We hope you will never be faced with a challenge as severe as Tim's, but you need to be able to put whatever challenges you do encounter into a *context for yourself* that helps you respond to them effectively. For example, if you don't have as much business as you need, how should you interpret this? If suppliers and potential customers are not taking you seriously, what meaning do you make of this? You can interpret these circumstances many different ways. You can take them to mean you're not suited to be on your own, or that you need to do something differently. How you respond will depend on the *context* you advise yourself to place these developments in.

That's what this chapter is about: providing a context for what to do when you don't know what to do, a context for knowing how you're doing and what you need to do next. We'll also provide a context for how to approach three of the most common problems most self-employed individuals face at one time or another:

- Getting the world to take you seriously
- Not having enough money coming in
- Feeling like you want to quit

Eight Things to Do When You Don't Know What to Do

If you knew you couldn't fail, your spirit would always be looking for success—and would find it.

ARNOLD AND BARRY FOX

Being self-employed presents numerous situations you don't immediately know what to do about. And when these situations arise, of course, you can't go to your supervisor. So what are you to do?

If you have a network of professional advisers (a lawyer, accountant, computer consultant, and so on), you can turn to them for help in their areas of expertise. But unless you have an unlimited budget and they have unlimited patience, you can't turn to them for advice on the majority of the decisions you need to make. For example, should you take on a particular client? Can you get a particular project done according to the proposed schedule? Can you bring it in within the quoted price? What should you do about an overdue bill? Do you use the same print shop you used last time even though you weren't totally satisfied with them, or do you take the time and the risk to find a new one? Do you use a consultant thousands of miles away whom you know to be good, or, to keep costs down, do you use someone local whose reputation you're not sure of?

The decisions we face when we're on our own are endless and relentless. And we have to resolve most of them by ourselves. Here are several guidelines we've found useful for those moments when you don't know what to do.

1. It's Okay Not to Know

Who doesn't have a memory of being called on in class as a child and not knowing the answer? Now, years later, when we encounter something we don't know, we may still get that sinking feeling because we believe that somehow we're always supposed to have the right answer on the tip of our tongue. Well, of course, we don't—and we don't have to. The first step to discovering anything is admitting that you don't know but would like to.

2. Assume Something Effective Can Be Done

No matter what situation you're presented with, if you start from the premise that *problems are solvable,* you'll get much further. You may not know what to do at a particular moment about a specific situation, but you will be able to find out what to do. You have a world of information at your beck and call. In other words, wherever there's a will there's a way, especially today. This is the information age, after all. And if you can't find what you need, an information broker can find answers to the most arcane problems, often for only a few hundred dollars.

3. Your Gut Will Guide You

Sometimes you want something so badly, or you're so afraid of losing out on something that looks good, that you make a snap decision even though the little voice in your head or the twinge in your stomach is whispering, "Don't do this!" At other times that little voice is saying, "Go for it!" but your mind is hung up on insignificant details. You probably can remember countless times you wished you'd heeded that little voice.

Ellen worked as a systems analyst but had been wanting to start a gift-basket service for years. Finally she decided to start the business on the side. She sold a few baskets here and there, but she wanted to sell enough so she could leave her job and devote all her time to her business. Then she met Suzanne. Suzanne had her own travel agency and told Helen she wanted to order one hundred baskets for a cruise that would set sail in two months.

This could be Ellen's big break! She was excited. But a little voice in her head kept telling her not to incur any costs on this project without money up front to cover her out-of-pocket expenses. Although Suzanne had promised that having these baskets was essential to the trip, she claimed that her cash flow wouldn't allow her to pay for them until after the tour was launched. In her excitement, Ellen decided to go ahead and make up the baskets. She spent many hours and, of course, incurred the full cost of all the materials. So you can imagine her horror when she called to arrange for delivery of the baskets only to have the office manager tell her that the tour had been canceled.

Suzanne took the position that since she hadn't used the baskets, she didn't owe anything for them. In fact, in the crush of her many other projects, Suzanne had conveniently forgotten about Ellen's baskets. Now a lawsuit is pending. Ellen may still get her money, but she's lost valuable time and gone to needless expense. She told us, "I knew I shouldn't have done that. Suzanne even told me about disputes she was having with other vendors. I knew I could have a problem. I just didn't want to pass up the opportunity."

The point, of course, is to trust your *gut*—that inner sense of knowing that the psychiatrist Eric Berne called "the little professor." And even then you will make mistakes from time to time, but at least they won't be ones you knew better than to make in the first place. And you'll get some vital gut training. As Nolan Bushnell, the founder of Atari and Chuck E. Cheese Pizza Time Theater, has said, "If you're not failing occasionally, then you're not reaching out as far as you can." Or as the creativity consultant Roger von Oech reminds us, "Errors are stepping-stones to new ideas." One way to do it right is to do it wrong but not for long.

4. Focus Your Attention Away from the Problem

When a problem develops, instead of focusing on the problem, focus on your desired outcome. Focusing on the complexities of the problem takes your attention and energy away from what you want to accomplish. It traps you in the details of the problem itself. For example, if you see a friend fall into an open manhole, you won't be of much help if you jump into the hole with him, will you? Well, that's exactly what happens when you get ensnared in the complexities of some problem you face. Focus instead on what you want to accomplish, and you'll know better what needs to be done.

Let's say you notice that your revenues are falling. Instead of focusing on this problem, you'll get better results by focusing on what you can do to increase your income. If a client is slow in paying, instead of focusing on your cash-flow problems, focus on how to motivate the client to send you the check quickly. Once you focus on your ideal outcome, you can work backward to where you are.

5. Generate Multiple Possibilities

Once you have a clear idea of where you want to go, start generating as many possibilities as you can for getting from here to there. Postpone evaluating these ideas at first. Just let your mind come up with as many options as you can. Sometimes the more bizarre an idea is, the better. Try using the tips below for generating a variety of workable possibilities. They are distilled from *A Whack on the Side of the Head*, by the creativity consultant Robert van Eck.

6. Grapple and Let Go

After you've grappled with your situation for a while, put it aside. Just let it go. Do other things you need to do. Let you subconscious mind work on it while you sleep or go to the movies. Often the decision, solution, or answer you've been looking for will come to you spontaneously in the midst of something else you're doing. You can get some of your most productive ideas and solutions this way.

7. Talk It Out

Sometimes you can struggle with something mentally and get nowhere, but in talking the situation through with someone else you may find that the

---

Thirteen Wacky Ways to Generate Workable Possibilities

1. Pretend you know what to do. Maybe you do.
2. Think of impractical ideas. They may lead you to practical ones.
3. Come up with illogical ideas. They may lead you to logical ones.
4. Come up with wrong answers; they may lead you to the right ones. In fact, come up with the stupid, foolish, and absurd answers. They may lead to smart, feasible ones.
5. Turn the situation into a metaphor: What if it were a contest? An elevator? A cowboy movie? A vacation?
6. Propose solutions that break the normal rules. As von Oech says, "You can't solve today's problems with yesterday's solutions."
7. Play *what if*. Pretend you're a wizard. What if things could be any way you can imagine? How would the situation you're facing get handled then?
8. When you find the right answer, look for a second one. It may be better than the first.
9. Imagine doing what needs to be done backward. This perspective may give you insight into how to move forward.
10. Consider how someone in another profession or field would approach this. What would an architect do in this situation? An actress? A farmer?
11. Pose the questions you're asking differently. What if the problem isn't what you think it is? As Emerson said, "Every wall is a door."
12. How would your idols handle this situation?
13. Turn what you're doing into a game. Play with it.

Questions That Help Solve Problems

When you don't know what you need to do, ask yourself these questions, or have a friend or colleague ask them of you.

1. How do you want this to come out?
2. What's important to you about this?
3. How will you know if you've found the answer?
4. When have you handled something like this successfully in the past?
5. What's an example of one possible way you could handle this?
6. How could you do that?
7. How do you know that?
8. What stops you from . . . ?
9. What would happen if you did (or didn't) do that?

answers emerge almost magically. The person you're talking with may offer a new perspective or see a nuance you've overlooked because you're so close to the situation.

This person doesn't even need to be an expert on the subject at hand. We're not talking here about getting someone's advice, although that is always an option as well. And certainly if you do that, you should seek the opinion of an expert. Here, however, we're talking about the value of articulating your situation to see if someone else can understand and relate back to you what he or she hears you saying. Having someone feed back what you're saying is like holding up a mirror in which you see your thought processes. From this new vantage point, you can better see what you need to do.

8. If All Else Fails, Act

As a rule, it's better to do something than nothing. So if you need to act and still don't know what to do, try something. Test out some approach in a small way if possible, and assess your results. If that doesn't work, the results may suggest to you what to do next.

Getting the World to Take You Seriously

> *To earn your own respect is to have the greatest respect of all.*
>
> PAUL AND SARAH EDWARDS

The most common complaint we hear from people who work from home on their own is that they aren't being taken seriously by clients, customers, family, or other business contacts. And this is not surprising because there is still some institutional prejudice against being self-employed, especially if you're working from home. For example:

- Many banks categorically refuse MasterCard and Visa merchant accounts to home-based businesses.
- Some temporary employment agencies won't send personnel to a home office.
- Trade suppliers sometimes won't extend credit or give priority to small businesses.
- Large companies may put a free-lancer or independent contractor at the bottom of their list of who gets paid.
- Unscrupulous individuals may even figure they can break contracts with self-employed individuals they don't think will have the funds to sue them.
- Sometimes potential customers assume home-based, free-lance, or single-person businesses are less substantial and reliable and require them to be twice as good as a larger business would need to be in order to convince them otherwise.

As the ranks of thriving, successful propreneurs continue to swell, we're confident these institutional barriers will come down. In the meantime, however, we each have to find ways to make sure that those we deal with do take us seriously. Therefore, we've been curious as to how the most successful self-employed individuals go about assuring that they are taken seriously.

Surprisingly, many of the most successful individuals we spoke with reported that they never have problems with being taken seriously. In fact, although it is the most common concern self-employed individuals have, it was actually a problem for only one out of five of those we spoke with. Here are some comments as to why they aren't having this problem.

The publicist Kim Freilich told us, "I've always been taken seriously by business contacts because I have a very expensive brochure and no one spends that kind of money on a brochure who isn't serious."

The private-practice consultant Gene Call reported, "I never have had a problem being taken seriously. I have never thought of working from home on my own as a negative. I keep a clear separation between home and office. I've always made housekeeping a priority, so everything is neat and clean. Between 9:00 and 5:00 my home looks more like an office. I always go out for breakfast, for example, so there will be no cooking odors or anything like that. I dress for business and return to the office after breakfast."

Wellness researcher Dean Allen said, "People take me seriously because I'm an expert. I feel like a recognized professional. In fact I think I'm one hundred years ahead of my time—and I project that. I won't let anyone treat me any other way."

The accountant Michael Russo has found that "to be treated with credibility, you have to be projecting credibility. You have to project that you're in it all the way."

The career consultant Naomi Stephan told us, "If I approach what I do seriously and I take myself seriously then they have to take me seriously, too. One bank told me I couldn't get MasterCard and Visa because I didn't have a bona fide office. So I changed banks." Not only did she get a MasterCard and Visa merchant account at her new bank, she also get a $10,000-secured loan to purchase her office equipment.

The bookkeeper Chellie Campbell has a different experience: "The big firms automatically think I'm the secretary, but I let it roll off my back. I make a joke out of it." They're surprised to discover she runs a five-person office and earns $36,000 a month.

The professional organizer Dee Behrman remembers that when she first went out on her own, she didn't have the confidence she needed to be taken seriously: "I felt like I was on shaky ground, and that affected my credibility. After building up my confidence, I've had no problem being taken seriously."

As you can see, the one theme that runs through these answers is:

If you take yourself seriously, you will be taken seriously.

But just what does that mean? It sounds so simple. Yet there's a lot that goes into simply believing in yourself. Here's an example of how it can be both complex and simple.

When Sarah was practicing psychotherapy, one of her clients was a young woman who had a lifelong history of emotional instability. Through their work together, the young woman began to feel better and better about herself, and as she felt better about herself, she felt better about her life and did better in her life. She felt so good, in fact, that she soon met and fell in love with a man from her church. This young man also had a history of many problems, both in school and on the many jobs he'd tried to hold. But he, too, was feeling better about himself and was changing his life—especially now that he was in love.

As the months passed, this couple grew healthier and healthier, and happier and happier. Within the year they decided to marry. Their families and friends in the church were all very happy for them. But before they could marry, they had to attend a prenuptial interview with the priest. They were both nervous about this meeting, and when the day arrived they were devastated by the priest's probing questions. He wanted to know if they thought they were now actually mature enough to marry, or whether they would be falling back into their many past problems. He wanted to know if they were certain they would be able to handle the responsibilities of marriage, which he enumerated.

Under interrogation, the couple's confidence collapsed. They became uncertain. She became tearful and inarticulate; he became angry and loud. The priest took this as an indication that perhaps they were not as prepared for marriage as they thought and invited them to think about their decision further.

Sarah's client called for an emergency session and arrived in tears. Clearly the couple had gone into the interview seeking reassurance from the priest—validation that they were, in fact, becoming the people they so desperately wanted to be. The priest, on the other hand, was wanting them to reassure *him* of their progress. He was pulling for them, hoping to see this progress confirmed by their answers to his questions. The interview was actually their chance to shine, but they had taken it instead as evidence of his doubting their abilities.

As the young woman came to realize this misunderstanding, her confidence returned. She left the session excited and clear about what she needed to do. She explained the situation to her fiancé, and they returned to talk with the priest with renewed confidence, eager to show him how happy and successful their lives actually were. As you can imagine, the priest was elated and their wedding was a marvelous celebration, not just of their marriage but of their victory over their pasts.

Of course, while most people going out on their own do so with a good and sometimes sterling past, we have nonetheless often thought how similar the plight of this couple was to that of a self-employed person who wants to be taken seriously. Underneath it all, the banks, the potential customers, the suppliers, and the many other people we have to deal with are usually actually pulling for us. They're predisposed to want us to be someone they can do business with. It's to their advantage. But they have to see this first. Others before us have let them down, and they don't want it to happen again. They want us to demonstrate that they can trust us, invest in us, and count on us to deliver for them.

We, on the other hand, as newly self-employed individuals venturing into unknown and potentially treacherous territory, are eager for any sign of support from those we must work with to validate that, indeed, we can and will succeed. The last thing we need is to be required to prove ourselves worthy to every supplier, lender, and customer. Yet, as with the young couple, that's exactly what we must do to seize the prize that's there for the taking. But we must believe in our own competency, reliability, dependability, and credibility sufficiently to find ways to demonstrate these qualities to others.

In many ways, being taken seriously is like a *rite of passage.* The tradition of going through a rite of passage traces back to the most ancient and primitive cultures. Throughout time, people have had to *stand the test.* Granted, sometimes the test may not be a fair one. It may even be an irrelevant one. But one way or another, if you want in you've got to pass the test. You've got to have one of the magic passwords.

Think about it. Chances are you routinely require such proof yourself from those you do business with. What criteria do you use to screen people before you hire or are willing to buy from them? If you read about a seminar on a topic of interest to you, what do you want to know about the instructor or the company before you pay several hundred dollars to attend? If you need to hire a consultant, or you're selecting a doctor, a mechanic, or a hair stylist, what criteria do you use? The size of their office? The location? Their written materials? Their academic background? Their list of past clients? A reference from a friend? Whatever you use to check them out, those are the magic *passwords* they must have to get your business.

Four Available Sources of Power

Fortunately, there are a variety of magic passwords and many different doors to being taken seriously. The psychiatrist and author Eric Berne identified four sources of power, any one or any combination of which can bestow you with ample credibility to be taken seriously. Understanding these four sources of power is very useful in explaining why some people have such an easy time establishing themselves while others struggle to be taken seriously.

The best password to anywhere, of course, is to have power from all four of these sources. President Franklin D. Roosevelt is an example of someone who had them all. But very few of us are so well endowed. The more of them you do have, however, the easier it will be for you to be taken seriously. Fortunately, most people can build enough of at least one to be able to succeed on their own.

As you read about these sources of power, you may find yourself feeling angry or resentful or even discouraged. They can serve as the root of prejudice and discrimination. They are undoubtedly the basis for your having missed out on past opportunities that went to others who you felt were no more qualified or even less qualified than you. But we would invite you to look at these sources of power with new eyes. You'll find you have strengths in some areas and not in others. Think about where your greatest strengths lie and how you can use those to build your sense of authority and stature.

Position Power: Using Your Title

Position power is authority and respect that you command because of the position you hold. The president of the United States, of course, is the ultimate example of position power in this country. Chief executive officer, chief financial officer, foreman, executive secretary, office manager—titles like these bring with them position power. In fact, any position of authority, however small, imbues those persons who hold it with the level of authority commensurate with their title.

As self-employed individuals, most of us have very little position power. This is especially true if you are changing fields. It can be particularly frustrating and even surprising for those who are used to the ease with which their previous position opened doors and produced results for them. To suddenly discover that you must build a new reputation before you can command the degree of authority to which you are accustomed can be disconcerting. But it can be done. You have other sources of power available to you, and even though you are on your own, there are ways to create the illusion of position power as well.

For example, you can refer to yourself on your card, letterhead, and stationery as president or founder of your own company. "John J. Callahan, President, Corporate Design Services," commands more authority than "John

President, Corporate Design Services," commands more authority than "John Callahan, Freelance Designer." There are actually many ways the business name you choose can build your credibility and help you be taken more seriously. For information, see Chapter 4 of our book *Getting Business to Come to You* (which we wrote with the marketing consultant Laura Douglas).

You can also capture a bit of the glow from any past position power you may have held by highlighting your previous position on promotional materials or in introducing yourself to others. This is of value, of course, only when your past position has some direct relevance to what you're doing now. For example, when Tom Drucker went out on his own as a management consultant, he always mentioned his prior position as an executive with the Xerox Corporation. And it did, in fact, confer upon him more authority than the average novice management consultant would otherwise command.

To enjoy the benefits of position power, some self-employed individuals have also taken part-time teaching positions at local colleges or universities. These positions enable them to say something like "I am a professional potter. I teach pottery at the art institute." Others have become active in professional or trade associations and have gotten elected to positions of authority within those organizations as a way of building their stature. Some individuals have even founded a trade or professional association as a way of enhancing their position power. Still other self-employed individuals have arranged to take positions as regular radio or television commentators or magazine columnists.

Historical Power: Using Your Past

Historical power is authority based upon your lineage or your family name. If you are the son or daughter of a respected prominent family or are carrying on a long-established family business or profession, you automatically inherit the benefits of historical power.

Of course, most people going out on their own do not have such an asset. And this is one reason some people buy a business, a practice, or a franchise from someone else who does have some degree of historical power. This is also why you will see slogans like "In Business for 35 Years" on promotional materials.

Sometimes you can gain some degree of historical power by having studied, apprenticed, or worked with historically prominent individuals in your particular field. Therapists, for example, who studied personally with the founders of various psychotherapeutic modalities such as Anna Freud, Carl Rogers, Wilhelm Reich, Eric Berne, and Ida Rolf will often include this fact in their biographical materials and introductions. One photographer we met made a practice of pointing out that she had studied with Ansel Adams and had become his protégé. Of course, getting references from long-standing leaders in your field is another way of mustering a degree of historical power you could not command on your own.

Cultural Power: Using Your Credentials

Cultural power arises from the values of the culture within which you work. The academic degrees you hold, the schools you attended, the past experiences you've had, the clients you've served, the money you have, the car you drive, the way you dress—these are all what we refer to broadly as your *credentials*, and they are all sources of cultural power. Each field and each community will have its set of expected credentials.

A diploma from the Harvard Business School, for example, has traditionally gone a long way in getting people to take you seriously in the business world, but it won't help much if you're trying to break into a career on the stage or in organic gardening. The formal academic or professional background that will provide you with cultural power varies widely from field to field. In some fields, having a certain degree, certification, or other credential is a mandatory ticket without which you simply cannot succeed—particularly on your own, where you are operating without supervision. Other fields are more open, and often people will forgo the time and expense of obtaining particular formal credentials. You will find, however, that being taken seriously will be much easier if you do invest in obtaining the expected ticket.

In an effort to enjoy the benefits a credential conveys without investing the time and money involved in obtaining further academic credentials, some self-employed individuals will earn a credential through their professional or trade association or an independent licensing body of some kind. The National Speakers Association, for example, has a certification process for its members. Insurance professionals and financial planners can obtain certification through their professional associations. Such credentials matter most to the members themselves, but with referrals accounting for a major percentage of many businesses, such respect can mean a lot.

Some colleges and universities offer certificate programs in fields like public relations, script writing, and so on. These are not full degree programs, but they do provide a credential upon completion. And often the greatest value in completing such programs is the important contacts you make in the process.

In addition to these more formal credentials, every field also has a set of informal credentials, which we call the *ideal image.* Successful people in any field look a certain way, act a certain way, drive certain types of cars, have certain beliefs, skills, and attitudes, and so forth. The better you fit that ideal image, the easier it will be for you to be accepted and respected in that field. John Malloy's book *Dress for Success,* for example, essentially describes the uniform or ideal image for corporate America.

Certainly dressing for success in your field is a simple and relatively inexpensive ticket that will help you get in the door. It's one that anyone can acquire, even on a limited budget. All you need to do is to take note of the most successful people in your field and follow suit, adapting their choices to your own style and preferences. Your goal here is to get past the doorman, not to become a carbon copy of someone else. And even if those at the top of your field have clothes, materials, and equipment you can't afford, you can usually acquire the look without necessarily paying an exorbitant price.

Some people rebel at the idea of dressing for success or otherwise putting on the trimmings of success. And, of course, as your own boss you are free to dress and conduct yourself however you please. Just be aware that how you dress and act can make the job of being taken seriously a lot easier or a lot harder.

Kathryn and Mark gave communications training courses for educators until government cutbacks dried up funds for teacher education. They quickly decided they would shift to offering their courses for corporate managers. But they were unable to even get in the doors of the personnel directors who could hire them. They recognized that they had little corporate experience, so they conducted a number of complimentary programs for executives from various companies to build a track record with corporate managers. Their evaluations from these programs were good, and they received some glowing references. They thought they had solved the problem of being taken seriously.

And yes, they were able to get appointments with several personnel directors. But still none hired them. "They still don't seem to take us seriously," Kathryn told us. Having done a lot of corporate training ourselves, we could see the problem. Kathryn and Mark did not convey the image of corporate trainers. They dressed casually, Mark in a sport coat and open collar, Kathryn in slacks and flats. Corporate culture, at that time, called for both men and women to wear suits, with ties for men and high heels and hose for women. We shared our observations with Mark and Kathryn. They were amazed at the altered reactions they got after making this one simple change. Suddenly they were being taken seriously.

And of course the way you dress has an equally powerful effect on how you feel about yourself. J. B. Morningstar, the founder of Natural Health Resources, found just how true that is. She saw a sign at her dry cleaners that read "Dress for the Success You Want to Have." And she took it to heart. She traded in her T-shirts, jeans, and sandals for a more professional look and considers this early decision to dress for the success *she wanted to have* to be a crucial element in developing the confidence she needed to go out on her own.

Another form of credentials involved in cultural power includes being able to talk the talk and walk the walk. Every field has a vocabulary and a set of concepts and issues that its members are expected to use and understand. Using the right vocabulary, so to speak, says you're one of the club. In any field there is also a certain way things are done and other agreed-upon ways that things are *not* done. These informal and often unstated rules may or may not actually be important to doing a good job, but they are the passwords. The best way to make sure *you* can talk the talk and walk the walk is by participating in the professional and trade associations or organizations of both your field and the fields of your customers and clients.

An aspiring professional speaker we'll call Joyce told us of an unfortunate example of how this aspect of cultural power works. Joyce wanted to speak to corporate management groups that hire outside speakers. So she paid to be featured in a showcase where corporate meeting planners came to see prospective speakers. Joyce gave an excellent presentation, and many meeting planners rushed up to find out how they could book her. One meeting planner asked her what she charged and she freely volunteered that she had spoken for many different fees so it all depended on what was needed.

Obviously Joyce had committed an unspoken no-no, because within minutes the many meeting planners who were clustered around her began drifting away, and she got no bookings from the showcase. She had no idea what she had done, but in talking with other speakers she discovered that the unwritten rule among these meeting planners was that professional speakers don't discuss fees in public and most certainly don't have flexible fees.

Joyce paid a very high price to find out the rules. From that point on, however, when she prepares to market to a new clientele she does her homework first so she can talk the basics of their talk and walk the path they walk without stepping on any unexpected land mines.

Personal Power: Using Your Charisma

Personal power is the authority you command by the force of your own personality, will, intention, and results. Here is where everyone can excel. This is the one most valuable source of authority you can have. It's why we can say with confidence that if you take yourself seriously, others will, too—at least over time. This power may be called *charisma,* and while that word is usually reserved only for those special individuals who can move crowds of thousands with simply a look or a word, we believe all people have the capacity for a charisma that comes from developing their own personal effectiveness to the fullest. All of us have our own unique personal qualities that can imbue us with influence and authority.

If we do not use or develop these qualities, of course, no one will perceive them. You may have had the experience of meeting people who made no particular impression on you whatsoever. They may have seemed like wallflowers receding into the woodwork. But when you met them again, perhaps years later, you were amazed at their transformation into impressive, unforgettable individuals. Whereas they once passed unnoticed in any crowd, now heads turned when they entered a room. Whereas once their voices were lost in normal conversation, now everyone listened to them with rapt attention. Whereas you once would have forgotten their names if you ever heard them in the first place, now their names remained emblazoned in your mind.

Such individuals are outstanding examples of the magnetism of personal power. And we can all command such power. We all have the ability to be stunning, awesome, arresting, prominent, sensational, noteworthy, and significant. We all have the capacity to inspire trust, confidence, dependability, legitimacy, authority, and credibility. But we must each develop these capacities in ourselves. The more competent, capable, and effective you become, the more you will reflect these qualities in everything you do—the way you talk, the way you walk, the way you dress, the way you conduct yourself. You won't need to affect credibility; you will simply project it.

It has always intrigued us how often highly successful individuals, when asked if success has changed them, will quickly say, "Oh, no. I'm just the same. Success hasn't changed me." Chances are they are not the same. Success has probably changed them considerably, in that they are probably much more of all they can be. You can't achieve success and maintain it for very long without becoming more of what you're capable of being.

Success demands more of you. To achieve success you have to bring out your best qualities. You have to overcome your worst qualities. You have to become a more effective, more capable, more caring, and more productive person.

But here's the best news. Your own personal power is the most valuable of the four sources of power. The other three can only get you in the door. Personal power, however, enables you to produce the results you need to make sure you can come back again and again. The offspring of successful entertainers and politicians are often asked if their family name helped or hindered them in following in their parents' footsteps. Usually they will say that yes, the name did help them, but only to gain access, only to get in the door. Once they got the audition or got into the office, they had to produce results or they didn't get to come back. Personal power is what enables you to produce results.

Nothing produces success like results. If you produce results for people, you will be taken seriously. You will get repeat business. You will get referrals. The better the results, the more seriously you will be taken. And the more your personal power will grow. Then you'll find people actually going out of their way to support you.

Developing personal power, however, is a process. When I, Sarah, opened my private practice as a psychotherapist, I had very little personal power. I had been accustomed to having the power of the United States government behind me when I spoke, and believe me, people listen to someone who holds the power to give or withdraw federal grant funds. But having left that power behind, how was I to get people to listen?

Without my title, I discovered people didn't even remember my name an hour after they met me. Usually they didn't recognize me the next time they saw me. Ideas I raised and comments I made during conversations were often attributed to someone else. Sometimes people had to ask me to speak up so they could hear me. I felt my lack of personal power dramatically. I felt like I had become an invisible woman.

But I began working with people who already knew and trusted me. I attended personal-growth classes, took lessons in projecting my voice, read books on self-esteem, took acting and improvisation classes, hired an image consultant, and forced myself to give speeches and seminars until I felt at ease speaking from a podium and could capture and hold people's attention.

As time passed I could literally feel my self-confidence growing. People I counseled were improving from our sessions. My personal power was building. I started to feel, look, and act like someone I would admire. Once I began to feel like the person I'd always wanted to be, people started remembering my name, recognizing me, and even seeking me out because others had told them about me. I began enjoying the strength and assurance that personal power imparts. And I can tell you with all confidence that if I can develop personal power, anyone can do it.

To boost your personal power, identify and maximize your talents, your strengths, the things you do well. Use them, develop them, refine them, and improve them. Begin working with people or companies that already know you and do take you seriously. Establish a history of results. This is exactly how Michael Cahlin built Cahlin Williams Communications. When Michael began his public-relations and marketing company, he worked with smaller companies that the larger agencies wouldn't take. Often he wasn't their first choice. He charged a lower fee with certain specified goals and an up-front retainer. The balance was due upon satisfaction after a trial period. He says, "After they saw the results, they were willing to pay the money. Now after seven years I'm getting bigger clients and I'm beginning to be their first choice." He has a thirty-to-forty page capability statement now. It's his track record, and when people see it they take him seriously.

You Don't Have to Fake It to Make It

So you see, to be taken seriously you don't need to put on a facade and hype yourself like a carnival pitchman. Quite the contrary. If you approach the hurdles people seem to put in your way to being taken seriously as part of the race, getting over them simply becomes a matter of taking them in stride.

Hurdlers expect the track to be strewn with hurdles, and they know that how they get over them is what will enable them to win. So if you think of being on your own as like running hurdles, you won't be surprised by the barriers you encounter. They're not obstacles; they're there to test and hone your skills. They make you a more accomplished runner, so to speak.

From this perspective, we no longer need to resent the demands suppliers, customers, and other institutions place on us. We no longer need to rebel against them or be intimidated by them. We can think of them as *rites of passage,* not as personal indictments of our abilities. They become a chance to show off, an invitation to dance. And they enable us to become much more effective, confident, productive, and capable.

As J. B. Morningstar told us, "We think we have to do a little dance and that if they don't like it, we have to keep trying harder until we get the dance right. We think we have to try to be someone we're not. But that's not it. It's about finding the best in yourself and showing that you can do what needs to be done in the language your marketplace understands."

In other words, it's not a matter of having to choose between doing it your way or doing it their way. You don't have to try to give people what you think they want. You can give them more than they've dared to dream. The screenwriter Quinn Redecker, who wrote the Academy Award–nominated screenplay for *The Deer Hunter*, put it this way: "You have to do what you care about passionately and make them like it. You have to show them something, something they like. Take them someplace they've never been. Show them something they've never seen."

It's been said that there are two sets of rules: the rules for people who want to get in, and the rules for people who are in. And it's certainly true that everyone gives you greater latitude once they trust you and believe in you based on a track record of success. But truthfully, people are willing to make exceptions, give a chance to the novice, consider the unusual, the new, the different, the untested—if you can make doing this so appealing and desirable that they can't resist it. And that's what personal power is all about. It's about developing and showing off your magnificence and excellence as only you can. And when you do that, not only will people take you seriously, they'll do so eagerly.

Five Attitudes That Get in the Way of Being Taken Seriously

There's one thing that will sabotage all your other efforts to be taken seriously, and that's having an MBA—a *Marginal Business Attitude.* Whether you're a free-lancer, an independent contractor, an artist, a performer, or a craftsperson, if you're self-employed, you are *in business.* And if you don't have an SBA—a *Serious Business Attitude*—ultimately no power base or amount of image building will convince your public that you're for real.

A Marginal Business Attitude will show through in your business dealings like a pot belly in a bathing suit. And just as when your fly is open or your slip is showing, chances are no one will point it out to you. Instead of wondering why everyone's looking at you so funny, however, you'll be wondering why no one is taking you seriously. This means you've got to be the one who makes sure your attitude is on straight. Here are five common signs of a Marginal Business Attitude and how to avoid them.

1. I'll work when and if I want to.   One of the benefits of being your own boss is the flexibility to work when and if you choose. But erratic hours coupled with excuses and exceptions sends a message that you're not serious about your work. Someone with a Serious Business Attitude puts business first during business hours.

Here's an example of what we mean. An event planner had been trying to get a contract with a certain corporation for many months. Finally they called her on the spur of the moment and asked if she would do a special event the following week. She told them she'd love to, but that she had houseguests that week and asked that they call her another time. To this day, she continues to complain that she isn't taken seriously. To be taken seriously, you have to be there and deliver when you have the opportunity.

2. I don't have the money for that.　Serious business owners realize that money begets money. The money you spend on your business allows your business to grow. Money reproduces itself. You invest money to make money. Too often self-employed individuals bemoan the fact that they don't have the money to do what they know they need to do. If you really believe in yourself and take your business seriously, however, you will have the confidence to use credit and profits to buy what you need to be taken seriously.

A home-based seminar leader, for example, aspires to big-time fees of $5,000 a day. His courses are excellent, so he could command such fees. But although he knows he needs a computer and laser printer to create topnotch handouts, he hasn't purchased one. Although he knows he needs exposure, he doesn't advertise in the trade journals, nor does he have a newsletter to keep in touch with previous and prospective clients. He wants to do all these things, but he claims he can't afford to and continues to complain that he doesn't get the respect or command the fees he deserves.

To be taken seriously, you have to throw what money you have in the direction you want to go. Your success will follow.

3. I can't charge that much.　Serious business owners charge what they need to charge in order to succeed. One of the most common mistakes propreneurs make is to underprice their services. It's almost like they have an inferiority complex because they're small or work from home. A good example is a home-based newsletter publisher who was just barely keeping his doors open when he finally hired a business consultant to help diagnose the problem. The consultant's advice was to triple the price of the publication. The owner reacted angrily: "Gee, I can't do that! People won't buy it at *this* price!" "That's right," the consultant replied, "a newsletter as cheap as yours can't be that good." The publisher tripled the price and tripled his subscriptions in three months.

To be taken seriously, your price must convey value.

4. Being on your own is so tough.　We've noticed that serious business owners love the challenge of being on their own and realize that ups and downs are part of the process. They take the fluctuations in stride and talk about what they're doing rather than what's being done to them. They have a "lucky me," not a "poor me," attitude.

Marginal business operators, however, always have a ready complaint, a catastrophe, or a slight to report. They give their power away by complaining. When we complain we assume that someone else can solve the problem, that someone else holds the power to make things better. *But you have the power.* So seize it. When times get tough, focus on your purpose and your goals, and get on with what you're doing. Complaining isn't going to change things anyway. When you hear yourself complaining, take some action right there and then to do something about whatever's bothering you.

It doesn't matter what field you're in: success flocks toward success and runs from failure. So you have to expect and project success.

5. I do a lot of different things. Those with a Marginal Business Attitude tend to dabble in multiple things at the same time on the grounds that if one thing doesn't work out maybe something else will. They try to be all things to all people in hopes of being something to someone.

We know an aspiring propreneur who falls into this category. Every time we talk with her she has some new direction for her business. First she was a free-lance foreign-rights distributor for publishers. Then she was creating greeting cards. Next she was starting a national association. As she speaks of these new directions, she also complains bitterly about how people never take her seriously.

One evening we met a professional organizer at a networking event. When we found out about her business we wanted to refer her to a colleague of ours who could use her services. But then she added that what she really wanted to do was build her real-estate business and that she was puzzled as to why she could get neither of these businesses going. She wanted to know if we thought she should try something else.

To be taken seriously, you need to decide what you want to do most and give 100 percent of what you've got to that for as long as you've got. That type of commitment says that you have a Serious Business Attitude. Is it any wonder that ads reading, "In Business for 25 Years" are taken seriously?

We have many other sad examples of how these five signs of a Marginal Business Attitude can work against people who are trying to make it on their own: the young mother who lost a project when she didn't meet her promised delivery date because her daughter developed a cold; the typesetter whose printing contractor always lets him down so he gets behind on his jobs; the electrician who can't afford an answering machine so his teen-age son forgets to tell him about calls from prospective customers; the musician whose music gets little radio play because he charges for his demo tapes to cover the cost of their production.

If you want to be taken seriously you have to take yourself and your business seriously enough to do what you know you need to do to succeed. And when you do, everyone else will, too. In fact, they'll start making exceptions for you. It's true that there are two sets of rules: rules for those who want in, and rules for those who have met the rules.

In *Working from Home* we identify a dozen money-saving ways you can give yourself a Fortune 500 image—simple things like using a federal ID number instead of your Social Security number on business-related forms, or using a check protector instead of writing your checks out in longhand. Taking steps like these helps to convey that you are serious about yourself and that you mean business.

What to Do When You Don't Have Enough Money

Man [and woman] was born to be rich or inevitably to grow rich through the use of his [and her] faculties.

RALPH WALDO EMERSON

People who have been on their own for more than thirty days will tell you that cash flow is the lifeblood of surviving and thriving. It takes the place of your paycheck, and without a reasonably steady flow of cash, your goals and dreams will starve.

Often when a business is slow in taking off or hits a stall, propreneurs will ask, in desperation, "Where can I get some outside money?" In most cases, however, this is the wrong question. Banks and investors are rarely interested in loaning money to self-employed individuals—especially when those individuals are struggling to stay afloat. Outside money from loans and investors can sometimes be a way to finance expansion of an ongoing single-person business, but it's not a reliable route for getting the operating expenses you need to get a business going or to keep it afloat.

Ninety-nine percent of the time you should not need outside money for operating expenses. You are not Donald Trump. You don't have a big payroll. Chances are you don't have much overhead. You need to make enough money to support your business and yourself. And if you are providing the right product or service, your clients and customers can provide you with that support. Ultimately your customers are your only source of funding. Even if you are able to get a loan, it's your customers who will enable you to pay it back.

If you discover there's not enough money coming in, don't start from the premise that you must find some outside money. And don't take it as a sign that you need to fold up shop and take another job. Start from the premise that there's a way for you to get enough customers to pay you sufficiently to support yourself adequately. In other words, when you experience a cash crunch, don't ask how you're going to find someone to loan you some money. Ask instead how you can get the money you need from increasing your service to more clients and customers.

Like it or not, when you're self-employed, money is a barometer of how well you're doing. And we can be thankful that it is. The constant feedback a bank balance provides means that we can't fool ourselves into complacency for very long. Jerry Gillies, the author of the best-selling book *Money-Love*, puts it this way: "Money is a vehicle to take you to your desires. It's an extension of your personality. So-called money problems are not problems at all, but results that are dissatisfying. If you get results that don't satisfy you, it is because you are doing something to achieve those results. Many people want to solve their money problems without changing what they are doing to achieve those results. You have to change what you are doing if you want to change the results [you're getting]."

So if you don't like the state of your cash flow, look at what you are doing that's resulting in less income than you want and identify what you can do differently to produce better results.

The Only Three Reasons for Not Having Enough Money

It's easy to come up with a myriad of reasons for not having enough cash on hand: your marketing let you down, people don't appreciate the value of your service, the competition is undercutting your price, your overhead is too high, the market is sluggish, and on and on. Most of the endless list of reasons we give ourselves for not making as much money as we would like, however, are simply excuses. When it comes right down to it, unless you are wantonly overspending, there are only three reasons for not having enough money:

1. You don't have enough business. This is the most common reason for not having enough money. If you were operating at your peak capacity and your time was filled with paying clients and customers, chances are you would have enough money.

2. You're not collecting the money you're due. This is the classic cash-flow problem many small businesses face. It happens when you're actually making enough money from the work you're doing, but you're not getting paid soon enough to have the money on hand when you need it.

3. You aren't charging enough. If you have plenty of clients to fill your time and you're collecting everything you're owed and you still don't have enough money, you are not charging enough or not packaging your products or services in a way that allows you to charge what you need.

There are a variety of ways to change what you're doing that will produce better results in each of these areas.

Diagnosing What You Need to Do to Get More Business

All the people we interviewed for this book told us that at one time or another they didn't have enough business. Although the solution to not having enough business is really a simple one—get more business—the question becomes why you don't have enough business and what you can do about it. Here are several questions you can ask yourself to determine what you need to do:

1. Is there actually a need for what you have to offer? If there seems to be little interest in what you're offering, see if anyone else is making money providing this product or service. If no one is, it could be a sign that you need to change the nature of your product or service to something for which there is more of a demand. This was the problem for Rosalind, a family counselor. She wanted to teach parents how to convey values to their children, but parents weren't interested in her classes. She did discover, however, that many parents wanted to learn how to teach their children to deal with sex, drugs, and potential child abusers. So she restructured her programs to meet that need, and her classes began to fill.

How can you determine whether there's an ample demand for what you offer? And if not, how can you repackage or redefine what you do to meet a more pressing need?

2. Are there too many other people offering what you do? Frank wanted to teach presentation skills to corporate managers. At first he thought his proposals weren't up to snuff. But by talking with some of the personnel buying these programs he learned that in his community there were at least five trainers for every company needing these programs. As a result of this glut, very few of these trainers were earning a full living from presentation-skills training. Given this reality, Frank had several choices. He could travel to other communities to offer training. He could come up with a strategy to beat out the competition. He could develop training programs on other subjects to supplement his income from presentation-skills training. Or he could offer presentation skills to some market other than corporate America. He decided to do the last and began offering presentation-skills training for professional nonprofit fund-raisers Although he could not charge as much per day, he got more work.

How could you carve out such a niche for yourself?

3. Are the people who need you aware of what you offer? If other people are succeeding at what you're doing and there's plenty of demand for it, this may be a sign that not enough people know about you. And that means you need to step up your marketing efforts. If people who need your product or service don't know what you have available, how can they do business with you? For example, in health-conscious Los Angeles there are plenty of people who would love J. B. Morningstar's healthy chocolates, but they're a brand-new product. People don't know about them yet. In order to get enough business, J. B. has to create a high profile for her delicious and healthy candy. The more she does this, the more customers she will have.

How could you make sure that more people know about you?

4. Is your offer desirable? People may need what you have to offer and they may know about it, but if they find your product or service too expensive or not in a form they can use, they will do without it or go elsewhere to buy it. You may remember that when Jean and Shaun started a referral service, they set their business up so that in order for them to make enough money, vendors had to pay to be listed with their service, and people who were interested in a referral had to pay a small fee as well. Vendors were willing and eager to pay for their listing, but individuals were not willing to pay for the referrals. In other words, their offer was desirable to the vendors but not to the customers. Other referral services that have upped their listing fee and given away the referrals have flourished.

How could you make your offer more appealing to a larger number of people?

5. Are you doing a good job? If you get business, but your clients or customers don't come back and don't send anyone else your way, it's an indication that you need to do a better job of what you're doing or you need to find a different set of customers who will be happy with what you're providing. You can use the criteria on the next page to honestly and objectively assess your performance.

Lifesaving Measures to Turn Tough Times Around

The key to dealing with tough times is to keep your energy and your efforts up. Slow times need not be fatal or even inevitable unless you succumb to them. When business slows down and money starts to get tight, it's not time to cut back on your sales, PR, marketing, and promotional efforts, although this may be what you're tempted to do. Slow times are a signal to move into high gear, to approach your situation as a challenge and call forth your greatest creativity and ingenuity.

There is always some way to approach a slowdown that will get you through it victoriously. We know propreneurs who have even had to declare bankruptcy; after regrouping and starting again, they still came out on top. In fact, in many such cases the bankruptcy was a turning point in their ultimate success. From prayer to promotion, the propreneurs we've interviewed all have their favorite strategies for turning slow times around. Here are several secrets from the source.

Kim Freilich (publicist): "Before my baby was born, I was turning business away. I didn't want to take on too much. But I hadn't done enough planning ahead, and after the baby was born I found myself without enough business. I made a vow I would never again turn down business unless I didn't want to do the work. I took the Scarlet O'Hara pledge: 'I will never go hungry again.' Now I will farm work out before I'll turn it away."

Gene Call (private practice consultant): "I view slow times as a chance to be creative. I have to plan for times of the year when business is slow. I offer discounts on seminars at the end of the year. I get out and talk to people. I create a new seminar I think my clients want. If they're not buying, I view that as meaning I haven't found the right vocabulary to motivate them. I view everything I do as practice. I'm always looking for ways to make it better."

Michael Cahlin (marketing specialist): "When business is slow, I remind myself that not all the rewards I get are in how much money I make. Any time I'm not having to work for someone else, things are pretty good. When times are slow, I target a market I think will take off and start going to trade shows and making cold calls. I will cold-call anyone. I find that nine out of ten people don't like their current agency."

How to Know If You're Doing a Good Job

Since no one else is there to give you a monthly or quarterly performance evaluation, how will you know if you're doing a good job? Here are some useful criteria. The more of these you get, the better a job you're doing.

- **Compliments, appreciation, and gratitude.** The comments of customers and clients are a great indication of how well you're doing. If they go out of their way to tell you how much your product or service has meant to them, you know you're doing well. If you get frequent complaints, however, you need to take the time to figure out why and make changes.
- **Repeat business.** When clients and customers come back again and again, obviously what you're doing is working for them. If they go elsewhere, you should look at what your competition is doing that you're not. If some people come back and others don't, take a look at how you are meeting the needs of some and not of others. You may be able to make a shift in how you serve those you're losing so that you can get them to come back, too.
- **Referrals.** When colleagues, clients, or customers send other people to you, consider it to be an outstanding performance evaluation. It says, "We think you're great." If they don't, it could be a sign that you need to improve. It could also be a sign that they're not aware that you would appreciate referrals or that they don't know how to go about referring others to you.
- **Meeting internal standards.** All of us have our own internal criteria as to what constitutes a good job. Honestly evaluating yourself regularly against your own greatest expectations is one way to keep track of how well you're doing. If you find yourself skimping and sloughing off, don't berate yourself; just do whatever you need to do in order to improve.
- **How you feel while working.** If you're eager to get to work, enjoy yourself while you're working, and feel pleased with your output, it's usually a sign that you're doing a good job.
- **Progress toward your goals.** If you can see steady growth toward your goals, you're on track even though it may be taking a little longer than you expected.

Avoiding Slow Times

The best way to deal with slow times is to take steps to prevent your business from slowing down in the first place. Here are several ways to protect yourself from that sink-or-swim feeling of suddenly discovering you don't have enough business.

1. When you're first starting out, line up several clients before you leave the security of your job.
2. Don't rely on one client as the primary source of your business. Even if you have to subcontract business out, build a base of several reliable clients.
3. If you must work with only one client at a time, make sure to set aside several hours each week to market for future business no matter how busy you are in serving that one client.
4. To avoid sudden dips in business, keep your advertising, networking, and other marketing efforts under way during even your busy times. If you wait until business is slow to get more business, you could find yourself without business for months, until your renewed marketing efforts can draw a response.

Cindy Butler (professional shopper): "I cut back staff and work longer hours. At times I've had to take on other kinds of work and limit expenses until companies are contracting out again."

Chris Shalby (public-relations specialist): "I had to get past the if-we-can-just-get-through-the-next-month mentality and start thinking of having a regular flow of income. I don't wait for my clients to ask for me to do other work. I propose things I think need to be done. They usually take me up on my proposals."

Ellie Kahn (corporate biographer): "I have to push myself to make calls and make contacts to increase my visibility. My business comes mostly from word of mouth, so I have to use every occasion in my life to connect. I also use publicity. I've had to shift my marketing to reach organizations who could pay my fees, and not focus on people who think what I do is a great idea but can't afford to pay for it."

Dean Allen (wellness researcher): "The best way to make sure I have plenty of business is to do such a great job that people can't resist coming back and referring to me. Also it's a matter of having the right contacts. I go to the people who could refer to me and demonstrate what I can do. I've spent eight hours just showing someone with influence what I do. When things were slow I'd talk about new things I was working on."

Michael Russo (accountant): "Because my business is cyclical, I don't expect every month to be high. I know where I stand in relation to last year at the same time. You anticipate the slower times so they're not a shock. And I'm always out there hustling. The bottom line is that you have to keep knocking on doors. You have to make people know you exist. There are people who need you as much as you need them."

Dee Berhman (professional organizer): "It's a myth that there's never enough business. No matter how much you earn it's always perceptual. I've learned to shift my thinking to believing that I always have what I need."

Sherrie Connelly (management consultant): "Success comes from responding from possibilities and creating from possibilities. When times are slow, I look for the prime possibilities."

Five Ways to Get Business Fast

The lead time for getting business in the door can be considerable—from as short as several weeks up to several years depending on the type of business you do. Lead time can be especially long if you're working with large companies that must go through layers of decision making. But if you need business fast and don't have time to wait for the normal marketing process, here are five stop-gap measures for getting instant business on an emergency basis. Just be sure you keep up your ongoing marketing efforts, however, so you won't have future emergencies.

1. Get on the phone. The quickest, surest way to get business is to get on the phone and call prospective customers or clients. Begin with your past-client list. Satisfied customers are your quickest and surest source of instant business. Then call contacts who have expressed interest in the past. Use the yellow pages or an industry directory, or draw up a list of names of other people who might possibly need what you have to offer. Although we know most people hate cold-calling, it does work. And once you get started, it's not nearly as hard as you might think.

Set a goal to make a specific number of calls every day. Just go down the list one by one. Reward yourself for the number of calls you make, not just the number of sales. It may take a lot of calls to get a sale, so the more you make the better. To make this process easier, use any of the following ideas as conversational entrées and as added incentive for immediate action.

2. Make a special offer they can't refuse. Virtually anything can serve as an opportunity to offer a special promotion. You can have a spring special, a New Year's discount, a free initial consultation, and so on. If, for example, you have a word-processing service you might offer every fourth page free or you might do a complimentary cover-page layout for reports of six or more pages. If you have a bookkeeping service, you might give away one month of service with each yearlong contract signed before a certain date.

A newsletter publisher used a similar promotion when one of his long-running weekly advertising accounts suddenly decided to take a three-month vacation. He called companies that had been hemming and hawing about advertising and told them a special one-time one-month opportunity had come along and he wanted to offer it to them first. He had three one-month specials sold in just two days.

3. Offer a pricing incentive. Some money beats no money. So offer a special price that's so tempting prospective clients simply can't say no. This can be one of the quickest routes to new business. For example, when Ben Rolada started a community magazine in the suburbs where he lives, he used a special pricing strategy. He needed revenue to cover the production costs of his first issue, which he wanted to be filled with advertising. So he offered his inaugural advertisers a chance to advertise at half the going rate. And he gave top service for that price: he prepared the ads for no additional fee; he offered to write a feature article sometime during the year about their product or service. This approach enabled Ben to break even immediately. His first issue was a success. And since he let the advertisers know how special and unusual this offer was, they were willing to renew at the regular rate. And, of course, having so many satisfied advertisers made it easier to get new ones.

4. Subcontract or do overload work. Your competitors can be an excellent source of quick business. Howard Shenson, the consultant's consultant, reports that from 11 to 21 percent of new business comes from the competition. So scout around and find out who's busy; call to find out if they need backup or if they've had to turn away any projects.

One instructional designer was able to get business quickly in this way when the project she'd been working on was suddenly canceled due to a hostile corporate takeover. She called other instructional designers who knew and told them her plight. Sure enough, one designer had just turned down a job that he didn't have time to do and she got the work.

5. Volunteer. There's nothing worse for morale than having no work to do. Therefore, doing some work beats doing no work at all. And any work tends to beget more work. Often what begins as a volunteer effort ultimately becomes paid work. Many volunteers are able to turn their experiences into future paying contracts or orders. At the very least, volunteer efforts can be a source of experience and references that you can leverage into getting additional business elsewhere.

What to Say to Others When Things Aren't Going Well

It's a proverbial dilemma we all face when business is slow. You're out with colleagues, customers, or prospective clients and they ask, as they always do, "How's business?" What do you say? Do you lie and say, "It's great"? Do you dare tell them just how bad things are? We've found that propreneurs have varied but strong feelings about this situation. Some are adamant that business is *always* good and sometimes *very good.* For others, honesty is always the best policy. Still others say that the health report you give on your business should depend on whom you're talking with.

Those who always say business is great believe that you have to put forth a positive, upbeat image no matter how bad things are. Some people feel this is true only when it comes to clients or prospective clients; they don't want to cast any doubt about their future reliability. As one person told us, "I would never let a client know my business is down. Who wants to do business with someone who may not be in business soon?"

Those who believe honesty is the best policy, however, usually claim that customers and clients know when you're putting them on, so saying things are great when they're not throws even more doubt on your credibility.

Actually, many of the people we talk with are conflicted about what to say when business is bad. "I think I should say that things are fine, but I don't," one person said. "I tell the truth." Another person finds that "I never know what to say, so whatever I say sounds pretty bad."

After listening to all aspects of this dilemma, we believe both sides are right. You need to be—and can be—honest and upbeat at the same time. Here are some truthful, upbeat answers to the question, How's business?, that not only inspire confidence but also may help you get business when you most need it.

Getting better.

About to take a definite upswing.

It's a little soft right now. I'm looking for it to get better. So if you can, send some people our way.

It's taken a little downward dip, but we're about to start a promotion.

We're creating more.

How'd you like to help us create more?

We're expecting a real good season.

It's been a little soft up until now, but let me tell you about this new thing we're doing.

Let me tell you what we're doing.

We're about to do something that's going to take us through the roof.

Business is as it needs to be. Right now it's slow, which gives me time to develop new material.

I'm busy.

I can't complain.

We're plugging along.

We're between clients.

I've got some time free.

Who to Pay When There's Not Enough to Go Around

1. When you are temporarily short of funds, pay the following bills first.
   - Expenses related to your bringing in more business—for example, advertising.
   - Suppliers whose services you depend on to continue offering your product or service—materials, electricity, and telephone service.
   - Bills that will pay for themselves—for example, a printing bill for a newsletter that will generate business.
   - Bills from people who are giving you referrals.
   - Bills from people who have gone out of their way to help you thrive.
2. Arrange to make partial payments if necessary.
3. Pay the minimum on credit-card charges.
4. Defer optional expenses—things you can do without or do yourself, like magazine subscriptions, airline clubs, memberships, housecleaning.

Collecting What You're Due

Many propreneurs have a casual attitude about collecting fees—at first. The prevailing paycheck mentality leads us to presume that people will pay their bills upon receipt. Sometimes it's a great surprise when the money you've earned doesn't come in automatically. Far too many self-employed individuals end the year with thousands of dollars tied up in outstanding bills.

Fortunately, this is not necessary. But you do have to put your foot down when it comes to getting the money you're due. If you do the following three things, you should not have a collection problem:

1. Accept only clients who can pay. We don't believe you're doing anyone a favor by allowing clients or customers to build up a debt they cannot pay. If people cannot pay your fee, we suggest referring them to a service or product they can afford.
2. Get clear payment agreements and make very few exceptions.
3. Follow up immediately on any late payment.

If you find these policies to be too hard-nosed for you, we suggest that you set up a sliding fee scale of some type for people who cannot afford your standard fee. Decide how many such customers you are willing to serve, and charge them only what they can pay. Be aware, however, that if you take on too many reduced-fee clients you'll develop a reputation for bargain rates.

Here are some additional guidelines for making sure you get paid with as little effort as possible.

1. Establish a payment policy and make it clear before you begin any work. Design a policy that best suits your needs. If you are to meet with someone and there is to be a charge for the appointment, make sure he or she understands the costs ahead of time.

2. Get a signed contract. Before starting any job, get a signed agreement as to what you will do, what the fee will be (sometimes this will need to be an estimate), and when payment will be due. This agreement can take the form of an order form, a letter of agreement, a contract, or a purchase order. For additional information on negotiating such contracts see *Getting Business to Come to You,* which we wrote with the marketing consultant Laura Douglas.

3. Get money up front whenever possible. Payment up front in full is preferable, but is not always possible. At least get partial payment up front for projects that will involve your efforts over a period of time. Make sure your up-front payment covers all out-of-pocket expenses. Professional speakers, for example, often require half their fee in advance in order to hold dates for their clients. Kim Freilich gets 50 percent up front for publicity tours she books for publishers. Michael Cahlin requires a monthly retainer that's applied to his fee. He tells his clients, "I'm a small business. I can't wait for a 30-to-60-day billing period. But I don't take a lot of other clients. You are always a top priority for me. And I work with you personally. You won't ever be working with some underling."

4. Collect payment in full upon delivery. Whenever possible require that your fee be paid in full at the time you deliver the service. Professional speakers, for example, usually require that the balance of their fee be paid on-site the day of the speech. Word-processing services usually require payment on delivery of the work. Psychotherapists and other health professionals usually request payment at the close of each session.

5. If you must extend credit, check it out and tie it down. We advise extending credit only when absolutely necessary and then only with companies that have an excellent credit rating. Credit is a privilege. Large companies are sometimes the worst in abusing this privilege and will occasionally delay payment three to six months. As a single-person business, you often cannot afford such a delay. So be sure to get written contracts, with payment dates clearly spelled out. Act immediately when a payment is late. Call the person with whom you have the contract. If you do work on credit with a company that has a bad credit history or appears to be having financial problems, acknowledge that you are not doing business; you are gambling.

6. If they don't pay, don't work. If some clients are behind in their payments, do not continue working. Stop working when they stop paying. If you do otherwise you are saying it's okay not to pay and you're setting yourself up for continued collection problems.

7. Establish a cancellation fee. When establishing your costs, get a clear agreement about your cancellation policy. Cancellation fees should cover any costs you've incurred and lost-opportunity costs.

8. Take legal action if necessary. Most states have some provision for adjudicating small claims. Usually the cost is small. Do not hesitate to take unpaid bills to court. Propreneurs have told us how surprised they were to discover how easy it was for them to recover money that was clearly due them and what a positive effect it had on their self-esteem.

9. Take 100 percent responsibility. Making sure you get your money is completely up to you. If you are not getting the money you're due, don't complain. Don't feel sorry for yourself. It means you took a risk. You worked without money up front. You extended credit. Look at the situation and acknowledge that you allowed it to happen, then see to it that it doesn't happen again. People respect people who respect themselves.

Can You Raise Your Prices or Fees?

If you are working full-time at capacity and collecting the money you're due, feeling like you are still not making enough money can be one of the most frustrating aspects of being on your own. It can eat away at your morale, create friction with family members, and generally erode your quality of life to the point where you may yearn for a return to the paycheck. But we find that the clearer you are about your financial expectations, the more likely you are to create self-employment opportunities that will actually meet them.

Obviously you need to cover your costs of doing business and keep your business running. Therefore, you need to itemize all your costs including your overhead, and make sure that your fees cover these costs with enough left over to *support yourself at a level that makes it sufficiently worthwhile for you to continue working on your own.* This is simple enough, but it's at this point that many people run into difficulty. What is the level that will make it worthwhile for you to work for yourself? How much is enough? When you can set your income goals anywhere you want, where do you set them? What can you expect? What should you expect? How do you make sure you don't get discouraged by setting unrealistic goals and yet still not settle for less than you have to?

In order to define precisely what you need and want to earn at any given time without limiting yourself, we suggest identifying three specific income goals as follows.

1. How much money do you need to make in order to survive? This is the figure you must bring in to keep a roof over your head, clothes on your back, and food on the table. This is an amount below which you cannot go. If the business is promising in the long run, you may be willing to subsist at this level for some period of time as long as you can see how building your experience and clientele will ultimately enable you to earn more. But if your business cannot provide you with this figure, you must make some fundamental changes in your business now.

It's very sad when people have struggled to make it on their own, gone into debt to keep themselves afloat, and then, psychologically exhausted from not having known what they were in for, had to give up before their venture could become viable. Therefore you need to know exactly what your subsistence level is and have some idea about how long you are willing to live at this level.

This survival figure, and the others that follow, are all completely subjective. Here are three hypothetical examples based on composites of actual individuals. Cheryl, who transcribes court reporters' notes, believes she can live on no less than $25,000 a year and says she would live at this level indefinitely if it meant she would never again have to work for someone else. Mark, an actor, can squeeze by on $15,000 a year as long as he sees himself making some progress in his career. Kyle, a management consultant, isn't willing to live on less than $35,000 a year, and he doesn't want to live at that level for any more than three years at the longest.

2. How much do you need to feel satisfied? This is the figure your business must be able to produce at some point in the foreseeable future. When you are busy full-time, working at capacity, the fees you charge will eventually need to be able to bring in this figure or beyond; otherwise you will start to feel resentful and bitter about your work.

For Cheryl this amount is $35,000, about $5,000 more than she was earning as a legal secretary before going out on her own transcribing court reporters' notes. Mark is more concerned about acting than he is about earning money; but he's married and he and his wife want to have a child. His wife works, too, however, so if he can ultimately earn at least $30,000 a year, he'll feel satisfied. Kyle won't be satisfied with anything less than $75,000 a year. And he thinks that by working full-time himself he could easily attain that in his consulting firm.

3. How much would you really like to make? Your business must be able to at least hold the potential of hitting this figure or you are likely to feel like you've created your own dead-end job.

If Cheryl has hopes of making more than about $35,000, she may well be in the wrong business, because working full-time transcribing court reporters' notes can bring in only about that much. Mark, of course, could make a fortune if he hit it big as an actor, so there's no intrinsic limit on his future. Kyle has expectations of earning over $150,000 a year, so he will have to add two associates in order to achieve his ultimate goals.

Having these three figures clearly in mind should help clarify what you need to charge and whether you need to raise your fees. Now let's talk about if, when, and how you can actually raise your fees. The amount of money you can charge as a propreneur is determined by three variables.

1. *Your self-esteem.* You have to be able to state your fees or prices with sufficient confidence and comfort to inspire acceptance of them.
2. *Your reputation, credentials, and results.* Your customers or clients must perceive you as being sufficiently skilled and capable to warrant the fee you're asking.
3. *The marketplace.* Your fees or prices must be within a range that keeps you competitive with others. Retailers and service providers alike have learned that if people can go elsewhere and get comparable results for much less money, they will.

In other words, there are limits to what you can charge at any given time for any given service or product, and you have to determine what those limits are in your field and in your community. First you must determine if there is the potential in your field to charge what you need to charge. If not, you must begin by planning how you can refocus or completely change your business so that you can at least potentially earn what you consider to be *enough* money.

If, for example, Cheryl eventually hopes to earn $50,000 a year, she must make other plans. Given that there are so many hours in the day and she can work only so fast even at her best, Cheryl will not be able to earn $50,000 a year at the prevailing rates for her chosen occupation. If she doesn't want to leave the field, however, she might meet her income goals by hiring others to work for her. Or to bring in additional income she might teach workshops on how to do what she does.

Once you determine that you can at least potentially charge what you need to, you need to determine if you now have sufficient stature to command that fee or price. For example, people expect to pay more for treatment by a psychiatrist that by a psychologist. Therefore, as a newly graduated psychologist, you will want to find out the going rate newly graduated psychiatrists are charging. You will also want to find out what the established and well-respected psychologists in your community are charging. You can then set your fees in relation to those at the level that your skill, credentials, and self-confidence justify.

If you can't initially command the fees you want, you can immediately outline for yourself a course of action for establishing the reputation, results, and self-confidence you need to raise your fees to the level you desire. In the chapter on pricing in *Working from Home,* we outline a variety of strategies and guidelines for setting your best possible price.

Do You Have to Cut Your Costs and Living Expenses?

You'll notice that we have not talked about cutting back your expenses. The reason for this is that we believe in starting from the premise that you deserve to earn the amount of money you aspire to earn—that is, enough for you to feel satisfied, well rewarded, and comfortable. As the bookkeeper Chellie Campbell says to her clients, "Don't ask, 'How can I cut back to live within my means?' Ask, 'How I can create the means to live as I desire?' "

Of course, once you determine how to create the means you desire, you must begin doing so within the means you have. But then, you are living at that level only temporarily. You are cutting back not because you don't have what you want, but because you want to do those things that you need to do to create what you want. For most people, these are two *very* different experiences.

For example, when John and Margaret started their balloon business they knew they couldn't immediately achieve the income they'd been earning as managers for a local retail chain. But they had developed a business plan that would put them at double their previous income within five years. Margaret recalls, "We felt like newlyweds again, starting out our lives together eating macaroni and cheese. It was fun even though we had some really tight months. We could enjoy those times because we knew where we were headed. We knew what we were working for. We didn't feel sorry for ourselves. We felt proud about having the courage to do this. It's taking longer than we'd projected, but we can see our progress and we know we'll get there. We even eat out once a week now!"

What to Do When You Feel Like Quitting

Feeling, from time to time, like you want to quit working for yourself is as normal as feeling like you want to quit your job. And who hasn't felt like that at one time or another? In fact, we found that most of the self-employed individuals we spoke with in writing this book had entertained the idea of quitting or doing something else at least once. Of course, none of them had actually quit, but we find that allowing yourself the option of quitting is actually very important for working successfully on your own.

Without the option to entertain the idea of quitting, you become enslaved to your own so-called freedom. Research studies of individuals who work from home clearly show that those who work from home because they choose to are much happier and more satisfied than those who work from home because their circumstances have led them to believe they have no other option. We're convinced the same is true of working for yourself.

So whenever you feel like quitting, we suggest responding the same way a manager would upon hearing that a valued employee is considering looking elsewhere for employment. Take your desire to leave seriously. Look into the source of your dissatisfaction and do what you need to do in your own best interest. For example:

Do you feel like quitting because you need a break? Often people feel like giving up when they're tired out, burned out, or bummed out. If this is your situation, give yourself a break. Get some sleep. Take a long weekend. Go on vacation. Do whatever you need to do to get refreshed and rested. Then you can reevaluate whether you still want to quit.

Do you want to quit because you don't like what you have to do in order to succeed? Since there is almost always more than one way to do something, if you hate the way you're doing it now, explore other ways you could do what needs to be done or consider how to refocus your work so that you will like it better. Jeannette loved making gift baskets, for example, but she hated selling them. She was about to give up when she called in to talk with us on our radio show.

We asked Jeannette this question: If you could run your gift-basket business exactly the way you would want to, how would you run it? She said, "Oh, I'd have someone else sell the baskets, and I would make them." So we suggested that she do just that. At first she wasn't sure this was possible, so we asked her to imagine how she would do it if it were possible. Immediately she said she would find a partner, and so that's what she did.

Do you want to quit because succeeding as your own boss is not what you thought it would be? Sometimes being out on your own allows you to discover just how much you enjoy working for and being part of an organization. And if that's the way you feel, that's okay. You know what you need to do. Being your own boss is often an ideal way to position yourself for a permanent job offer. It provides you with more status and makes you more desirable. So parlay your situation into a job you will enjoy more. Deciding you want to take a job again is not a sign of failure; it's simply a sign that you've realized what you really want to do.

Do you want to quit because it's time to expand or move on to something else? Sometimes if you've been doing the same thing for several years you can get burned out even though you're doing well enough at it. The dissatisfaction you feel may be a sign that you've settled into your comfort zone and are no longer growing. Why not diversify, try out a new side venture, expand, or take on a whole new direction for your business?

Do you want to quit because you don't feel like you're succeeding? If making it on your own has been too hard for too long, it's easy to feel like throwing in the towel. When that's the way you feel, it's time to take an objective look at what you're doing. You don't have to keep going. How much do you want this? How long are you willing to continue? Consider the following insights into why making it on your own is sometimes so difficult and why it can take so long. Then follow your heart.

Does It Have to Take So Long and Be So Hard?

Most of us go out on our own with visions of sugarplums dancing in our heads. We may fear failing, but we don't expect to fail. We expect success to be right around the corner. And society encourages our optimism. Movies and television feed our expectations. In one movie Dianne Keaton plays a divorced woman with low self-esteem who decides to start her own business and becomes an overnight millionaire—in less than thirty minutes of screen time. Patricia Wettig, of television's *Thirtysomething*, plays the role of Nancy, who decides to write a children's book and, after minor setbacks, gets it published within the thirteen-week season. Magazines and newspapers feature inspiring stories of immigrants and high-school dropouts who have built successful businesses overnight.

We love these stories and thank goodness for them. They tantalize us and make us think we can do it, too. They give us the courage to rise above our doubts and limitations and go for our dreams. They help us believe that dreams come true. Sometimes, however, it doesn't go like it does in the movies or the books and magazines. Sometimes it's hard, very hard. And sometimes it's not around the corner or even around the block. Sometimes it takes what feels like a long, lonely lifetime. And it's at those times that we most need to understand why it's taking us so long, why it's so hard for us while it seems so easy for others.

The two of us know a great deal about times like those. In 1980, we had a dream that involved writing best-selling books, speaking, and doing seminars around the world, appearing on radio and television, writing magazine columns and articles, and much more—all to tell people about the joys of going out on their own and working from home. In our mind's eye, we saw crowds of men and women packing into our seminars, lines of people forming to get our books. We saw their faces excited and eager to learn about the positive changes they could make in their lives.

That was the dream. It burned in our very souls. It lit those early days with intoxicating determination. The reality, however, tested us to our very core. It took us five years just to get our first book published. No one showed up for our first publicly advertised workshop—no one. There were many long, dark years, and hours of despair and dejection. Seven years later, however, the dream began coming true. Now, ten years later, we're living the lives we imagined in 1980. In the midst of the worst of those years, however, we learned several important things that helped us understand why pursuing our dreams was more difficult than we had expected, and that helped us to continue with renewed resolve.

Success Has a Schedule of Its Own

We've learned that in making it on one's own, each person is truly traveling his or her own path to success, and each journey takes as long as it takes. For some it's short and fast; for others it's long and tedious. The rate of success, however, has nothing to do with the ultimate outcome—unless, of course, you quit before you finish. Here are four common patterns of success rates.

1. The fast start. Tova Borgnine enjoyed instant success. Forget that Tova is married to a famous and wealthy movie star. She had found a rejuvenating facial mask and on a whim decided to take out an ad to sell it. The orders flooded in. She was overwhelmed with the response. It came before she'd even made a full commitment to her business idea. From that one ad has grown a multi-million-dollar business, Tova Beauty Products.

Sandy Gooch also had a fast start. She opened one of the first truly natural health-food stores in Los Angeles. She had to cancel the ads she placed in the local paper even before they all ran: there were more people coming to her store than her employees could handle.

Such fast starts are like fairy tales that come true for real-life Cinderellas. Peggy Glenn was making more money from her typing service within her first six weeks than she'd been making on her job. Ann McIndoo made over one-hundred-thousand dollars within a year of opening her computer training service. The accountant Michael Russo brought in 240 percent more business during his first year than his initial projections. In 1988, thirty-one-year-old Lisa Lamee was laid off from her thirty thousand dollar-a-year job as an import buyer. Instead of finding another job she decided to turn her love for cooking into Le Saucier, a mail-order and retail business that distributes over five hundred exotic sauces. She installed a toll-free number and was almost immediately drowning in orders.

We know of many such instant success stories. They're a real inspiration. Of course it's what we all want. But know this:

You don't need instant success to succeed!

While it's tempting to drop what you're doing and take off on a wild search for instant success, that is a mistake. *Most successfully self-employed individuals did not have a fast start.* And fast starts pose their own challenges. For example, when a woman we'll call Jill started her business, offering human-potential seminars, she had such an immediate rush of business that she was overwhelmed: "I didn't feel I deserved it. I don't know why people flocked to me in such numbers. Frankly, I couldn't handle it because I really didn't know what I was doing. The business took over my life." Finally she moved to another city and started over again. This time, since no one knew her there, she was able to start more slowly.

2. The slow and steady route. Many very successful businesses start out more like marathons than sprints. They build momentum over the long haul instead of igniting on the spur of the moment. In fact, this is a more commonplace experience than the instant success. Most propreneurs gradually build their businesses week by week, month by month, and year by year. As one caterer told us, "On New Year's Eve I realized I'd made it. I'd been on my own for five years! It sort of sneaks up on you." As long as you can see the gradual progress you're making, this pattern can actually be more comfortable than, and certainly as rewarding as, a fast start.

3. The roller-coaster ride. Some people discover that making it on their own is a series of peaks and valleys, feasts and famines. Michael Cahlin, for example, finds that "one month you may bring in seven thousand dollars, the next month seventeen thousand dollars." While you're riding high in a business like this, it's tempting to think the highs will last forever—and, of course, there's no reason not to enjoy them while they do. It's useful, however, to plan ahead financially for the valleys. And when they hit, it's important to realize that they don't mean that you're going under. In businesses like these, the valleys don't last forever, either. You can use these downtimes to gear up and build for the next climb.

4. The endurance trials. As was the case with us, some success comes after years of perseverance and determination. When this is your situation, it's particularly important that you be highly motivated. If you don't want to do what you've set out to do *a lot,* you'll have a hard time remaining positive and continuing on doggedly. Three years passed, for example, before wellness researcher Dean Allen broke even. But now he has all the business he can handle; he doesn't even have to market. He says, "Even when I was starving to death I never seriously thought of quitting, even though I was pressured by girlfriends to get a job. I felt like if I gave up I would die. Doing something else would be the kiss of death."

In addition to being highly motivated, it's also important to keep your eye on your ultimate goal and not get bogged down in your current reality. Look, instead, at the progress you have made and keep taking steps forward to where you want to be. It's especially important not to compare yourself with others, especially fast starters. That's just too demoralizing.

Two Factors That Determine Your Success Rate

Achieving success out on your own is a process much like growing up. As you think back to when you were twelve or thirteen years old, you'll undoubtedly remember that some kids matured much more quickly than others. Girls fill out their sweaters at different rates. Boys' voices deepen at different times. If you've had children of your own, you'll undoubtedly remember that they all walked and talked on their own schedule. Each did ultimately walk and talk, however, just as each of us did ultimately mature. Our unique genetic composition and social environment combine to determine the rate at which we achieve various developmental milestones.

So it is with being on your own. Instead of your genetic heritage and social milieu determining your rate of success, however, two other primary factors combine to influence when and how you will succeed: the receptivity of the marketplace, and the resources you bring with you when you start out on your own. Just as child-development experts agree that it's unwise for parents or teachers to try to force a child to develop more quickly, it's equally unwise for us to try to force ourselves to develop our businesses faster than our circumstances will support. But just as there are things parents can do to nurture a child's development, there are also steps we can take to work within the circumstances of the marketplace and our resources to nurture our journey to success and make it as quick and easy as possible.

Is Your Market More or Less Receptive?

Your *market* is the body of existing or potential buyers who need or want your product or service. Most propreneurs don't think a lot about the market before going out on their own. They start out with either an existing skill, an idea, or a desire they want to pursue. This is one of the characteristics that sets propreneurs apart from classical entrepreneurs, who are more likely to tailor what they set out to do to market trends and patterns of what, when, and how people are spending their money.

If you think about the fast-start success stories we described, they were all examples of individuals who were in the right place at the right time. The market was ripe for their products. People who tried to do what they did before or after them most likely met with different responses. For example, in any particular venture or type of work you undertake, you may find yourself in one of the following situations.

- **Ahead of the market.** This was our situation. We were seven years ahead of the market. In this case you have to have patience, and do a lot of educating and hand-holding to help people get on board. Your growth will be slower and perhaps even an endurance trial while the market catches on. When it does, however, you may become the leaders in your field and even be in a position to be acquired.

  Case in point: When Sue Rugge started Information on Demand, one of the first information-brokering companies in the country, few people knew what information brokering was. She had to literally define that business, educating people about her service and showing them how it would benefit them. It took her eight years, but ultimately she thrived, and as the market caught up with her she sold her company for a substantial profit.

- **Right on the market.** In this case, your business will take off like a rocket. There will be lots of immediate demand for what you do. As our fast-start examples illustrated so well, all the business you need will be there for the taking. You can count on other people jumping on the bandwagon, however, and you will have to stay alert to keep up with your competition.

  Case in point: Sometimes people hit on a hot idea. Twenty-four-year-old Keri VanderSchuits certainly did. She loved to dance to live rock music, and to create firm and attractive support she would sew appliqués on her bras. Every time she wore one of these bustiers, other young women would go wild, so she decided to invest $500 dollars in creating a line of ten bustiers. She put them in a shopping bag and went from boutique to boutique. Putting another $500 dollars into her business, she hired help, and her fledgling business has grown into a $200,000-a-year proposition.

■ **In a growing market.** In this case, you can actually see that a particular business is already in demand and taking off, so you can join in to share in the profits by starting such a business yourself.

Case in point: Forty-one-year-old Robert Dobnick was working in showroom design when he saw that showroom construction was booming. There was clearly a demand for specialists in this field, so he became one. He started Robert F. Dobnick Design Consultants two years ago. He designs and plans wholesale showrooms and earns $150,000 a year.

■ **In a stable or declining market.** In this case you will have a lot of competition right from the start from others who have already captured most of the business. Therefore, unless you can find a special untapped niche, you will have a battle on your hands. To break into this type of market, you will need to be better or cheaper in order to take over business from others.

Case in point: Ann MacIndoo was one of the first to begin computer training in law offices, and her business took off like a flash. She was making over $250,000 a year within only a few years. By the time Jerry Conklin graduated from college, however, many businesses were already computerized. The demand for computer training was far less than when Ann began. And companies like Ann's had a corner on the existing markets. But Jerry wanted to do computer training and he was good at it. Therefore he had to find a specialized niche, that had not yet been tapped. He chose publishing, because publishers were slower to adopt new technology and his family had connections in that industry.

■ **Dealing with a fad.** In this case your venture may take off like a skyrocket and then peak fast. So you will have to use some of your profit and resources to expand quickly into other ventures before your original idea fizzles out.

Case in point: When women's clothing began to feature shoulder pads, a Midwest-based woman saw the opportunity to start a mail-order business selling shoulder pads in various sizes and shapes. The business took off fast because the demand was high and she was one of the only sources. But soon fashions changed. In order for this business to continue, the owner had to look for new products. She chose headbands, which were just coming into fashion as shoulder pads were about to fade.

■ **Entering an evergreen.** Certain types of work are always in demand and may well always be: accounting, bookkeeping, and secretarial services of various kinds are a few examples. In this case, with the right credentials and connections, you will usually be able to break into such a business at a steady but perhaps gradual pace. Or if you want to speed up the process, you can specialize in an untapped market, offer a new approach, or apply a new technology to existing markets.

Case in point: There were many dentists in practice in Pasadena, California, when Craig Scheele graduated from dental school. He wanted to build his business as quickly as possible, however, so he decided that he would specialize in the patients other dentists hated to see. He specialized in *difficult* patients: people with heart conditions and dental phobias, and hospitalized individuals. Needless to say, his business grew quickly. Fortunately these people had friends and relatives, and ultimately he had a well-rounded general practice.

■ **Without a market.** Sometimes your idea or skill has no existing market, in which case you have to create one. You have to convince people that they want or need what you have to offer. And once you do, you will have created a new industry, a new field, in which you will be the leader. As with being ahead of the market, this is usually a long, involved process, but once you begin doing well you will be joined by others. You may also be in a good position to be acquired.

Case in point: Boyd and Felice Willat were the first people to create a personal time-management system, the DayRunner, a system for managing your life. No one had ever heard of such a concept before. Reps didn't know where to place it; stores didn't know where to display it. Boyd and Felice built a market for the DayRunner, however. They convinced the reps of its viability and showed the stores how to merchandise it. They've built a multi-million-dollar industry, which now includes many competitors.

Evaluating the market conditions for your business can help you understand what you're up against and give you insights into why you're encountering whatever challenges you are. It is senseless, for example, to attempt to understand your rate of progress by comparing it with that of someone who is dealing with an entirely different market. Propreneurs often do this, however. But, to take one of the above examples, why should Jerry measure his progress in offering computer training by comparing it with Ann's? Such comparisons would be useless. The businesses were started under two completely different market conditions.

Sometimes, in looking realistically at market conditions you will decide that you want to rethink the type of product or service you offer simply because you have taken on more of a challenge than your available time, money, or energy can sustain. Many librarians, for example, wanted to do what Sue Rugge did with Information on Demand, but very few were willing to go knocking on doors the way Sue did. She had to go door-to-door calling on potential customers and educating them as to the value of information research. To this day Sue says, "If I hadn't been laid off, I am not sure I would have had the guts to quit and start my own business. Doing the work was the easy part. It was selling a service no one knew about that was hard."

Now many researchers work free-lance for companies like Sue's. Others waited until the pioneering tasks of educating the market were well under way and are starting out on their own now that their services are beginning to be more in demand.

Barbara Cooper is a marvelous songwriter and singer. Her style, although New Age, is reminiscent of the big-band era. Her albums are all done with a full orchestra. This sound is not the norm in New Age music. The big-band sound peaked in the forties and has yet to return to popularity. But Barbara is determined to find a niche for her music. It has been and will be an uphill battle for Barbara, but it's one she is willing to undertake.

Cheryl Miller is also a singer and songwriter. Her style is reminiscent of the folk songs of the sixties. Like Barbara she has been committed to her style, and it has been a long, hard struggle. Now the market seems to be receptive once again to folk music and her sound is beginning to take off at last.

Like Cheryl and Barbara, you have a choice about what type of work you want to do and how you choose to focus on it. Some people have taken on more difficult tasks than others. But too often our choices as propreneurs are made unknowingly. Evaluating your market can assist you in knowing just what you're up against and what you'll need to do in order to survive and thrive. With this knowledge you can decide what you're willing to commit to and can proceed accordingly.

Are You More or Less Ready?

Just as we don't all start out in the same market conditions, we also don't start out with the same degree of personal and professional readiness. The resources we each bring to self-employment vary greatly and affect how quickly and easily we will succeed. Here are six resources that can help you survive and thrive on your own. The more of these you have, the easier it will be. The fewer you begin with, the longer it will take you to acquire them or to succeed without them.

1. Your experience level. The level of experience you have in what you do and in managing yourself as a business will determine how long your learning curve will be. If you have been doing what you do for many years, know your field well, and have experience in marketing and managing yourself, your learning curve will be much shorter than that of people relatively new to their field who have little marketing or self-management experience.

Mike Greer had worked for several firms as an instructional designer over several years. He had become very good at his work and knew the ins and outs of bidding, pricing, billing, negotiating, and delivering his product. Melissa was also a good designer, but she was new to the field and had always worked under another designer. Whereas Mike was profitable from day one when he went out on his own, Melissa barely survived the first year. By the third year, however, she was doing fine.

2. *Your contacts.* Who you know and their willingness to serve as gate-keepers or mentors can greatly enhance the ease with which you move into self-employment. The more contacts you have, the less time it will take you to get established.

The publicist Kim Freilich and the PR expert Chris Shalby both had major clients already signed up before they left to go out on their own. Kim had been working as a publicist for a midsize publisher and had valuable contacts already in place. Chris also had a host of valuable contacts from his having done PR in-house for a large organization. Libby Goldstein, however, had just moved to Baltimore and knew not a soul when she started her PR firm. As you can imagine, getting started for Libby took more time and a lot more effort than it did for Kim and Chris.

3. *How much money you have to capitalize yourself.* While having lots of money isn't necessary, it can certainly help get things moving more quickly. If you don't have experience, you can buy it. You can hire a marketing consultant, a PR firm, or an ad agency. You can attend top-notch courses and classes. If you don't have contacts, you can buy advertising to get the exposure you need. Or you can buy access to contacts through club and organizational memberships, donations, and fund-raising activities.

When Naomi Stephan left her position as a university professor to become a career consultant, she took a six-month leave of absence and worked for a yellow-pages company to learn about advertising, sales, and direct mail. She used savings, a loan from her parents, and a ten-thousand-dollar bank loan to purchase her office equipment. This capital provided her with the cushion she needed to be debt-free and supporting herself in her brand-new career within eighteen months.

Marie Wallermeyer, however, had been working as an employment counselor when she was laid off. She had to bootstrap her career-consulting business. She had to live off of, and finance her business with, the fees her first clients brought in. Things were very tight. She had to take a part-time job for three years, but ultimately she made it, too. It just took longer.

4. *Your credentials.* As we discussed earlier in this chapter, credentials open doors and smooth the way. You don't always need them, but having them makes your job easier.

As a psychiatrist Tom went directly from his psych residency into private practice. With his credentials, he was able to quickly get referrals from several agencies and from the hospital with which he was affiliated. Terry, on the other hand, had no counseling, ministerial, or psychotherapy credentials, so when she started offering personal-growth classes, she had to build her enrollment strictly with her personal power. It was a slow process. Recently divorced, she also had very few funds. In fact, at first she had to hold her classes in a library and split the fees with the library while she lived with friends. Then for five years she held her classes in the living room of her one-bedroom apartment. Now, however, she has a thriving practice. Her classes are full. Her calendar is full with private appointments, and she has recently built a new home and studio for her work that she and her new husband have jointly financed.

5. Your results. The more dramatic your results, the quicker and easier you will be able to become established.

When Cyril came to the United States from Australia, he had two hundred-fifty dollars in his pocket. He knew not a soul in this country. He'd been a typesetter, and typesetting jobs were few and far between. But he loved people. He saw an ad for a multilevel marketing company and started selling its health products. He loved the products and found he could sell them to anyone. Soon he began teaching others to sell them. The people he trained were so excited about what they learned from him that before he knew it he was teaching sales skills for other companies. Within a year he was doing sales-training programs for major corporations. All this was based on the results he was able to produce.

Jeffrey also became a sales trainer. He'd been selling on commission for a manufacturing company. His own sales record was marginal, but he thought it was the product, not his skills, that were holding him back. He discovered how much money sales trainers can make and decided he could do that. People who came to his classes, however, complained that they hadn't gotten much. Some even asked for their money back. But Jeffrey kept at it. The promise of future fees motivated him to stay with it. As his skills improved, so did his results, both in the field and in the classroom. Ten years later he was making the fees he had initially aspired to.

6. Time. As you can see from the above examples, even if you don't have any of the other resources, you can still make it. Lots of people do. But you will need time—and patience and determination—to complete your learning curve.

Moving Mountains

We hope that after reviewing the preceding discussion of personal resources and market issues, you are feeling pleased with your own progress in view of your particular circumstances. Certainly that is our goal in having described them. You undoubtedly have certain assets that are enabling you to succeed, and which you can capitalize on even further. You also undoubtedly have some limitations that are making your progress slower or harder than you might like, and which you must work around and compensate for in some way.

As your own coach and mentor, you need to play up your assets, acknowledge yourself for them, and take pride in having acquired and used them. It's important not to take them for granted. There are people who must struggle desperately for the very things that come so naturally to you. So point out these strengths to yourself frequently, especially when you are feeling discouraged or doubtful. Make sure you lead with your strengths and encourage yourself to continue empowering yourself by fully developing your talents and resources.

This is exactly what every good coach and mentor does, no matter what the field. Every top athlete and every top performer in every field has certain strengths and weaknesses. The coach's job is to bring out the strengths and shore up and overcome the weaknesses.

Taking a Personal Inventory

You are the best you've got. But you are enough, and you can be even more. Give yourself time to develop the resources you need, even if you must redirect your efforts or even start over. As long as you are still breathing, there is no end to your capacity to grow and to develop. Every day you can be more, do more, and have more of what life has to offer.

Resources

Getting Business to Come to You. Paul and Sarah Edwards and Laura Clampitt Douglas. Los Angeles: Jeremy Tarcher, 1991. Identifies the marketing methods of the most successful home-based businesses. See especially chapters 4 and 15.

Money-Love: How to Get the Money You Deserve for Whatever You Want. Jerry Gillies. New York: Warner Books, 1978. Teaches you how to rethink self-defeating attitudes about money. It shatters myths our culture and families teach us about money and provides a new outlook on prosperity and how to achieve it permanently.

Money Is My Friend. Phil Laut. New York: Ivy Books, 1989. Provides methods for eliminating financial fears and making money a fun, fascinating, and creative enterprise.

Working from Home. Paul and Sarah Edwards. Los Angeles: Jeremy P. Tarcher, 1990. See especially chapters 14 and 21.

CONCLUSION

■■■■■■■■■■■■■■■■■■■■■■■■

Enjoying Your Success

Success is really a dreamlike experience.
BRUCE JOEL RUBIN

Congratulations! You're doing it! You're living the dream of seven out of ten Americans. You are on your own. You are your own boss. You are a success! Have you noticed yet?

Some highly successful people we've met tell us, "Oh, I'm not a success yet! I'm not going to be successful until . . ." For them success is reserved for the things they haven't yet attained. Actually, success is a process. There is no finish line; there are only milestones. As you achieve one set of goals, you set new ones in an ever-unfolding journey.

From our perspective, if you're on your own, you are already successful, right here, right now. You have had the courage, ingenuity, and confidence to do what you've done to get as far as you have at this moment. And that makes you a success.

Take, for example, the story of the scriptwriter David Mickey Evans. Evans's script *Radio Days* was sold to Columbia Pictures for a record $1.2 million. Evans disagrees, however, with references to his so-called overnight success. He points out that *Radio Days* was his twenty-second screenplay. He had been writing scripts for low-budget horror and western films to pay his way through college. The most he had ever made for any of these scripts was thirty-five hundred dollars, so he had to work as a bartender, security guard, and phone installer to stay in school.

When he graduated from college, he owed $50,000 in student loans and had nowhere to live. For three years he lived at his brother's home, isolated in a small room with a bed and a computer. He was lonely and discouraged. At one point he needed money so badly that he called the navy recruiting office to find out about officer training. When he signed the Columbia deal he had $4 in the bank.

So when did David become a success? Was it when he signed that $1.2-million deal? We don't think so. We think David became successful the moment he began steadfastly pursuing his desire to write screenplays. He was a success at each step in his struggle to stay afloat throughout those many years. Yet how easy it is to overlook all the success along the way and focus on some specific desirable outcome.

The Five Stages of Success

Actually, the process of being on your own involves at least five major stages, each of which is a victory in and of itself. Getting through these stages can seem frustrating and discouraging if you concentrate strictly on getting to the end. But if you can acknowledge and enjoy each stage en route, the journey can be as rewarding as arriving at your ultimate destination. Where are you along this success continuum?

Stage One: Exploration

The journey to anywhere usually begins with deciding where you want to go. And in making it on your own this means exploring what you want to do. Many propreneurs feel like they're responding to some type of calling, which makes this stage a short and easy one. These fortunate individuals seem to have been born knowing what they wanted to do with their lives. Like the world-famous ballerina Suzanne Farrell and the choreographer George Balanchine, they don't feel they've chosen to pursue their work so much as that it has chosen them. Farrell told the *Los Angeles Times,* "[Balanchine] was meant to do ballets. I was meant to dance. Call it Providence. We had no say in the matter."

Others of us, however, find the exploration stage to be much longer and more difficult. Many aspiring propreneurs are fraught at first with a lack of clarity about what type of work they want to do and how to proceed on their own. This was a particularly difficult problem for me, Paul. I had been raised from the time I was four years old to believe that I would become a lawyer. And I did. But once I began practicing law, I found it was not how I had wanted to spend my days. I was not enjoying the career my mother had chosen for me. One day I was eating lunch with a wealthy and respected attorney who asked me how I liked practicing law. I guess my response was less than convincing; the attorney picked up that I wasn't really satisfied. He proceeded to tell me that he, too, would rather be doing something other than practicing law and that if he had it to do over again he would pursue something else.

This candid revelation stuck in my mind. I was haunted by the possibility of being in the same situation as this lawyer after a lifetime career: successful perhaps in the eyes of the world, but a captive of an erroneous decision made long ago. Within the year I decided to leave my profession. Having no idea what I wanted to be now that I was really on my own, I had to spend several years searching for a new direction for my career.

So who's successful? The prominent, affluent man who works a lifetime wishing he was doing something else, or the young man who drops out of a promising career to struggle with what he really wants to do? It's all in the way you choose to look at it.

I found that like other aspects of success, the process of determining what you want to do can't be hurried or forced, whether you like it or not. If you allow yourself the time to explore and discover, to mentally try on and investigate the many possibilities open to you, ultimately you will identify what you want to do. And when you do, you'll know it. You'll find yourself feeling committed to a specific line of work.

Your success begins the moment you begin the process of exploration, however. Even if you must explore for some time, even if you are trying out one thing after another and seemingly getting nowhere, even then, and throughout the entire exploration process, you should consider yourself successful because you've had the courage to set forth on a journey to find yourself.

Stage Two: Preparation

Once you know where you're headed, the next stage involves preparing to undertake the journey. Many people attempt to bypass this stage. They jump right into doing what they want to do, with little forethought or preparation. Of course, as your own boss, you can proceed any way you choose. Research shows, however, that individuals who take six to nine months to prepare themselves for self-employment make it more frequently than those who jump in unprepared.

The preparation one needs to do, of course, varies from person to person. For some it's a matter of learning—reading about their field or taking marketing courses. For others it's a matter of money—saving enough to have a financial cushion before leaving the paycheck behind, or cleaning up past debts and establishing credit. For still others, it's a matter of lining up initial business or setting up a team of professionals to support their ventures.

Usually people who don't take steps to prepare for going out on their own end up taking the needed steps later. Fortunately, it's never too late to undertake whatever preparation you need, even if you have to start over again after an initial attempt. And even when you must start over, you should consider yourself a success because you are continuing to move toward your goals. On your own, success lies in running the race, not in finishing first or even in finishing the first time.

Stage Three: Start-up

Actually, starting out on your own is probably the most exciting and energizing of the stages. You not only have formed your dream and committed to it, but have taken action and turned it into reality. It can be exhilarating. But this can also be the most frightening stage, because you are leaving behind the world as you know it in exchange for a future you can only imagine.

Although you may feel like a greenhorn and may be living on a shoestring until things get going, many people look at you and see someone who is doing what he or she wants to do. Your tomorrow holds unlimited potential. Any day could bring you your break—not by happenstance, but as a result of your own efforts from today and yesterday.

Starting Again with Confidence

When things don't work out, you can go home and tell your spouse you've failed and you're going out of business, or you can go home and tell your spouse you're starting a new business.

JAMES SIRKIN
CERTIFIED MANAGEMENT CONSULTANT

Along the way to your goals, if you've found yourself going down a road that is not taking you where you want to go, the following thoughts can be useful in getting started again.

You are not alone. Most successful individuals have turned down one or more dead-end streets on their journey to success. It's disappointing, but you have undoubtedly learned a lot along the last path that better prepares you for the next one. Your chances for a future more to your liking have just gone up immensely.

Don't give up on living a glorious dream. There are many roads to the same destination, so don't settle for less than something marvelous for your life. With the knowledge you now have, you may want to reshape and redefine your dream; you may even want to replace it, but don't settle for less. Continue dreaming great dreams.

Wipe your slate clean. Start afresh. Dump the old baggage and throw out or wash the dirty laundry from previously unsatisfying forays. Each day is brand-new. Anytime you are reminded of a previous situation which didn't go well for you, remember that this is a totally new situation. You can never stand in the same river twice.

Use what you've learned. While you may still not have it all figured out, proceed confidently with what you now know and pay attention to the results you get from everything you do. Your results from day to day will point you to what you need to do to get where you want to go.

Stage Four: Survival and Growth

Unless you are fortunate enough to have a fast start, this stage of success is probably the most challenging. It's the time during which you discover all the things you didn't expect, all the things you didn't know about and therefore couldn't prepare for. During this stage it's easy to get so fixated on all the things that aren't working yet that you forget to notice that you are making it.

Everything may not be going exactly the way you want it to, but since completing this stage may take you weeks or even years, it's important to keep in mind that *you're doing it!* And as long as you keep on doing it, ultimately you'll get where you want to go.

Stage Five: Bull's-Eye

When you finally attain your full dream, when you are actually living life the way you want to, what a moment! Celebrate and enjoy. Of course, sometimes the reality of your dream is as full of surprises and challenges as the journey you took to get there. You may be astonished by what you encounter once you achieve your goals. And you may quickly dream new dreams. But before traveling on, let yourself enjoy what you've worked for. Don't let anything interfere with the pleasure of what you've achieved.

Success Is Supposed to Feel Good

Despite all the changes and surprises that it brings, *success is supposed to feel good.* It's what you've worked for. Yet few of us are particularly well prepared for success. As the actor Charlie Sheen pointed out in a television interview, we learn as children how to work hard toward some future possibility of success and we even learn how to deal with failure, but we're rarely taught much about how to live with success.

In actuality, the price of success must be paid in full in advance, so whatever success you've achieved, you've already paid the price. Now it's time to enjoy the prize. You should do whatever you need to do to make sure that you can enjoy what you've worked for. Here are some ideas for overcoming five of the most common problems people have that prevent them from fully enjoying their success.

Keeping Success in Scale

Success acts as a magnet. It attracts more of everything your way—money, business, phone calls, mail, bills, and opportunities. So whether success turns out to be all it's cracked up to be will depend in large part upon how ready and willing you are to handle the abundance it brings.

When you have very little coming into your life, orchestrating it is relatively easy. The more that comes to you uninvited or without any effort on your part, however, the more important it becomes to let in only those aspects you want so success won't litter your life. Never think that you must accept everything success brings simply because it has come to you.

As we mentioned in Chapter 2, in order to seize the reigns of their success many propreneurs consciously decide to limit or even cut back their businesses. They choose not to expand. They choose not to complicate their lives. This is one example of how you can shape your success into a way of life that makes having achieved it worthwhile.

You also can elect to take on only those clients, customers, projects, and jobs that you enjoy, and refer others elsewhere. You may be able to raise your prices as a way of keeping your business manageable. And you most certainly can use the resources success is bringing you to make sure you don't become enslaved by your success. As you grow, for example, you can hire administrative personnel and outside services. You can purchase and use technology that was once beyond your budget to help keep your day, your desk, and your disposition clear for what's most important to you.

Knowing Your Success Is Here to Stay

Nothing can ruin the satisfaction of success quicker than an ever-present lingering fear that it will all disappear tomorrow. Sometimes people subconsciously imagine that if they notice and enjoy their success it will somehow magically go away. Some people even seem to believe that if they're sufficiently miserable or drive themselves relentlessly they can ward off future misfortune.

In actuality, you've created whatever success you've achieved from the events and circumstances around you. As the bookkeeper Chellie Campbell says, "You've made it up." Every day brings a completely new set of ingredients for you to create more with, so you might as well approach each day from the premise that you can do it again. You might as well expect your success to continue. We've found that the more you enjoy success, the more it enjoys you and the more it just keeps hanging around.

That does not mean, of course, that you can take your achievements for granted and assume that, having achieved what you have, you're all done. We're never done! Every day is a new chance to play. And if you drop out of the game, of course you can't win. But playing doesn't have to be a grind or even difficult. It doesn't mean you can't take a rest or relax. In fact, the most successful people we know are the most relaxed. They take more vacations and have more fun than anyone else we know. That's because the more momentum you build up for your business, the easier it is to keep going and the less energy it takes to create more.

Adjusting Your Relationships to Your Success

Certainly success brings changes in the way people relate to you. In some ways, these changes make your life simpler. Your calls may be taken more eagerly. Doors may open more readily. In other ways, your life becomes more complex. You may experience an influx of people who see you as *their* opportunity. You may find yourself besieged by salespeople and other solicitors. Friends and family may become jealous of you or make new demands on you. And you may find yourself the target of people who are not pleased with your success. But you need not let these changes stand in the way of enjoying your new life.

While there may be those who are jealous or resentful of your success, there are many others who genuinely enjoy associating with successful people. So spend your time with people you enjoy who enjoy you. Cultivate a habit of generosity. As Phil Laut, the author of *Money Is My Friend*, reminds us, the more willing you are to prosper others, the more willing others are to prosper you. Enjoy giving freely of your time, knowledge, money, and energy to individuals, projects, and causes that you admire and wish to support.

Feeling Worthy

Sometimes people feel undeserving of all the bounty success brings. This is especially true when the degree of success you've achieved seems disproportionate to the amount of effort you've put out. And if you've achieved success far beyond that of others around you, you may feel somewhat embarrassed or guilty about having so much.

In some ways our culture reenforces a sense of ambivalence about success. Even though this is the land of free enterprise, where the entrepreneurial spirit abounds, there is also an underlying implication at times that people who do well are somehow doing so at the expense of others.

But you deserve whatever rewards you can create for yourself from your honest labor. So it's important to come to peace with your good fortune. We've found that one of the best cures for feeling unworthy is *gratitude*. Simply allowing yourself to feel grateful for what you've been able to accomplish may allow you to accept and enjoy your success more fully.

We realize that some people have a problem with the idea of gratitude. In the process of growing up, many parents and teachers were a bit too eager to remind us that instead of wanting something more or being disappointed about something we don't have, we should feel grateful for what we do have. That is not what we're talking about here. From our perspective you always have a right to want more. The desire for more of life is what keeps us alive and growing.

We believe it's equally important, however, to let yourself enjoy what you have, to allow yourself to fully savor the feeling of satisfaction that comes from having accomplished something you've wanted. So while you undoubtedly have even greater things to do, go ahead and let yourself revel a bit in the pleasures of what you have already created.

Acknowledging Yourself

And while you're at it, acknowledge yourself for what you've accomplished. You probably deserve a medal of honor for getting where you are today, but there are few outstanding-service awards for self-employed individuals. So we suggest that you give yourself one. Find some way to demonstrate to yourself just how much you value your perseverance, dedication, and willingness to sacrifice for your goals.

For Jean Zalinsky, it was a gold ring she bought herself the day she reached her financial goal. Three years later Jean says, "I love this ring because to me it represents the commitment I made to myself. Every time I look at it I feel a sense of self-satisfaction that makes everything I've gone through to get where I am worthwhile."

Like Jean, all the people we interviewed for this book told us that no matter how difficult their journey was, they would do it all again in a minute. In fact, the more challenging it was, the sweeter the joy of accomplishment, not just because it was so hard, but because success demands that we go beyond what seems possible and become more than we thought we could be. "It's all mine!" Chris Shalby told us. "It's like giving birth," Ellie Kahn claims. "I feel very lucky." Chellie Campbell put it this way: "The best part is knowing that I'm totally the master of my own fate."

Success Is a Beginning, Not an End

We've found that once you begin to enjoy the sense of mastery success brings, you want to succeed all the more. You begin to have a sense of the magic you can make. It's the magic of life. It's the intoxicating force that has driven the creative powers of humankind throughout the ages. We all crave it, and as your own boss you're free to pursue it throughout your lifetime.

We urge you to let your natural desires direct and motivate you to increasing levels of success in your life so that each day may become more rewarding and fulfilling. Each day can hold a new opportunity for us to participate in creating a world we'll all find more to our liking—a world in which all of us are free to pursue our creative talents and abilities to the fullest and to live well from them. We're delighted to be sharing this journey with you. Here's to your success!

INDEX

■ ■

80/20 rule, 65–68
Activity centers, 77–79
Administrivia, 87, 88–89, 100, 108–115
Ambition, 181–182, 186, 187, 189
American Business Management Association, 97
Amos, Wally, 58
Anger, 159–161, 186
    role models, 160
Answering machines and services, 87, 111, 139
Anxiety, 186–187. *See also* Fear
Artists, 24
Assumptions, 190
Authority, 52–54. *See also* Power, sources of *and* Credibility

Backlog. *See* Cleaning
Balancing work and personal life, 84–86
Benefits, thinking, 39
Billing, 100, 222–224
BIS CAP, 23
Bookkeeping with computer, 109
Boredom, 168, 181–182, 187
Breakthroughs, 44–48
Business plan, 21, 32, 36

Cameron-Bandler, Leslie, 153, 158, 175
Capable, 171–178, 182
Capital, 236
Cash flow, 222–224
Charisma, 53, 207–210
Children, 86, 139
Cleaning,
    clutter, 68, 74–78, 100, 116
    routines, 100
    shortcuts, 115–117
Coaching, contextual, 194–195
Collections. *See* Money
Color, 58, 117, 141

Commitments, 123, 130
CompuServe Information Service, 97, 113
Computer, 92, 108–110
    consultants, 97
Concentration, 138–139, 143–146
Confidence, builders, 175. *See also* Self-confidence
Confusion, 34
Copiers, 91, 111
Credentials, 37, 205–207, 236–237
Credibility, 199–213
Credit,
    extending, 223
    sources of, 51

Decision-making, 70
Delays, handling, 42
Depression,
    emotional depression, 161–162, 186
    the Great, 9
Determination, 176–177, 181, 189
Disappointment, 156, 162–163, 187–188
Discouragement, 164, 186, 189
Disruptions, 139

Emotional road map, 158–183
    handy guide to, 184–185
Emotional throttle, 186–189
Emotions, 151–193
    designer, 190–191
    preselecting, 190–193. *See also* emotions by name
Encouragement, 161–162, 164
Energy, 129, 134–138
    colors for, 141
    drink, 138
    emotional, 155–158
Entrepreneur,
    definition of, 13
    new breed, 10, 12–18

Environment. *See* Office environment
Equipment, 90–92, 98
  do-it-yourself office, 108–113
  deducting, 115
  financing, 115
  for under $2500, 114–115
Exercise, 137
Expectations, 190
Experts, using, 94–96

Failure,
  as a stepping stone, 39–42
  changing feelings of, 165–166
  contributing factors to, 2–5, 8–10
  fear of, 9
  rate of, 8–10, 24
Family and friends, 51, 58, 85–86, 139
Fatigue, 154. *See also* Lethargy
Fax, 91, 111, 112
Fear, 20, 25–26, 34
  of failure, 9, 169–170
  of mistakes, 40, 166
  of rejection, 171–174
  of success, 170–171
  turning into confidence, 166–174
Fee setting. *See* Pricing
Feelings. *See* Emotions
Fight/flight reaction, 154
Filing, 76, 100, 116
  archives, 79
  filing center, 79
Financial
  cash cushion, 48
  reasons for problems, 49–51
  safety net, 47
  spending to earn, 48–51
Focusing, 83–84, 129
  lack of, 212. *See also*
  Concentration
Follow-through, 121–123
Food, for energy, 137
  for relaxing, 133
Friends. *See* Family and friends
Frustration, 156, 162–163, 186, 188
Furniture, 58, 117, 141

Gatekeepers, 92, 94, 103
Getting business. *See* Marketing
Goals, 22, 58, 70
  goal-setting, 80–84
  goals vs. commitments, 123
Guilt, 85–86, 174–175, 188

Helmstetter, Shad, 58
Help. *See* Support
Hiring help, 87–93. *See also* Support
Hopefulness, 163–163
Hopelessness, 176–177, 186
Humor, 58

Image. *See* Professional image
Impatience, 189
Inadequacy, 177–180, 188, 189
Information professionals, 97
Inner dialogue. *See* Self-talk
Institutional barriers, 200
Interruptions, 87
Irritable, 189

Laser printers, 91, 110, 115
Laughter, 58
Learning curve, 46, 47
Leisure time, 61
Lethargy, 181–182, 187, 189
Lighting, 58, 141
Loans, 51

Mail, center, 78
Mailing, joint, 92
  lists with computer, 109
Marginal Business Attitude, 210–213
Marketing, 4, 36–39, 51, 100
  critical mass, 102–107
  diagnosing need for, 214–216
  evaluating market conditions, 232–235
  finding your unique advantage, 105
  getting business fast, 219–220
  in tough times, 216–219, 220–221
  mindset, 36, 37–39
  platform for, 106
  samples, 106
  self-generating, 105
  self-liquidating, 105
  showcasing, 106
Meditation, 134
Mental shifts, 9, 22–57
Mentors, 92, 103, 119–120, 122
Mistakes, 3
  handling, 39–42, 166
Modems, 111, 112–113
Momentum, 45–48, 90–91, 104
Money,
  attitudes toward 48–51, 211
  billing, 222
  collecting, 214, 222–224
  how much you need, 224–225, 236
  money processing center, 78–79
  not having enough, 213–227
Morale, 56–58
Motivation, 4, 121–128, 181–182, 189
  staying up, 58, 134–138
Music, 58, 132–133, 138, 143, 144

Naisbitt, John, 24
Negative feelings, 58, 154.
  See also emotions by name
Networking, 58, 103
  electronic, 97
  professional, 96

Newman, Jim, 152

Office supplies, 98–99
Optimism, 140–143, 189.
    See also Positive attitude
Organizing work, 74–78
    activity centers, 77–79
    archives, 79
    files, 79
    supplies and equipment, 98–99.
    See also Filing
Overwhelmed, 182
Overworking, 84, 135

Pareto Principle, 65
Patience, 162, 189
Paycheck mentality, 9, 19, 20–21, 22, 37,
    49–50
Peak performance, 128–148
    characteristics of, 129
Pep talks. *See* Self-talk
Performance anxiety, 168–169
Performance reviews, 58, 217, 238
Perseverance, 32, 33–34
Personal organizers, 76–77, 113
Planning your day, 77
Positive attitude, 2, 10, 129, 140–143,
    211–212
Positive illusion, 140
Possibility test, 163
Power, cultural, 205–207
    historical, 204
    personal, 52–54, 207–210
    position, 52–54, 203–204
    sources of, 53, 203–210
Prejudice, institutional against self-employed,
    200
Premise, 189–193
Pressure, performing under, 168
Pricing, 211, 214, 220, 224–227
Priorities, 70, 83
Problem-solving, 196–199
Productivity tips, 99–101
Professional image, 92, 205–207
Professional organizers, 97
Profit, 24
Propreneur, 12–19, 20–22, 200
Psychoneuroimmunology, 140, 155
Public relations, 103
Purpose, 68–74
    finding your, 70–73
    poster, 73

Quitting, 227–237
Quiz
    for propreneur, 17
    for success, 130

Reassurance, 159, 165, 174, 176, 183
Referrals, 103
    cross-referring, 93
Rejection, overcoming, 171–174
Relationships, 86, 244–245
Relaxing
    colors for, 141
    under pressure, 129, 131–136
Responsibility, 180–181
Results, 32–36, 79–84, 237
    quadrupling, 67–74
Resume, 37
Right of passage, 202
Role models, 160, 179, 180
Routines, 64, 100–101
Rules, 32–36

Sales personality, 36, 37
Scheduling, 68, 79–84, 130
    activity blocks, 84
    time for personal life, 84
Scheele, Adele, 37
Security, 25–29
Self-confidence, 160, 166–178, 183, 189, 242
Self-discipline, 19, 29–31
Self-employment, 23
    a hybrid, 11–12
    average hours worked, 62
Self-liquidating marketing, 105
Self-management, 4, 29, 56–58, 119–120,
    122–128, 194–238, 217, 238
Self-reliance, 2
Self-supervision. *See* Self-management
Self-sustaining business, 46
Self-talk, 126–127
Serious Business Attitude, 210–213
Seriously, being taken, 199–213
Single parents, 86
Sleep, 136, 137
Slow times. *See* Marketing
Small business, definition of, 12
Small Business Administration, 12, 24, 97
Small Business Network, 97
Software
    bookkeeping, 109
    file-management, 110
    mailing-list, 109
    phone-dialer, 110
    time and expense, 110
    time-management, 77
    voicemail, 112
Soundproofing, 141
Starting over, 242
Staying up, 194–238
Storage, 79, 117
Stress, 45, 62, 131–134
Success
    as a joint venture, 54–56, 94

Success *(Continued)*
  as an experiment, 32–33
  attitudes for, 9–10
  building a history of, 168
  characteristics of, 2–5, 8–10, 25, 32, 34
  developing feelings of, 165–166
  enjoying, 5, 239–246
  managing, 242–244
  quiz for, 130
  rate of, 8–10, 24, 36
  readiness for, 235–237
  relationships and, 244–245
  stages of, 240–243
  time frame for achieving, 46, 228–237
  versus being right, 41
Supplies, cleaning, 116
Support,
  getting, 54–56, 58, 92–96
  group, 148, 173
  services, 4
Survival rate, 8

Technology, 4, 91
  do-it-yourself office, 108–115
  for cleaning, 115–117
  overcoming resistance to, 113–115
Telephones
  calls, 87, 100

center, 78
equipment, 98, 111
software, 110.
  See also Voicemail
Tension. *See* Stress
Time management, 4, 61–87
Time off. *See* Vacation
Time planners. *See* Personal organizers
Time savers, 100–101, 110, 115–117
Tiredness, *See* Lethargy
Trust, 28–30

Undercapitalization, 46

Vacation, 58, 132, 136
Visibility, 37
Voicemail, 87, 111–112
Volunteering, 220
Von Oech, 198

Waking up, 133
Working From Home Forum, 97, 113
Worry
  how not to, 143
Wall Street Journal, 23–24